*f*P

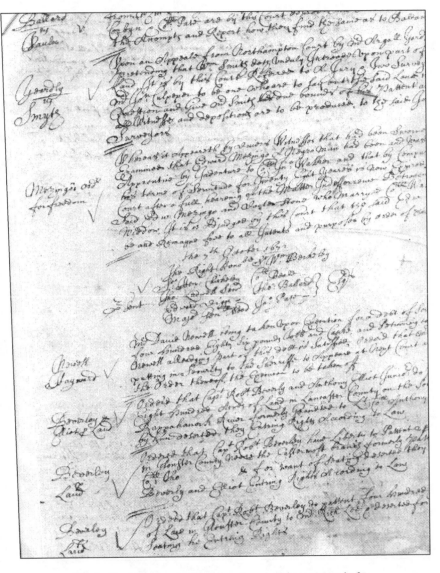

The handwritten entry in the Jamestown colonial court record of
October 5, 1672, noting the judges' ruling that Edward Mozingo
should be freed after twenty-eight years of "indentured servitude."

The Fiddler on Pantico Run

An African Warrior,
His White Descendants,
a Search for Family

JOE MOZINGO

Free Press

New York   London   Toronto   Sydney   New Delhi

Free Press
A Division of Simon & Schuster, Inc.
1230 Avenue of the Americas
New York, NY 10020

First Free Press hardcover edition October 2012

FREE PRESS and colophon are trademarks of Simon & Schuster, Inc.

Permission, 190–91: Excerpt from "My Dungeon Shook: Letter to My Nephew on
the One Hundredth Anniversary of Emancipation," © 1962 by James Baldwin.
Copyright renewed. Collected in *The Fire Next Time*, published by Vintage Books.
Used by arrangement with the James Baldwin Estate.

For information about special discounts for bulk purchases, please contact
Simon & Schuster Special Sales at 1-866-506-1949 or
business@simonandschuster.com.

The Simon & Schuster Speakers Bureau can bring authors to your
live event. For more information or to book an event contact the
Simon & Schuster Speakers Bureau at 1-866-248-3049 or
visit our website at *www.simonspeakers.com*.

Manufactured in the United States of America

1 3 5 7 9 10 8 6 4 2

Library of Congress Cataloging-in-Publication Data
Mozingo, Joe.
The fiddler on Pantico Run : an African warrior, his white descendants, a search for
family / by Joe Mozingo.—1st Free Press hardcover ed.
p. cm.
Includes bibliographical references and index.
1. Mozingo family. 2.Mozingo, Joe—Family. 3. Mozingo, Joe—
Travel—Africa. 4. United States—Genealogy. I. Title.
CT274.M73M69 2012
929'.20973—dc23
2012008971

ISBN: 978-1-4516-2760-2

For Noaki and our children,
Blake and Lucia.
And for my mom and dad.

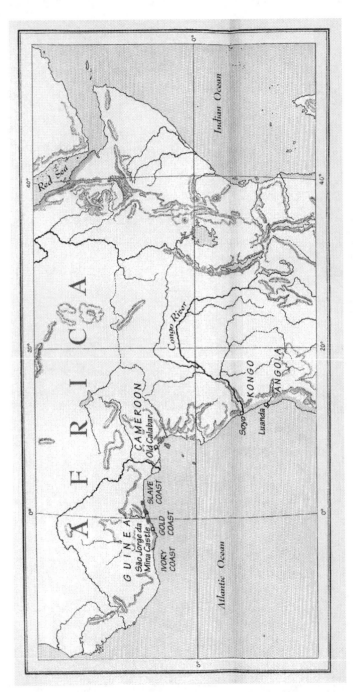

University of Texas Libraries. Adapted by Doug Stevens, from the map of Africa in Cambridge Modern History Atlas, 1912.

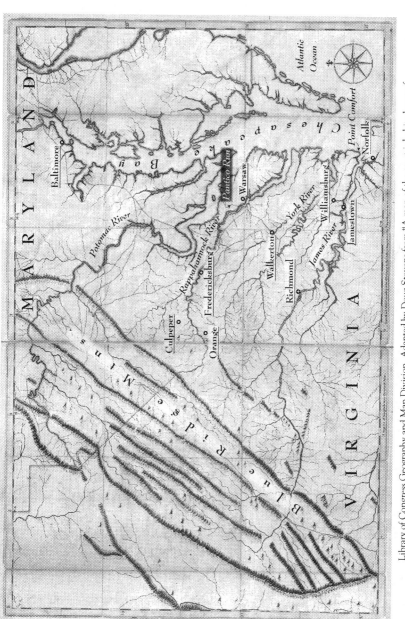

Library of Congress Geography and Map Division. Adapted by Doug Stevens from "A map of the most inhabited part of Virginia containing the whole province of Maryland with part of Pennsylvania, New Jersey and North Carolina." Drawn by Joshua Fry & Peter Jefferson in 1751.

Contents

Contents

The Fiddler on
Pantico Run

Chapter 1

The Strange Twist of History

This was where the thread first came into view, an old stone palace miles up a rutted dirt track, alone in the gum resin trees and elephant grass. We parked next to the wives' quarters, a small village of soot-blackened walls and peaked zinc roofs. Young men in frayed clothes guided us through a twisting corridor to the king's court. My friend Walter and I waited on benches until the eighty-year-old king, the *fon*, beckoned us from his wood throne in the fading gray light. We crossed the courtyard in an extended bow. The *fon*, wearing a black skullcap and a light blue *boubou* robe, sat rigidly erect in his chair, sipping a local liqueur called Marula Fruit Cream from a Baltimore Orioles mug. His face was long and stolid, thin clenched lips and cold rheumy eyes. He spoke haltingly in his language, showing teeth like weathered pickets. Walter translated that the king was welcoming us, and I nodded and smiled as the palace guard hissed at me to take my hands out of my pockets. After further formalities, I was told to kneel before the king and cup my hands at my mouth, as he poured a blessing of the liqueur so copious it streamed down my right arm under my jacket. Walter whispered to me that this was the highest honor, to show effusive gratitude. I sighed, knowing my sleeve would be stuck to my skin until my next shower, whenever that might be. As evening came, the young men, whom I had taken to be street hustlers and now realized were princes, guided me to a perch in the canopy on the high ridge. I let them walk off so I could have a moment alone.

As I listened to the dry rasp of the elephant grass, I gazed out over the Kingdom of Kom. A narrow gorge threaded through the lush terrain below, opening into a smoky blue chasm in the distance, the Valley of Too Many Bends. A cluster of white streetlights hovered on a dark crest a few miles away—Njinikom, a town to which earlier kings once banished sorcerers and foreign missionaries. The crumpled topography of these mountains had long repelled invaders, colonists, and change. Many villagers still lived in red earthen huts with grass roofs, collected firewood before dusk, and poured libations of palm wine on the ground for their ancestors. The view from this spot had not changed much in centuries. Only that tremulous constellation of electric lights broke the deepening shades of blue.

The footpath wended down into the darkness, almost two thousand feet below, where I was told a momentous baobab tree stood near the river. The story is that it fell one day, years ago, cried and cried all night, and the following morning was standing again. Villagers call it "the talking tree."

Mythical stories abound up here, filling the void left by an unwritten history. It is said the Kom were led to this very spot by a python. But the story that no one talks about is the true story of the people removed from this land. This belt of fertile savannah in western Cameroon rested at a terrible crossroads, with no forest to hide in when the marauders arrived. The kings may have been safe in their fortified isolation, but their people were not. They were taken first by Arab invaders in the Sudan in the north, and then by the southern peoples who found that humans were the commodity Europeans most desired.

Captured and bound together, they were driven on long marches, some south across the sweltering lowlands to the mangrove estuaries of the coastal kings, some west through sheer mountain rain forest to the Cross River, where merchants loaded them onto canoes and rowed three hundred miles south to the port of Old Calabar. Those who survived had been handed from tribe to tribe, through too many hostile foreign territories to dream of escaping and returning home. And then off they went, into the sea.

High on a ridge, three hundred miles by road from the Atlantic, I sat at the headwaters of that outward movement, imagining the people flowing away like the rivers below. I pictured a boy, gazing down into that blue mountain cradle, the grass dry-swishing in the breeze, the drums coming up with the night. A boy suddenly pulled into the current and scrambling to reach the bank. A boy unable to imagine the ocean and sickly white men in big wooden ships and the swampy, malarial settlement called Jamestown where he would be sold to a planter in the year of their lord 1644.

This is the beginning, I said to myself. The beginning of my family's story, the point just after which my forebears obscured the truth—and nearly buried it forever.

A few days later, on the coast, I caught a motorcycle taxi to a ferry terminal late at night. The air was fresh and fragrant as we sputtered along the edge of an old botanical garden where the German colonials tried to find tropical medicines. At the port, the driver dropped me at a hulking stone warehouse, where I had bought my ticket that afternoon. The boat was to leave at three-thirty in the morning. Passengers milled about or slept on straw mats under high ceiling fans. Bleary and dry-eyed, I handed my passport to an officer behind a desk. He inspected it briefly, then leaned back in his chair, arched his eyebrows, and opened his palms in mock challenge. "Mozingo. That is your name?"

"Yes."

He smiled and shook his head. "That is not an American name."

"I know."

He turned to two women behind him and showed them my passport. They joked in the local pidgin language, and he turned back to me. "That is a Cameroonian name. How do you have it?"

"I might have had an ancestor from here."

"So your father came from Cameroon?" he asked, rightfully dubious.

I am white, with straight, light brown hair and blue eyes. No one has ever mistaken me for anything else.

"Not my father, an ancestor. Way, way back," I said.

"Your grandfather?"

"No, long before him." I had already come to realize that the past here, unrecorded almost until the twentieth century, was somehow compressed. When events beyond memory were not fixed in writing, they swirled about, unmoored from linearity, and 358 years didn't mean too much more than "a long, long time."

"But who gave you the name?" he asked.

"Well, it's different in America," I said. "We just get whatever name our father has. It just goes down the line. Automatic."

He still seemed unconvinced. Our accents muddled our points to each other, and I didn't think explaining further was going to clear things up. But I took it as a good sign that I had come to the right region of Africa, that he, of all people, had that spark of recognition; every day he took several hundred passports, stamped them for the trip to neighboring Nigeria, then called out for the owners to take them back. He must have known the names of this region like few others.

"Let me ask you, which part of Cameroon does this name come from?" I asked.

"That is Kribi, east province," he said definitively.

I thanked him and wrote it down. I'd have to look that up on my map.

We boarded a modern, air-conditioned ferry and took off in the dark along a desolate coast for Old Calabar, about a hundred miles west in Nigeria. As we left the port, we passed under the bulk of Mt. Cameroon, hidden in the night, rising thirteen thousand feet straight from the sea. Long before any Europeans saw the great volcanic massif, one of earth's great migrations set off from the other side of it, peopling most of southern Africa. The Bantu Expansion.

The captain read a bit of scripture as we set off, Psalm 91:9–16, something about "crushing fee-yerce lions and sare-punts under your feet." I fell asleep and came to after dawn to see a distant gray sliver of treetops between gray water and gray sky. This was the view that the slave captains and crews would have seen, an endless knotted line of coast where a good portion of them would meet their death.

The shore slipped in and out of view for an hour or so. At one point, an armada of fishermen in canoes sailed past for deep waters, rising and falling on loping swells. With tattered plastic tarps strung between bamboo poles, they caught a light offshore wind from the lowlands. Some were father-and-son teams, the boys mending the nets as they traveled. Other canoes had five or six people. Ahead of them lay no horizon, only a gloom of ocean vanishing into a gloom of air, with the vague outline of a thunderhead to the west. Far out in the gray murk, orange flares burned in the oil fields of the Niger Delta. The fire flickering in the vaporous abyss was dreamlike, and somehow disturbing in my sleep-deprived state, as if the fishermen were ferrying souls to Hades. I'd never had such an unsettling reaction to a seascape.

We came into the wide mouth of the Cross River, rocking sideways on a beaming sea. The engines wound down sharply as we approached a reef or shoal, and the captain turned hard left and then right to maneuver. Two sticks with red rags hanging from them apparently marked a channel. The move felt panicked, and I braced for impact, thinking of all the African ferry disasters I'd read about. The exit door was right behind me, and I thought, *At least the water's warm.* But the captain threaded through the sticks and throttled the engines back up. The outgoing current was running fast, breaking white off the channel markers and crab trap buoys. This must have been a nerve-racking entry for the slavers. The Dutch sailors largely avoided Old Calabar for this very reason, but the English learned its ways, and in the mid-1600s developed a brisk trade of slaves between the Efik chiefs and the planters in Barbados.

An English captain, William Snelgrave, traded regularly in Old Calabar and left a rare account of his transactions:

> As soon as the natives perceive a ship on their coast, they make a smoke on the seashore as a signal for the ship to come to an anchor, that they may come and trade with the people aboard. As soon as we are at an anchor, they come to us in small boats, called *Cannoes*, being made of a single tree, and bring their commodities with them.

Like most Europeans, Snelgrave figured he would be killed if he ventured inland and set foot ashore only on a few occasions. He knew nothing of the continent—three times the size of Europe—beyond the impervious thicket of foliage backing the beach.

> In those few places where I have been on shore myself, I could never obtain a satisfactory account from the natives of the inland parts. Nor did I ever meet with a white man that had been . . . up in the country; and believe, if any had attempted it, the natives would have destroyed them. . . . However the trade on this part of the coast has been exceedingly improved within these 20 years past. It consists in negroes, elephants teeth, and other commodities; which the natives freely bring on board our ships, except when any affront has been offered them.

The affronts, he explained, had occurred when the ships took away not just the goods and people being sold, but the sellers too.

He called the natives here "barbarous and uncivilized" mainly because they had had such limited interaction with the Europeans, compared to those at points west and south, who had dealings with forts and trading depots.

> I have, in my younger years, traded to many places in this tract, especially at Old Calabar, where, in the year 1704, I saw a sad instance of barbarity. The king of the place, called *Jabrue,* being fallen sick, he caused, by the advice of his priests, a young child about ten months old to be sacrificed to his god, for his recovery. I saw the child after it was killed, hung up on the bough of a tree, with a live cock tied near it, as an addition to the ceremony.

The odd thing about Captain Snelgrave was that he conveyed deep objections to such scenes, even as he took a leading role in a wider atrocity. On his thirteen trips between Africa and America, including three to Virginia, he carried nearly five thousand slaves away, and over nine hundred of them died during the crossing. The paradox was particularly vexing when he sailed the *Anne* from London to Old Calabar in 1713. A new king, Acqua, sat on a stool under some shade trees, and the captain took the stool beside him. Ten armed sailors accompanied him, standing off to one side, while fifty of the king's guards stood across from them with swords, bows and arrows, and barbed lances.

The captain noticed a baby boy tied by one leg to a stake in the ground, with "flies and other vermin crawling on him, and two priests standing by." He asked the king why the child was bound there. The king said "it was to be sacrificed to his God Igbo for his prosperity."

Appalled, Snelgrave ordered his men to remove the child. A ruckus ensued, with weapons drawn all around. The captain told the king he meant no harm, to relax, and they sat back down. The king averred that the child was his property. "This I acknowledged," Snelgrave wrote, excusing his actions "on account of my religion, which, though it does not allow of forcibly taking away what belongs to another, yet expressly forbids so horrid a thing as the putting a poor innocent child to death. I also observed to him, that the grand law of nature was to do to others as we desired to be done unto."

Snelgrave offered to buy the boy, and much to his delight, the king agreed to sell him for a mere bunch of sky-colored beads, worth half a crown sterling, bringing us to one of the most profoundly deranged happy endings ever written:

> The day before I went on shore to see the king, I had purchased the mother of the child (though I knew it not then) from one of his people; and at that time my surgeon observing to me that she had much milk in her breasts, I inquired of the person that brought her on board, whether she had a child when he bought her from the inland trader. To which he answered negative. But now on my coming on board, no sooner was the child handed into the ship, but this poor woman espying it, run with great eagerness and snatched him out of the white man's arms that held him. I think there never was a more moving sight than on this occasion between the mother and her little son (who was a fine boy about 18 months old) especially when the linguist told her I had saved her child from being sacrificed. Having at that time above 300 negroes on board my ship, no sooner was the story known amongst them, but they expressed their thankfulness to me, by clapping their hands, and

singing a song in my praise. This affair proved of great service to us, for it gave them a good notion of white men, for that we had no mutiny in our ship during the whole voyage.

Snelgrave leaves his account of the trip at that, with the slaves singing happily across the sea.

The mercantile records of the voyage cast a pall on this party: he picked up more slaves before he left Africa, ultimately setting off for Antigua with 395. The chorus lost plenty of voices. Ninety-five Africans died during the crossing—one out of four. Two corpses a day on average were thrown overboard. There is no record of whether the mother or her child survived the passage.

I gazed through the salt-smeared window of the ferry, half-listening to a Nigerian sitcom about two hustlers, Silas and Titus, on a TV mounted to the ceiling in the cabin. We'd come closer to shore, which appeared as a low colorless ribbon of palms and mangrove now. Villages of thatched and clay huts dotted it here and there, and smoke unspooled from settlements hidden up the creeks that tunneled through the canopy. The river narrowed and then divided into numerous channels that joined again farther upstream. The water grew thick and brown with silt. Bottles and bags and water hyacinths swirled in foamy gyres. We passed an island where the mottled trees of an abandoned rubber plantation tilted with the prevailing wind in neat rows. Heading up a tributary to the right, we slowed before a high bluff. The closer we came through the haze the better I could make out the glinting gray-brown lines of a city. We pulled up along a wharf with little warehouses and the hulks of half-sunk ships.

"There were some very strong currents today," the captain said on the loudspeaker. "That is why we are late. But it is better late than never. That is why we must pray to Jesus Christ." Which he did. The strange twist of history—and this story is all about strange twists of history—was that the solitary white man on board was not among the converted.

I disembarked down the gangway to the quay. The air was wilting and smelled like diesel and pond dredge. Old Calabar was a modern city of 1.2 million people, and any glimpse of the traditional village life that Snelgrave encountered here had long been paved over. I walked past money changers and hustlers and cell phone card hawkers to a spot where I could look up the river. Silos and tanks and concrete wharves continued up to a hard bend west, and mangroves obscured the opposite bank.

In the seventeenth and eighteenth centuries, the slave traders paddled here down the Cross River from the interior in fleets of twenty or more canoes, each carrying twenty or more slaves. The captives often came originally from the Grassfields and were marched to the jungle village of Mamfe, 250 miles upriver from here. Illustrations from the time show the captives' arms tied behind their backs, with wishbone branches and ligatures binding them together by the neck. The river cut a long arching course to the coast, like a shepherd's staff, through rain forest that is now home to some of the last gorillas in West Africa and that still boasts chimpanzees, hippopotamuses, crocodiles, forest elephants, and drill monkeys. As the canoes neared the coast, Efik traders purchased the slaves to sell, in turn, to the whites, mostly for bars of copper, iron, guns, ammunition, and liquor.

The boy whom I and every Mozingo in America appear to have descended from might have come this way to the Atlantic. Mosingas were certainly taken out of the nearby Rio del Rey, where at the moment the "creek tribes" were kidnapping outsiders, putting a damper on my prospects of going there. I had set out to trace the story of that boy's origin, but I was beginning to wonder if I would ever really know where he came from. He may have lived nowhere near here. He may have embarked from a point a thousand miles south, in Angola. After months of research, I was still left weighing mere bits of the evidence on the two sides of a balance: Old Calabar in one pan, Angola in the other.

If he had come from Angola, he had likely seen and dealt with white people before; European traders and soldiers set up their first colony there in the 1500s. He may even have been of mixed race. But arriving in Old Calabar from the interior, he would probably never have seen a white person and might have thought they were buying him to eat; slaves were said to have thought the red wine the sailors drank was Africans' blood and that the cheese of the captain's table was made from Africans' brains.

The captains inspected the slaves and sorted out the infirm, the deformed, the weak and aged. Bad eyes, feeble joints, slender frames, and rotten teeth were grounds for rejection. Those purchased shuffled aboard, the men shackled together, and waited for weeks and even months until the ship was full and ready to set sail. Those rejected suffered their own terrible fates.

"The traders frequently beat those negroes which are objected to by the captains," wrote Alexander Falconbridge, a British surgeon on slave ships to Calabar and elsewhere in the 1780s. At a nearby port, "the traders have frequently been known to put them to death. Instances have happened at that place, that the traders, when any of their negroes have been objected to, have dropped their canoes under the stern of the vessel, and instantly beheaded them in sight of the captain."

I walked along the quay to the immigration office. Two men struggled to row a canoe filled with sand, the river rising up to its gunwales. Sand was big trade all along the waterway. Merchants bought it and sold it to Chinese road contractors to be mixed with concrete.

My mind kept going back to that gray abyss with no horizon I saw from the ferry. I struggled to fathom what the kidnapped people thought as they set off into that void in a state of pure unknowing, going farther and farther into the featureless Doldrums, crammed together so tightly they struggled to breathe and could barely turn, their excretions, stench, and disease suffusing the airless swelter. They watched the bodies of those who died simply heaved into the void. Once out at sea, many actually thought this *was* the white men's world, "this hollow place," in one man's account. They had been condemned to a sort of wandering hell, outside of space and time, where the newly dispossessed souls murmured in the minds of the barely living and perhaps only a fear of eternal exile from the soil of their ancestors, from all humanity, would steel their will to survive.

The slaves were usually kept belowdecks in shackles until the ships moved out of sight of land and the prospect of their hijacking the vessels and returning home had vanished. From Old Calabar, this may have been more than a week into the trip, as the ship first sailed a thousand miles west along the coast to Cape Palmas, before moving into the open ocean as the coast turned north. Some captives required a week or more to regain the use of their limbs after being unshackled. To try to tamp down disease, some crews let the slaves up on deck for sun and fresh air and had them clean their quarters with vinegar. Others did not. The month-long crossing killed an average of one in five, claimed by dysentery, smallpox, suicide, yaws, and all manner of unknown afflictions. On some voyages, half the captives died.

Falconbridge described compartments so cramped the slaves could only lie on their sides, and had to scramble over each other in shackles to reach overflowing waste buckets. Many just relieved themselves "as they lie."

"The exclusion of the fresh air is among the most intolerable," he wrote. Most ships had a half-dozen air-ports, four-by-six-inches, on each side of the ship. "But whenever the sea is rough, and the rain heavy, it becomes necessary to shut these. [The] negroes rooms very soon grow intolerably hot. The confined air, rendered noxious by the effluvia exhaled from their bodies, and by being repeatedly breathed, soon produces fevers and fluxes, which generally carries off great numbers of them."

The most emaciated of the slaves, lying on bare planks,

> frequently have their skin, and even their flesh, entirely rubbed off, by the motion of the ship, from the prominent parts of the shoulders, elbows, and hips, so as to render the bones in those parts quite bare. . . . While they were in this situation, my profession requiring it, I frequently went down among them, till at length their [compartments] became so extremely hot, as to be only sufferable for a very short time. . . . [The] floor of their rooms was so covered with blood and mucus which had proceeded from them in consequence of the flux that it resembled a slaughterhouse.

The ships sailing from Angola to Brazil had it relatively easy, with a shorter distance and favorable winds. Heading to the Caribbean proved to be deadlier as ships often stalled in the stagnant air over the equator. For the English, Barbados was usually the first stop, the farthest east of the Antilles. But its profile was low and easy to miss. The Dutch had to make their way another six hundred miles to their colony of Curaçao or four hundred to St. Eustatius, while the Portuguese and Spanish traveled even farther, to their ports in Cartagena, Havana, Panama, and Veracruz. The sailors usually spotted gulls, seaweed, and other ships before seeing land, then could smell wafts of grass and sun-beaten earth.

A small handful of the first slaves brought to the New World were delivered from the Caribbean to the starving, wretched outpost of Jamestown, where the story of Mozingos in America begins.

I was standing over a copy editor in the *Los Angeles Times* newsroom one afternoon two years before my first trip to Africa, going over an article I had written, when the managing editor, Davan Maharaj, stopped by. He was new to that position, and I had met him only briefly. "So where's that name Mozingo from?" he asked.

"We think it's Central African."

"I knew it," he shot back. He said he'd first heard my name years back, when I was an intern and he was a reporter in another bureau, and he had asked his friend Ken about me. "Is he a black guy?"

"No, he's white."

"Really?"

"Yeah. He has blue eyes."

"He's got to be black."

I was asked about my name about every other day of my adult life, and reactions to my response swung widely. A black colleague scoffed. A Rotarian the color of mayonnaise winced as if I were confiding the particulars of a bad circumcision. A prize-winning colleague with a Germanic last name sidled up to tell me Bantus danced with their butts sticking out. A female Haitian American friend asked me why I couldn't dance. Some people nodded as if I were bullshitting them. A beautiful young cashier at a coffee shop tapped her fingers, dying for me to stop talking. Soldiers of political correctness stood in uncomfortable silence, well tutored not to ask the obvious follow-up, about why a white guy bore the name. Plenty of people found it fascinating. One *Times* editor started calling me Mandingo.

"It's a long story," I told Davan, hoping he would have the patience to hear it. I had been planning to pitch an article about my lineage as a first-person feature for the paper, so that I could devote myself full time to investigating this long-buried family history I had become enthralled with.

Davan grew up in the racially split Caribbean nation of Trinidad, the descendant, I would later learn, of an Indian preacher who went there to minister to indentured servants the British had imported from India after the African slave trade was banned. He was a foreign correspondent in Central Africa for a spell before he became an editor and moved back to L.A. Surely he would be interested in the thread of European imperialism that resulted in a white man bearing this name.

He vaguely recalled having come across the name in the Caribbean, where some African names survived. I told him that most recently I had heard that the earliest known ancestor in the lineage, Edward Mozingo, had likely come from what was then the Kingdom of Kongo, which straddled the border of today's Angola and the Democratic Republic of Congo. One of Edward's living descendants, Melicent Remy, a dogged researcher of his African origins, had tracked this down, but I wasn't sure from where or whether her research was reliable.

"I think he married a white or light-skinned woman, and their sons married white women, and pretty soon they looked white," I said. "But I hear there are some black Mozingos still."

"We're cousins, I bet," he joked.

I laughed, not quite sure I understood, and made my final selling point on the rich tensions in this story: "There were Mozingos in the KKK."

At that he laughed in delight.

"What does your dad think of this?" he asked.

"That's a tough one," I said. "He laughs. I don't really know. I'm not sure he thinks it's all true.

"I've wanted to write this story for years," I added.

"You have to," he said.

Chapter 2

A Man Named Edward Mozingo

My father's family landed in 1942 Los Angeles as if by immaculate conception, unburdened by the past. Growing up, I heard all about how my mother's grandparents had come to California from southern France and Sweden. But my dad's family was mentioned only obliquely. My grandfather Joe died before I was born, and I heard only a few stories about his youth in Hannibal, Missouri, how he once found a tarantula in a shipment of bananas at his dad's corner store, how he explored the same caves where Tom Sawyer and Becky Thatcher ran from the fugitive Injun Joe. As an adult, friends called him "the Sheik" because he looked like Rudolph Valentino, handsome, with dark swept-back hair and an olive complexion. I didn't know much more, and the only image of him I had in my mind came from a single photo I had seen of him, standing, gray hair combed back loosely, suavely smoking a cigarette. I knew absolutely nothing about his ancestors and might never have given the subject any thought except for our strange name.

When I was in grade school, on the first day of class my teachers always looked at the roster inexplicably stumped, as if my last name wasn't pronounced exactly how it was spelled. "Joseph Ma . . . ma . . . monzeen . . . Uhm, is . . . where's Joseph?" Even then, I registered how foreign everyone in my peripheral world thought it sounded.

My parents always said they thought Mozingo was Italian, but this was offered only as theory. At the time it didn't really strike me as odd that such a basic piece of our identity could just vanish. We lived in a place where history had a way of getting lost. There were no family cemeteries or homesteads, no old money or old buildings, no pedigrees or legacies, no families we should or should not associate with based on bygone behavior. Life imitated a marketing scheme: southern California was a *new* place, truly a novelty by that late stage of human civilization, a place where you invented yourself.

My dad grew up in Hollywood, and a movie studio sat next door to his apartment building. The parallel universe of celebrity bubbled into his real childhood. My grandmother got to talking to Harriet Nelson at a sewing shop on Sunset Boulevard one day, and my dad and Uncle Joe ended up playing with Ricky a bunch of times at his house after school. Annette Funicello went to my dad's middle school, and numerous child actors populated his high school. But my grandfather wanted his children taking no part of this world, which he viewed as predatory and perverse. When my dad came home one day when he was about ten years old and said a man in a convertible had stopped to tell him he should try out for a spot in a commercial, his father said, in one way or another, "No way in hell."

When my grandfather saved enough money from his job at Hughes Aircraft Company, he bought the family a 1947 gray Buick Super and they moved over the hills to one of the new suburbs rising up all over the San Fernando Valley. My dad and uncle shared a room in a little wood-sided ranch house with a front lawn and a split-rail fence—the first land the family had owned, as far as they knew. The boys found high adventure exploring the swath of condemned homes—less than twenty years old—where crews were building the new Ventura Freeway. The Valley was the very epicenter of America's new suburbia, exploding out of a patchwork of dust-blown agricultural towns. Between 1945 and 1960, the population rose from 230,000 to 840,500. Forty-five percent of families there had two cars by 1959, according to the historian Kevin Starr, and in the next two years, "permits were issued for six thousand residential swimming pools."

I suspect my dad's family felt a bit like interlopers. They knew their neighbors but didn't have a wide group of friends or any extended family. I think a little dysfunction drifted along with them from a harder past. My dad never liked to talk about such things, but he'd offer glimpses: the time his mom waxed all the windows, then lost interest before cleaning the wax off and kept all the curtains closed for a year. He claimed they ate hamburgers nearly every night for a good portion of his childhood. These weren't the ways of a sociable lot.

My mom's side was different. Her parents had big families and circles of friends with deep roots to their old countries: France, and Sweden via Minnesota. Her grandparents were immigrants, and their late nine-teenth-century crossing of the Atlantic served as a baseplate of their family history. My grandmother Madeline and my great-aunt Louise grew up at the turn of the century on a rented bean farm in the hills southwest of Los Angeles. Their parents were southern French, and the community was rural and poor, with French, Basque, and Mexican farmers. Madeline and Louise spoke French and Spanish before they ever spoke English. Their mother, Amelie, was dark and homely, from a Basque family, and had worked as a maid before getting married to their father, Jean, who died when they were young. She bought a house in the fast-growing town of Inglewood in 1928. The grant deed from the J. D. Millar Realty Company stated on the first page, "Said premises shall not be leased, sold, conveyed or rented to or occupied by any person other than one of the Caucasian race." Apparently, brownish and Basque fit this designation well enough.

Inglewood had briefly become a hub for the Ku Klux Klan, which posted "Whites Only" signs all over downtown in the early 1920s and paraded at least once down Market Street in full white wizard regalia. Black people were migrating to Los Angeles from the South, but the Klan of that era focused their ire just as much on immigrants, Catholics, and bootleggers, which didn't make it resoundingly popular in that part of the county. In 1922, Klansmen raided the home of the Elduayer family, Basques from Spain, whom they alleged were bootleggers. The white knights got in a subsequent shoot-out with police. A grand jury indicted thirty-five of them, and the group was outlawed in the state.

My grandmother married the son of Swedish immigrants, Elmer Ternquist, who grew up in Minnesota and California's San Joaquin Valley. He attended UC Berkeley for a year, majoring in forestry, but had to drop out for lack of funds. He did some logging of redwoods on the North Coast, then got a job at Standard Oil in Los Angeles. During World War II, Elmer and Madeline bought a little bungalow in Inglewood, which was increasingly encroached upon by the ethnically diverse neighborhoods of South Los Angeles. My grandfather leased a Richfield gas station on Manchester and Normandie avenues, just east of their home, in an area then becoming predominantly black. By the time my mom was a teenager, racial tension was approaching the snapping point of the Watts riots in 1965.

With *Brown v. Board of Education* and a Supreme Court ruling that made racist real estate covenants unenforceable, Inglewood was the obvious next step for upwardly mobile African Americans looking for nicer neighborhoods. The whites scrambled to keep them back. Realtors refused to show them homes, and the schools would resist integration until the 1970s, well after it was rammed through in much of the South. The sense of the inevitable must have stoked the fierceness of their resistance in ways not felt in more distant suburbs. I can't say that alone pushed my grandparents to move to the working-class beach town of Oceanside in 1962, when my mom was seventeen. For years they had rented a clapboard cottage there in summer and had always dreamed of living there year-round and fishing on the beach in the early mornings. But I can only imagine that in the mind-set of white America at the time, they foresaw their neighborhood going to hell.

For a time, you could always move somewhere newer in California. My parents met at UCLA and were the first in their families to graduate from college. My dad got his dental degree, after which they moved to Tustin, in the southern suburbs of Orange County, where my brother and I were born. We were surrounded by orange groves and could smell the dry sage of the mountains when the Santa Ana winds funneled through the canyons in fall. We could watch the summer fireworks burst over Disneyland seven miles away from the cool surface of my friend Erik's brick front porch.

When I was four, we moved even farther south, to a shinier place. Dana Point was a town first conceived in 1926 by Los Angeles's oligarchs. The group had just launched a Mediterranean-themed development in the Hollywood Hills, with fifty-foot letters above Beachwood Canyon that would come to be recognized around the world as the Hollywood sign. They now formed the Dana Point Syndicate and ran innumerable ads: "The New Recreational City on California's sunny south coast, midway between Los Angeles and San Diego. . . . See the Golden Beauty of the South Coast at Autumn Times. When we say the delightful, ALL-YEAR-ROUND Climate of Dana Point, we mean just that. Golden Autumn Days . . . Mild, Mellow Winter Times . . . Gentle Smiling Spring . . . Refreshing, Exhilarating Summer." This ad had the gumption to tell readers in Los Angeles that the climate just sixty miles south was more blessed than theirs, that the very light had a different cast. But I would have been sold. The illustration was idyllic: a young family standing next to their new Ford Model A on a bluff overlooking the sea, the man wearing a suit, the woman in a fur stole and a cloche hat. With their backs to the continent, they watched the sun set over the sheltered waters of Dana Cove—a vision of absolution, the dark damp past behind them.

The developer sought to invent a past with a "hacienda-style plaza" and adobe walls. The streets were lit by wrought-iron ship lanterns with glass of different colors, which were said to evoke an era when ships pulling into the harbor used such illumination to signal their fares.

The realization of this vision of Dana Point sputtered to a halt in the Depression. For decades, the development amounted to a square mile of paved streets and weedy vacant lots, with a couple dozen homes scattered about. Basque shepherds roamed the hills beyond, and tenant farmers grew dry crops of barley, sugar beets, and lima beans in the valleys. Lobster and abalone fishermen lived in a squatters' camp of tar-paper shacks in the cove. The neglected bit of coast still remained a scruffy vestige of the frontier.

By the time we arrived in the 1970s, scrapers and bulldozers were just getting a new bite into the clay earth. The development boom had reared up, and the shepherds and tenants and coastal squatters had cleared out. The quaint old Spanish homes of Lantern Village quickly found themselves in the shadows of cheap stucco apartment buildings, favored by people who actually spoke Spanish. The plaza became a glorified strip mall, with Vic's Market, Raymar Cleaners, and a Christian Science reading room. The copper lanterns had mostly vanished, used as scrap metal during World War II. And new subdivisions, without the charm and vision of the original, mushroomed up all over.

We moved to a master-planned community that sat on the undefined edge of Dana Point and another town, conjured in a boardroom in the 1960s, named Laguna Niguel, supposedly after an Indian village that had vanished in the Spanish era. The developer had a document printed in grandiose calligraphy: "Chain of Title from the King of Spain to Laguna Niguel Corporation." Our house was an eighteen-hundred square-foot, Brady Bunch–style ranch near the highway. It had rust-colored carpet, avocado tile, a wet bar with reflective wallpaper, and a bidet in the master bathroom that my brother and I liked to turn on and watch spray the ceiling. My parents owned the house but leased the land from the developer, AVCO, which made the deal more affordable, though not a particularly sound investment. They had to be interviewed by the Monarch Bay Association before they could buy, which undoubtedly was the developer's way of keeping out blacks, Jews, Asians, and whoever they saw as Mexican ever since the Supreme Court outlawed redlining the old-fashioned way. The association probably just wanted to get a look at my parents, what with a name like Mozingo.

The area was still mostly undeveloped but changing fast. The janitor at my elementary school had to check for rattlesnakes under the bushes every morning. Pets regularly disappeared to the coyotes and mountain lions that still roamed the hills. Cattle grazed along the roads, and tumbleweeds bounced across the parkway and blocked the automatic sliding glass doors of the new Alpha Beta supermarket.

We settled into a life that, on the surface, wasn't too far off from those old ads. Freckles expanded out from my nose every summer and retreated in winter, and my bottom lip was constantly split from the sun. I had towhead blond hair in a 1970s bowl cut with a tenacious cowlick no amount of spit could keep down. One day not long after we arrived, my mom dragged me down the street, round the corner, and over three speed bumps to meet another freckled little boy, Richard Fox. His mom answered the door and talked to my mom, and he peeked out from behind a sliding door.

"I've got homework," said Richard, age four.

"You do not have homework," his mom said.

We became best friends. We shot BB guns in the drainage easement next to my house, launched off speed bumps on skateboards, built a motorless go-cart with no brakes, rode our dirt bikes in the vacant lots and empty hills, played soccer and baseball.

I could be an introverted kid, and I also spent lots of time alone in the wild triangle of my back-backyard that we called "the Way Back." It was a castoff part of our wedge-shaped property, below street level, surrounded by oleanders and an overgrown bougainvillea. One day I dragged some splintery, dirt-coated boards from the drainage easement that I'd been pondering for months, wondering if the cowboys, or the Spanish, had left them there. The two planks were about as tall as I was, connected by one bolt in the center. They swiveled like scissors, chafing soft splinters, and had two rusted caster wheels attached to the bottom. I painted part of this contraption blue when my dad gave me some paint. I thought I could make it into a land cruiser, like Luke Skywalker's, and glide around the neighborhood amazing my friends.

The Way Back was my domain of escape. No doors opened directly to it, and my mom usually just called out through the louvered window of her closet to tell me to come inside for dinner. This was where I jetted off to the moment I got off the school bus to work on whatever project my imagination conjured. I stayed out there as late as I could, but an eeriness always set in about an hour before sunset, and there was always a feeling I shouldn't dwell there too long.

When I was eleven, I found a less solitary refuge in surfing, the dominant lifestyle on the coast since the 1960s, the Beach Boys, Jan and Dean, and all that hype. There was no way to avoid it, and I didn't try to. Once I got the knack of it—no easy feat—I found that gliding down the face of a wave, trying to duck in and out of its watery throat, was pure reckless joy. I never had a stray thought or outside worry riding a wave, and as I grew older I appreciated the invigorating elements of the Pacific in fall and winter—the frigid water trying to drown you, the wind, the rain, the freezing headaches, the slogging paddle through oncoming waves and entangling kelp. The battle against the cold washed away any psychic dreariness settling down on late adolescence. And in high school, surfing offered a ready-made package as I hashed out an identity. It had its own fashion and pidgin language. "Tzuupbra? . . . Bro, it's toadly blown, victry at sea. . . . Ded, tsoff the rick!" (In college, a phonologist who had never heard the high nasal accent of this dialect wanted to study my voice.) Surfing presented an entire self-contained society. "An esoteric statusphere" is what Tom Wolfe called it in *The Pump House Gang*, all very white, exclusive, and snotty, in retrospect. We called people who lived five miles inland "quebs."

In this place where new cities and cultures and pastimes just boiled up, your narrative felt like it was yours alone. There was no sense of a longer one, threading through generations, whose struggles, secrets, failures, ambitions, and dreams propelled the epic to your moment on stage.

But there was this name everyone kept asking about. Mo-ZEENG-go. No corporate committee at AVCO invented that. It did *sound* kind of Italian.

Then one day my dad came home with news that he'd had lunch with an attorney near his office named Glen Mozingo. We all talked it over at dinner. I was about twelve and couldn't believe there was another Mozingo in town. I thought we were a lone tribe. What did he know about our history?

"He said he was down in Calexico and the phone book was filled with Mozingos," my dad told us. I knew vaguely of Calexico, sitting on the California side of the Mexican border, with a twin on the other side called Mexicali. "They're all Basque sheepherders apparently."

Sheepherders, I thought, stricken. It sounded so Old World.

I never questioned the underpinnings of the story. Did the white pages list a *Tomas Mozingo, shepherd, Basque*? Or was this discovered in the yellow pages section between "Shelving" and "Shingles": *Sheepherding, Mozingo*? It didn't matter. We'd heard the Basque country as a possible origin once before, vaguely connected to a rumor espoused by my dad's mom that the name arose from Mont Zingeau, a French or Swiss mountain so discreet as not to be found on any map. And we knew my mom's side had lots of Basque, so it was no big leap. My dad was even writing a novel set in the Basque country.

So we were Basque, not Italian. That easy.

But in the ensuing Basque phase, I never really felt Basque. Italian was already imprinted on my psyche in that nebulous way you can associate a feeling with a single word. I had flashes of understanding of what being Italian meant, mainly based on one of my baseball coaches, Joe Sarlo, who was stocky and tan, with a Brooklyn accent and wavy silver hair combed back in a fifties kind of way. People's names were our only reference points in Orange County. History just had no other hold. Richard Fox was German Jewish on one side and Irish Catholic on the other. His grandmother escaped Hitler's Germany before the Holocaust. Yet I knew none of this growing up. The only obvious vestige of his ancestry came on Sunday, when his dad dragged him to church. My other best friend, Erik Hilde, had Mexican ancestry on one side and Norwegian on the other. His great-grandparents came to southern California during the Mexican Revolution. Yet he didn't think of himself as Latino, or Scandinavian. He was just from Tustin.

This vacuum of history left me subconsciously groping around for a connection to the past, which I realized only later. The destruction of the natural landscape where I grew up initially fixed my focus on the history of where I lived more than on my family origins. My childhood attachments to cattle ranches and orange groves and hawks circling in the canyons felt like fading dreams of some deep truth.

I began to seek out old photos of the area and studied them. I read accounts of the old ranchers and drew pictures of an abandoned train station near my house. When I visited my great-aunt Louise in Oceanside, I'd ask her about growing up with Grandma on their bean farm. She told me that all the famous boulevards—Santa Monica, Wilshire, Pico—were just rutted dirt roads back then, cutting through bean fields, citrus groves, and truck farms. She told me that hemp grew on the empty hillsides, and when the horses ate it, they went crazy. The people called it "locoweed." She still spoke fluent Spanish and French.

I read and reread *Two Years Before the Mast* by Richard Henry Dana, who sailed the California coast on a Boston brig trading cattle hides when the area was still a Mexican territory, about sixty years before my grandmother's parents got there. The hides from this desolate coast supplied the Yankee leather industry on the other side of the continent. Dana's ship, the *Pilgrim*, anchored one spring day in 1838 in the lee of the point that was later named after him. His account was enrapturing: sperm whales breaching in the channel, surf crashing against "grand and broken" rocks. "The only habitation in sight was the small white mission of San Juan Capistrano, with a few Indian huts about it, standing in a small hollow, about a mile from where we stood. . . . There was a grandeur in everything around, which gave a solemnity to the scene, a silence and solitariness which affected every part. Not a human being but ourselves for miles, and no sound heard but the pulsations of the great Pacific."

I hiked out on that perch, now above a sheltered harbor with a replica of the *Pilgrim* at dock. Looking out over the water gave me the sensation of a new dimension opening up, the past suddenly visible, just inches out of reach. The feeling of connectedness to nature and time was a euphoria I had never felt.

This obsession with history stayed with me through college in San Diego. I studied biology and shared a house with nine guys, mostly surfers, who became close friends. Toward the end of high school, I had taken up oil painting, and in college I did more of it, starting to think it might be my calling. This created a relentless tension with my studies and a constant struggle in my mind over whether I would pursue a responsible career like medicine, or take a risk and be an artist. I reveled in moments alone now, hiking in the chaparral, mountain biking in a nearby canyon, surfing during bad weather when no one else was out. Sometimes I felt isolated, but at other times a sharp sense of harmonic convergence with the outside world overcame me. It was bliss.

Those moments fed the artist in me. But by the time I graduated with a pre-med degree in biology, I had doubts about my painting abilities, though I was still desperate to have a career with a creative core to it. Throughout my childhood, my dad had made it quite clear that he felt stifled with dentistry, and he took any chance he could to hole up in his back office and work on his novel. I didn't want a job where I always felt torn from what I really wanted to be doing. But what was that?

I considered every imaginable career option. To stall and make a living, I got a job laying tile in custom homes. The physical work—dragging fifty-pound buckets of cement in each hand up the stairs over and over—kept my mind away from my increasingly regurgitated and depressed thoughts. I loved the work, but soon the tedium gnawed at me. What's more, a quietly ambitious upstart named Rufino, recently arrived from Oaxaca, began outpacing me. The way things were headed I was soon going to be the college-educated underling of an illegal immigrant who started with nothing in life. I woke up with a shudder one night, having dreamed I was at a local pub with friends, and grabbing a nacho, suddenly realized it was a shard of paver tile, dipped in grout.

The downward pressure on my ego caused it to bulge out in strange places. I started writing a novel with no plot or point or characters, except for a deity worshipped by the Indians of San Juan Capistrano named Chinigchinich. At the time, I suspected this might be the beginnings of a masterpiece of some sort, while today I can only pray that the hard drive of that computer was put through a wood chipper.

If I wanted to write, I needed to learn the craft and for God's sake find subjects outside of my own head to write about. Journalism had bumped around my mind for a few years. My mom had been a reporter for a spell, and she and my dad nudged me with "Hemingway started out as a journalist." It suddenly clicked that this was what I would do. I launched into grad school in journalism as if I had leapt for the landing skids of the last helicopter off the embassy roof in Saigon.

On the first day of grad school in Los Angeles, I found myself, remarkably, in the office of a broadcast journalism professor named Sherrie Mazingo. She was short and gruff and black, with a low nasal voice, a great cackle, and an unnerving way of pausing for extended periods of time in conversation. She said her name was a variation of ours. "I went to a family reunion in North Carolina and I met this woman named Melicent Remy, who'd done all this research on the family name. You need to talk to Melicent. She said we all descend from a man named Edward Mozingo, who was living in Virginia in the 1600s. He was black."

"Hmm," I said, in the high arching tone in which you might say, "I'll be damned." My language skills had deteriorated sharply during my tile years, and I had developed anxiety about speaking not just in public, but in any circumstance where being intelligible was reasonably expected. With these journalism professors, who knew big shots like Dan Rather, I was a virtual mute.

She continued. "She said he was a warrior from the Congo and that our name is Bantu."

This came so out of nowhere I struggled to find an appropriate response. "We always heard it was Basque," I managed.

She shrugged, bored with me no doubt, and looked to someone waiting outside her office. "Well, there you go."

I called my parents to tell them to prepare for the Bantu phase. They laughed, dutifully noting, "Grandma Helen would roll over in her grave." The news jogged a memory from my dad: soon after he opened his dental practice in Tustin with a friend named Tony Mumolo from UCLA, a black woman was waiting at the counter of Mumolo & Mozingo, DDS, when my dad came out of the operatory. "He's the dentist?" she asked angrily, and stormed out. "What was that about?" my dad asked the receptionist. Colleagues took to calling them "the witch doctors."

The Bantu news felt like a lark, too strange and lacking in context to take seriously.

At the time, I had been living for a couple weeks with my uncle Joe at the old home in the Valley he'd inherited. My uncle was a leisurely man of more than leisurely girth, who was as unbothered and genial as anyone I knew. He was a manager in the City of Los Angeles information technology department. He'd bought a giant RV and parked it in his backyard, ceding the stale-smelling house to his two springer spaniels and his ever-growing piles of impulse buys: coffeepots, steam irons, Montblanc pens, travel kennels, binoculars, badminton rackets, exercise equipment, camera lenses, socket wrench sets. We ate dinner every night in that immaculately clean, air-conditioned RV. One night before I retired to the stuffy hoarder's cave that was once our family's mark of having made it in America, I told him about the man in Virginia and our Bantu roots. He embraced the story and the next day would tell his two black secretaries that he was descended from an African warrior.

"You know," he said, "Dad always said the Mozingos came from Virginia back in colonial times."

I had never heard this and hadn't thought any lore had passed down about our ancestry. Maybe Sherrie was right. Why couldn't we have a black ancestor? Ten or so generations had passed since then.

One day, I grabbed a pen and a pad of paper and calculated the number of direct ancestors I had ten generations back—multiplying two and two, ten times over—to be 1,024. So one of them was black, big deal. Based on photos of my mom's brown relatives in once-Moorish southern France, we had certainly gotten a much healthier dose of African blood from them.

But over the next year or two, this Bantu thing began to take root in my imagination. An African name had survived the entire span of American history—and I had it?

Sherrie gave me copies of some papers she got from Cousin Melicent, who had indeed done vast research tracing Mozingos back to this Edward. Sherrie's line had moved to North Carolina by the early 1800s and was one of several that stayed on the black side of the color line.

I started poking around on the fledgling Internet, visited the Mormon family history center in Westwood, and holed up with the homeless people sleeping in the genealogy department of the Los Angeles Central Library. I looked through book after book documenting the passenger lists of ships arriving in America, and at census, tax, and court records.

A reference librarian handed me the *Minutes of the Council and General Court of Colonial Virginia*. The book was seventy-two years old, with a grimy canvas binder, faded olive cover, and brittle pages the color of weak tea. I opened it delicately, but even so, each turn set off a flurry of paper flakes. On page 316 I found the heading "Mozingo's ordr for freedom."

Whereas it Appeareth by divers Witnesses that had been Sworne
and Examined that Edward Mozingo A Negro man had been and
was An Apprentice by Indenture to Coll Jno Walker and that by
Computation of his terme of Servitude for Twenty Eight year's
is now Expired, the Court after a full heareing of the Matter In
difference Betweene the Said Edw: Mozingo and Doctor Stone who
married Coll Walker's Widdow, It is Adjudged by this Court that the
said Edw: Mozingo be and Remayne free to all Intents and purposes
by order of This Court.

I grasped the back of my head and leaned back. Reading the name
Mozingo on those old pages gave me that same feeling of a new dimension opening up. First, somewhat inanely, it shocked me simply that
there were Mozingos so far back, that we didn't arise from spontaneous
generation on a petri dish at the turn of the century. Then the real shot
of awe: we really might have come from Africa, not sixty thousand years
ago, like everyone on the planet, but with this very man fighting for his
freedom in a Virginia court.

Over the next few months, I read as much as I could about the
first Africans in Virginia and learned that though they left Africa as
slaves they did not always remain slaves in the Chesapeake. Some were
indentured servants who got their freedom and even married and had
children with poor whites. I had so many more questions but had to
let them go. I was finishing school and needed to get my career going.
I couldn't keep indulging my imagination, even though that's what I
really wanted to do.

I started working at the Los Angeles Times, then moved to Florida to
work for the Miami Herald. Little moments kept my curiosity about our
name smoldering. White people who commented about it assumed it
was Italian. Black people tended not to volunteer opinions, until I went
to Haiti to cover one of its perennial rounds of instability in 2004. In
that country, with its tenacious African customs and language, I got an
invariable response when I introduced myself: "That's an African name."

Then one day, snooping around online, I came across an interesting
article in Wired magazine that featured two cousins, Reese and Thomas
Mozingo, who were using DNA to solve the riddle of their ancestry. The

writer interviewed them in Tennessee at a conference about preserving the heritage of the Melungeons, a dark-skinned group of mysterious origin who had settled in the isolated hollows around the Cumberland Gap. Reese and Tom had gone there to see if Mozingos were among them.

Reese struck quite a figure in the photo, built like a pickle barrel with a huge gray beard and suspenders over a flannel shirt. He was from Fayetteville, North Carolina, and if you were going to learn the secret of your own past, he seemed the perfect man to deliver it, perhaps stumbling down from a mountain cave with it seared onto an animal hide.

The pair told the writer that all Mozingos in America descended from Edward, who may have been a "Native American, Italian, or Negro."

"Wouldn't you love to find the Mozingo fiddle?" Thomas asked Reese. "God, I'd love to find that fiddle."

They said they had submitted their DNA for analysis to find out once and for all if they descended from Edward, and had received the results, but needed more "conclusive evidence" before they shared them publicly.

By this time I'd met my future wife, Noaki, who was mixed race, her mom born in Japan, her dad in Ohio of German Jewish and Irish stock. When we had our son, Blake, in 2006, we moved back to California to be near our families. Blake took much coaxing to get to sleep, and I began making up nonsensical songs and phrases as I rocked him. Sometimes, around when he was learning to talk, I would regale him with the most nonsensical word I knew: Mo-ZEENG-oe. He would laugh at that fly-away ZEENG, and sing it back to me. I pictured it ricocheting around the room, like a trapped bat trying to get out a window. As the chair creaked on the floorboards, I would think about the children he would have, and their children, and so on, until I faded from memory, and then Blake did, and all that would be left was this funny name that came with no family history, that no one knew how we got. I couldn't leave the mystery to my descendants.

Chapter 3

Middle Passage to Jamestown

The natural starting point to unearth my roots was Reese Mozingo, who had already done so much research on his own similar quest. He knew what his DNA had revealed, and his interest in connecting himself to the mixed-race Melungeons suggested his mind was open, even if he felt he had to protect others from what he found. I wanted to hear more about that fiddle. But a quick search online ruled him out: he had been shot to death in 2003 by his wife in a domestic dispute; no charges were filed against her, if that says anything about him. So went my hope in the bearded oracle from Fayetteville.

I located his distant cousin mentioned in the article, Tom Mozingo, a retired nuclear power plant operator living in Florida, who responded quickly to my email. "I have been researching the Mozingo surname for approximately 40 years," he began. All lines went back to Virginia, and Mozingos had fought in all of our wars. He asked me who my grandfather was so that he could find out what line I came from; I suspect he was also testing my legitimacy as a member of the tribe. He continued, "I wear the name, as do you, as many of our cousins also do, as our children and grandchildren do; these cousins and their families are now truly part of my extended family, and I respect their right to privacy; and since you work for a very large newspaper company, I am going to be cautious and try to balance the information I provide to you with the promises I have given to my extended 'families' concerning their right to privacy. I will promise you total honesty and if I cannot divulge something, I will tell you so. I hope you are not offended by my caution."

This was intriguingly strange.

He referred me to Samie Melton in Dallas, a Mozingo by marriage and the keeper of a Mozingo database. "Samie and I work closely together and she shares my 'Mozingo' obsession and concerns," Tom wrote.

Concerns? I imagined a cabal of gray-bearded southern gentlemen wearing purple robes and miter hats sitting me down to explain in sepulchral voices why the three-hundred-year-old secret must be kept. "We all wear the name, son, as do our children, and *your* children."

I emailed Samie the name of my grandfather and his hometown, and she responded with a list of names asking if it was the right one. Grandpa Joe and Grandma Helen appeared at the bottom; what once would have taken decades to research took only a few minutes on the Internet.

There was my line, right back to revolutionary Virginia. How had I never seen this? Only six generations separated me from my oldest documented ancestor, Spencer Mozingo, who headed a household in Orange, Virginia, in 1782. Samie said no one had found the records showing his exact connection to Edward, but he was assumed to be a great-grandson. She explained that most, maybe 90 percent, of the several thousand Mozingos alive in America today have been traced directly to Edward. The others could be traced to areas of Virginia where Edward's offspring settled, and they were naturally presumed to be descendants too. (Vast troves of records were lost when mobs and soldiers burned courthouses across the South during the Civil War.) No one had found evidence of other Mozingos arriving in America during the seventeenth, eighteenth, or nineteenth century.

From Spencer onward, my line was clearly documented: he begat Joseph, who begat Joseph, who begat Joseph, who begat Ira, who begat Joseph, who begat Dave, who begat me, another Joseph. Six people between me and the American Revolution. With brothers included, every generation had a Joseph. I looked at the list in silence, trying to grasp how that vast gulf of time encompassed so few lives.

Samie referred me to the database she had set up, and I started clicking madly through it, looking for relatives, making note of where each of my ancestors was born, when and where they died. The family seemed to have followed the receding frontier, from Virginia to Kentucky to Indiana to Illinois, the same route Abraham Lincoln's family took.

Spencer was listed as white in the census of 1782 and had four sons and two daughters. There was no indication of who Spencer's parents or wife were. The family had moved to Kentucky by 1808. Spencer showed up as a "poor person" in the care of a neighbor in 1827, then dying in poverty four years later, even as his sons Joseph and James still lived and owned land in the area. Joseph, my great-great-great-great-grandfather, even owned a slave, a female between age ten and twenty-four.

But where had Spencer been born? Was he really considered white by his contemporaries, or just white enough to persuade the census man? How was he related to Edward?

I had to learn more of Spencer's story, and I had to find his link to our enigmatic forebear freed in Jamestown. I needed to understand how Edward could sue for and win his freedom, and when his descendants crossed the color line. I'd have to go to Virginia to see what I could find.

Governor William Berkeley, a friend of the late, beheaded King Charles I, presided in court on that Saturday afternoon, October 5, 1672, in the new brick statehouse on the James River. Edward's master, Colonel John Walker, had died, and Edward had sued for his freedom from Walker's widow and her new husband, a big landowner named John Stone. The panel of judges listened to "divers Witnesses" and rendered their decision. The clerk dutifully recorded it in his big-looped court hand: "It is Adjudged by this Court that the said Edw. Mozingo be and remayne free to all Intents and purposes by order of This Court."

A man of African descent had won a lawsuit against a powerful member of the white gentry.

The clerk's notation that "his terme of Servitude for Twenty Eight year's is now Expired" suggested that Edward had a definitive agreement with Walker, who had served on the court and known its members.

Some of the witnesses must have testified to such. Perhaps they were friends of Walker who came to know and like Edward. No doubt they included Walker's daughters by his earlier marriage. Within a month of losing the case, Walker's widow, Sarah, rescinded the will that gave the daughters a substantial inheritance, including "certaine young Negroes." "I am for my good will and affection to them condemned and despised and rewarded with contumelious words and opprobrious actions," she wrote, "and my loving [new] husband John Stone molested by litigious lawsuits and daily threatened by more suits."

The politics and deliberations of the judging panel have been lost to time.

Edward Mozingo first set foot on the piney, white-clay banks of the James River when the settlement of Jamestown, founded less than forty years before, was still only a rugged outpost of the nascent British Empire. Initially the local natives, loosely banded together under the Powhatan Confederacy, had hoped to barter for guns and ammunition from the visitors to conquer enemy tribes and subdue rebel vassals. Before long, however, they realized that the English posed the more insidious threat. The English coerced them for corn, encroached on their gaming areas, raided their gardens, and swindled them out of their land. The tension between the two groups periodically ratcheted up into horrible violence. The very year of Edward's arrival, a guerrilla campaign led by the aged warrior King Opechancanough left five hundred settlers dead, a twelfth of the colony's population.

Christians had long salved their conscience over the slave trade with the balm of belief that the Africans were being released from the evils of a savage land and delivered to a civilized, God-fearing society. But it's hard to overstate the brutality and misery of the Virginia colony. The first settlers had landed in the Chesapeake in April 1607, a motley mix of marginal aristocrats, cashiered officers, adventurers, losers, and laborers looking for fortune. They had squabbled across the Atlantic, with one of the leaders, Captain John Smith, under arrest, having been spared the gallows at an island stop in the Caribbean. In Virginia they were attacked by Indians at Cape Henry the day they landed, escaping with two men wounded. They spent two weeks surveying the vast tidal basin at the mouth of the James River, then decided to settle upriver on a low island connected to the mainland by a narrow neck of sand. They set up rough shelters and tents while Captain Christopher Newport and some men continued exploring. They first met friendly natives eager to trade, but within days some two hundred warriors stormed through the settlement at night, shooting their arrows through the tents. The ship's cannon scared the Indians away, but only after two Englishmen were killed and ten wounded. After that, the settlers hastily built a triangular palisade, eight feet high, of logs stuck vertically in the ground. But they feared another enemy who could blow through those logs with ease: the Spanish fleet. They had picked the island, in part, because it sat on a sharp elbow of the river with a good view downstream. Spain and England were at a tense peace after years of wars on the sea, but Spanish warships could snuff them out in a blink, as they had a budding French colony in Florida in 1565.

By the time England decided to build colonies, Spain had already constructed an empire, extracting vast wealth out of Mexico and South America. King Philip III got more personal profit out of the Americas alone every year than twice the entire annual income of England's King James I. But after failing to install a Jesuit colony in the Chesapeake, very near the spot where Jamestown would sit, Spain had lost interest in the east coast of North America above its backwater post in San Agustin, Florida. England, with a rising merchant class eager for trade, slipped into the breach, sending its colonists to the territory christened Virginia, after the Virgin Queen. The settlement was mainly a commercial venture, conceived by the newly chartered Virginia Company of London to look for precious metals and a passage to the East Indies. The company picked a seven-man council to govern the colony and hoped to exploit the native kingdom that the earlier Roanoke colonists had reported on Chesapeake Bay, in the way the Spaniards had usurped the natives in Mexico and Peru. Unfortunately, the locals knew nothing about gold or silver. The preacher William Symonds, a Virginia booster back in England, lamented that the indigenes were not nearly as useful as the ones the Spanish had subjugated. They were an "idle, improvident, scattered people, ignorant of the knowledge of gold and silver; and careless of anything but from hand to mouth, but for baubles of no worth." The colonists, however, were greatly impressed with the fertility of the land, or at least wanted to convey to investors that they were. Colonist George Percy wrote that vines grew "as big as a man's thigh" and "goodly and fruitful trees and . . . strawberries, mulberries, raspberries . . . a great store of deer . . . bears, foxes, otters, beavers, muskrats and wild beasts unknown." The Spanish were going to be jealous, he surmised, when they saw this river England had found, where ships of "great burden may harbor in safety."

They were starving by August.

"The sixth of August there died John Asbie of the bloody flux," Percy wrote. "The ninth day died George Flowre of the swelling. The tenth day died William Bruster, Gentleman, of a wound given by the Savages. . . . The fourteenth day, Jerome Alikock Ancient, died of a wound, the same day Francis Midwinter, Edward Morris Corporall died suddenly. The fifteenth day, there died Edward Browbe and Stephen Galthrope. The sixteenth day there died Thomas Gower, Gentleman. The seventeenth day died Thomas Mounslic."

The men perished of inflammations, bloody dysentery, burning fevers, and Indian attack, "but for the most part they died of mere famine": "Our food was but a small can of barley soaked in water to five men a day." They drank from the river, which, being tidal, was salty at high tide and "full of slime and filth" at low tide, the "destruction of many of our men." Of the 104 who stayed on when the supply ship left, twenty-one died that same month.

Emaciated, weak, sick, and hunger-addled, some survivors fled into the wilderness to join the natives. The others turned against each other, with different factions scheming to take over the council and rumors running rampant that there was a spy among them. Suspicions first turned to a member of the council, George Kendall, then to the council president, Edward Maria Wingfield. Both were confined to the ship, which was found shortly thereafter marooned on a sandbank upstream. Kendall was accused of trying to hijack the vessel and sail to Spain and tell King Philip "all about this country and many plans of the English which he knew." He was condemned to death for treason and executed by gunfire.

That first fall, Captain John Smith set off on the James River in a small open boat, hoping to secure food from the natives and learn of rumored mines in distant mountains. When locals did not run to the boat with food in hand, he shot at them to demonstrate the power of his weaponry. Tribes began trading him corn for beads and copper—peacefully, according to his account, which is the only account to survive. He certainly might have just been pillaging the Indians' fields or pointing guns at them as his soldiers hauled away their crops. Throughout the fall, he made his way up the labyrinthine tidal inlets and bays, showing force and procuring corn. Then one day in December he paddled up the Chickahominy River, thinking it might lead to the Pacific (though it peters out less than forty miles from Chesapeake Bay), and was set upon by the warriors of the Pamunkey tribe and its warrior king, Opechancanough. In Smith's telling, the natives delivered him to the king's older brother, Emperor Powhatan, encamped on the Rappahannock River, where the Englishman was treated like a prince until the moment he was to be brained by a large stone. The emperor's beautiful young daughter Pocahontas intervened to spare him, and he returned to Jamestown, claiming to have a new understanding of the Indians' scheming ways. His return was greeted with great suspicion, but he emerged as the effective leader of the colony.

The bit of the story that never made it into American lore is the case of George Casson. Before Smith was captured, as he was making his way up the Chickahominy, the captain feared running the boat onto a shoal, knowing his detractors would use any such misstep against him. So he decided to anchor it near an Indian village and leave Casson to watch over it while he hired a canoe with two Indians to row upriver with two other crew members.

Soon Casson ventured off the boat, or was lured off, and the Indians seized him. He was taken to Opechancanough's camp, where one of the runaway colonists, William White, was living among the natives. Casson had evoked a fury among his captors that has led to later speculation he may have tried to rape one of the women before he was caught. Using White to interpret, the king began to interrogate the captive. The king knew an English captain was still bumbling through the forest, scattering bird and game, and that this same man had conducted raids for food up this river before. Casson refused to answer the questions about the captain's intentions, and begged for mercy.

The Indians calmly stripped Casson naked and stood him before the fire. They bound his wrists and ankles to two stakes in the ground on each side of him. A man approached bearing mussel shells and reeds. Using the shells as blades, he began to cut into the flesh around Casson's joints, then used the reeds to saw through the sinew, until each tendon popped and his limbs were removed and thrown on the fire. A gathering of men, women, and children watched.

Casson lived long enough to see much of his own dismemberment, writhing on the ground as much as a torso and head could. Then the executioner cut a line around Casson's neck and eased a shell under the skin and worked it around until the entire scalp and face peeled off cleanly, leaving the eyes. Then he slit open the belly of the faceless slab and extracted his stomach and intestines.

White was forced to watch this and return to the colony to relay what happened. Smith wrote about it in his autobiography, as did the colony's secretary and White himself. We might assume the English exaggerated the savagery. Accounts of Virginia vacillated between two extremes, idyll and dystopia, depending on whether the goal was to impress investors in London or keep the Spanish from swiping the colony like a gnat from its eye. In this case, one assumes the tellers just rendered the violence with a level of detail that they never used to describe their own savage acts: scalping, beheading, keelhauling, burning people at the stake, breaking them on wheels, nailing their ears to the floor, drawing-and-quartering them. There is a story of an English captain who cut open the belly of an insubordinate sailor, nailed the end of his intestines to a rail, and chased him with a flaming torch until all thirty or so feet of intestines unspooled on deck.

The seventeenth century was cruel wherever you were.

Prospects for the English began to look up briefly at the end of fall. Geese and duck and all manner of bird flying south for the winter filled the estuaries. Supplies and more settlers also arrived on the river, and Smith's meeting with Powhatan led to a fragile détente. The emperor even offered to adopt Smith as a son and make him a powerful member of his dominion. (Smith never recorded his response to this.) But he had no plans to let the English establish a permanent presence in his land unless they became his own subjects. What he most certainly coveted was their cannons and guns, which would give him absolute power. Historians suspect that while he pledged a wary acceptance of the English, he saw the threat they posed and played an artful role of gamesmanship in keeping them hungry, paranoid, and desperate for his help.

When the colonist Gabriel Archer returned to Jamestown in August 1609 after a year in England, he found the colony "in such distress" that many of the men had dispersed "in the savage's towns, living upon their alms for an ounce a day." The government ceased to function, as a new drought depleted food supplies and the infighting continued. In September, Smith got into a spat with a rival trying to build a fort thirty miles farther up the James River. His detractors accused him of having the Indians attack the fort. He lost the argument, and started back to Jamestown furious. As he slept on his boat, something or someone ignited his powder keg, tearing the "flesh from his body and thighs nine or ten inches square in a most pitiful manner." He leaped in the water to stop the burning and almost drowned. The wound was so grievous that it was rumored he had lost his genitals, and he ultimately returned to England for treatment, never to set foot in Virginia again.

With Smith gone, Powhatan saw a chance to smite the colony and had the tribes seal off the island, killing any livestock and settlers they came across on the periphery. Nearly a third of the settlers, about 130 people, were slain or fled into the wilds. The desperate new council president, George Percy, sent out two expeditions to trade for food with the Indians. One was lured into a massacre and its leader dismembered by mussel shell. The other crew managed to fill their boat with corn and escaped with the colony's best ship back to England. With no supply ship coming in the foreseeable future, the English faced another catastrophe.

The settlers ate corpses, horses, cats, dogs, snakes, mice, rats, roots, and toadstools. They boiled and ate their boots and shoes, and sucked the blood from the wounded. A gentleman named Henry Collins bludgeoned his pregnant wife, ripped their child from her womb, and threw it in the river, then chopped his betrothed into pieces, which he salted to preserve. This was not discovered, wrote Percy, "before he had eaten part thereof, for the which cruel and unhuman fact I adjudged him to be executed, the acknowledgment of the deed being enforced upon him by torture, having hung by the thumbs with weights at his feet for a quarter of an hour, before he would confess the same." Whether Collins himself was consumed thereafter is lost to history.

When two makeshift English vessels arrived in spring after being shipwrecked in Bermuda, only sixty settlers survived at Jamestown. Those who could get out of their beds ran out naked, crying, "We are starved!" The fort was in ruins, the palisades torn down, the church destroyed, houses dismantled for firewood.

Reinforcements came and rebuilt the fort, but the colony teetered on the brink of extinction, with the bulk of its inhabitants desperate to go home. Company leaders and boosters in London argued over what the objectives of the colony should be: Mine precious metals? Establish a base from which to attack the Spanish fleet? Convert the Indians to Protestant Christianity? Build a permanent settlement to ease unemployment in England and bring back commodities like silk, sassafras, hemp, timber, potash, fish, wine, fruits, and salt?

They sent new military leaders to wage war on the Indians, burning their crops and villages, killing men, women, and children, and instilling harsh discipline within the colony. Executions became common. Deserters were hanged, burned, or "broken at the wheel," a public spectacle in which the executioner would break the condemned person's limbs with an iron bar until they were as pliable as tentacles, and the gasping, dying man would be braided into the spokes of a wheel and propped upright for all to see. Men who stole from the store were hung from trees until they starved to death.

The English built new outposts up and down the James River in a show of strength, while Powhatan's dominion was weakening. The vassal tribes saw that the emperor failed to evict the interlopers, and now his people were suffering under the white men's attacks. The colonists had even kidnapped his favorite daughter, Pocahontas; for whatever reason, she agreed to marry John Rolfe, a settler whose wife had died shortly after arriving in the colony. Powhatan had little choice but to strike a peace deal, which he did in 1614, consummated by his daughter's wedding in Jamestown.

Rolfe had been experimenting with a Caribbean tobacco he would call "Oronoco," and other planters followed suit. In London, tobacco had become a mania, smoked in pinches in slim clay pipes. But the exotic leaf was expensive, coming via circuitous routes from Spanish America, and the English craved a direct supply. By about 1617 they had it, and the colony had finally found its gold. Settlers scrambled to plant enough of the sweet, luminous green leaf. But for this to pan out, the financially beleaguered Virginia Company needed more workers. Peace with the Indians opened a window to offer new land as an incentive. The company established the headright system, by which a planter would get fifty acres of land for any other person he paid to transport across the Atlantic. The newcomers would in turn work for the planter as indentured servants, from four to seven years, then be free to work as tenant farmers. If they managed their affairs well, they might eventually get their own servants and piece of land. But the company first had to fight the accurate perception that Virginia was a "slaughterhouse."

Of the fifteen hundred settlers who had landed in Virginia between 1609 and 1616, fewer than four hundred remained. In the next few years, three quarters of the indentured servants who came to the colony died within a year of their arrival. Only the lower class's grim lot in England, where periodic outbreaks of plague killed upwards of thirty thousand people at a time, kept them coming. The city of London even began rounding up hundreds of street children and forcibly shipping them to the colony.

Opechancanough took control of the Indian confederacy when Powhatan died and sought a more active friendship and reconciliation with the English. He agreed to the colonists' tribute payments of corn, conceding that his people were subjects of the English king. He sided with the colonists in a skirmish with the Chickahominy, accepted an invitation to visit Jamestown, and asked to be instructed in the Christian faith. The circles of English and Indian life increasingly intersected. The tribes whose land had been taken now had to rely on the colonists' provisions and moved about the English settlements, trading furs, deer, meat, and turkey. Some Indians even lived among the settlers.

On the clear, cool morning of March 22, 1622, Indians approached the settlements up and down the river with trade items. In gardens and on front doorsteps and market spots, they struck—slitting throats, clubbing in heads, hacking limbs, shooting arrows. They killed men, women, and children, burned all crops they could, and slaughtered all livestock they came across, the goal to mortally wound the colony, forcing the survivors to starve or leave. Over 340 settlers were killed, about a quarter of the total at the time, and the following winter twice as many died of starvation.

News of this massacre orchestrated by Opechancanough caused an outcry in England, with rage directed not just at the "savages" but at the drunken, indolent settlers who had ignored warnings of such an attack. The fiasco somehow sharpened the English resolve to see the colony succeed. More settlers arrived, along with hundreds of muskets, halberds, pistols, and suits of armor. The English king revoked the company's charter, and Virginia came under the direct authority of the Crown.

The English launched expeditions to kill Indians and burn their fields. The Indians retaliated, as more destitute Europeans streamed in, mostly to meet their demise. Yet by the sheer number of arrivals, success tilted toward the English, and the Indians backed into the margins.

As the colony grew, water remained its vasculature, allowing movement and trade in a nearly impenetrable wilderness and coursing with fish, shellfish, and waterfowl. Four great rivers sliced through the coastal plain, flowing sluggishly southeast: the James at the bottom, then the York, then the Rappahannock above that, and the Potomac at the top. All were navigable to the limestone shelf called the "fall line" and drained myriad tributaries that coiled through low clay hills and the ancient canopy of trees. By the 1630s, the English possessed all the lands along the James River and much of the York River, and were mounting in numbers to cross the Rappahannock into the Northern Neck. Nearly a hundred years old, Opechancanough staged one last-gasp attack, the siege of 1644, wiping out a twelfth of the colony's population. But he could not stop the flood of white people to come. The English quickly routed the Pamunkey and executed the old king, shooting him in the back while he sat in a cage. They coerced a peace treaty that cleared all the Indians out of the land between the James and York rivers in exchange for stopping the northward expansion, which they would quickly renege on.

Edward was probably between ten and fifteen years old when he arrived in the year of the attack or maybe before. That he kept his own name suggests he was old enough to assert himself and may have been Christian, for the English briefly afforded more rights to the converted. It was very rare for an African to retain his own name in the New World. Most were listed on arrival by a Spanish, Portuguese, or English first name, followed by the word "Negro" or the country of origin: "Antonio a negro . . . Angela a negro." And as they were sucked into the gathering stream of chattel slavery and became little more than property, they fell under their master's name.

Young Edward became a servant of Colonel John Walker, one of the "great planters" and a member of the colony's legislature. Walker lived in Warwick County, just downriver from Jamestown, near the open mouth of the Chesapeake Bay. The circumstances by which he bought Edward are a mystery.

Virginia planters were in dire need of labor at the time and taking anyone they could get. "Our principal wealth . . . consists of servants," wrote one English colonist. White indentured servants worked out the terms of their service with a broker or captain in England. At the end of their transatlantic voyage, they bathed, brushed their teeth, and combed the knots out of their hair and beards. The captain then paraded them on the docks at Jamestown to sell to the highest bidder. Potential buyers checked their teeth, made them walk and twirl and jump to see how healthy they were, and started haggling.

African slaves of this early era came through illicit channels, and the records of them are scarce. The settlers were supposed to get all goods and workers from the Crown, but the honeycomb of tidal inlets allowed for a vigorous untaxed trade between settlers and foreign sailors. Some slaves were brought by Dutch traders, particularly when Edward landed during the English Civil War, which constricted British trade on the high seas. At the same time, the expansionist Dutch had captured many of the Portuguese slaving forts in West and Central Africa, including Angola's, and the biggest sugar colony in Brazil. The Dutch West India Company sent at least twelve thousand African captives across the Atlantic in 1643 and 1644, and more shipments likely went unrecorded. They had delivered slaves to its northernmost colony on Manhattan Island, as well as to their colonies in South America and the Caribbean, and sold enough to the English planters in Barbados to ignite a "sugar revolution" there. The British themselves were just getting into the slave trade. We know that the English ship *Lucas* delivered 188 slaves from Old Calabar to Barbados in 1645, but it is not clear how many undocumented trips came before that.

Barbados became a conduit to the rest of the British colonies. Due to prevailing winds and currents, ships sailing from England often stopped on the island before proceeding to Jamestown, and some of the early slaves that trickled into the mainland came from there. Virginians also traveled to the Dutch island of Curaçao to trade at the slave market there. Fewer than three hundred blacks were in Virginia when Edward arrived there. By 1661, desperate to get more, the Virginia legislature reduced the export tax for any planter selling tobacco to the Dutch for "negro slaves."

So Edward could have come from Barbados or from the Dutch.

Another possibility centers around the namesake of the county Edward lived in, the second Earl of Warwick, Sir Robert Rich. The earl had inherited Britain's largest private fleet of ships from his father in 1619, making him one of the most powerful men in England. He was a member of the Virginia Company, heavily involved in the affairs of British colonies from the Caribbean to Massachusetts, and had acquired his own plantations throughout. He was a roguish sort, whose unscrupulous ways were often at odds with the Puritan cause he championed, and much of his wealth derived from robbing Spanish ships on the high seas. This had been illegal since Queen Elizabeth died in 1603. Her successor, King James, bowing to Spanish pressure, condemned piracy and even had Sir Walter Raleigh beheaded for it in 1618. Undeterred, Rich equipped at least two ships that very year to plunder Spanish galleons in the West Indies.

His captains set out to seize silver and gold, but often loaded up with African slaves. Rich had the captives distributed to his own tobacco plantations in Bermuda, Trinidad, and elsewhere, or sold to other planters in the colonies. The very first slaves to land in Virginia, "20 and odd negars" at Cape Comfort, as recorded by John Rolfe in 1619, were Angolans stolen from the Spanish in the waters off Mexico by Rich's ship the *Treasurer*, working in concert with another English vessel, the *White Lion*. Rich claimed these seizures amounted to legal "privateering" against a hostile nation. The problem was that King James's peace deal with Spain had technically ended the maritime war many years before. So Rich had to get commissions from principalities that were at war with Spain to have any type of legal protections; the *Treasurer* flew the flag of the Duke of Savoy in Italy, and the *White Lion* flew under the Dutch flag. Rich's many critics saw the practice as a loophole for piracy, and Virginia leaders feared he invited attack by the fearsome Spanish fleet. The governor of Jamestown complained to London that Rich's close friend, Captain Daniel Elfrith, was trying to make Virginia a base for raiding the Spanish Main.

But colonists began to see how those who got some of Rich's Angolan slaves were able to acquire larger and larger plantations. In one letter to Rich's cousin, a farmer in Bermuda complained that his neighbor, Captain Elfrith, was trying to procure more land than he could possibly cultivate based on the assumption that Rich would give him "his shares of negroes this next year, which perhaps is the reason the man would enlarge himself." Other planters bought the slaves with tobacco. A report from 1628 noted that another ship, the *Fortune*, had taken an "Angolan" vessel "with many negroes, which the captain bartered in Virginia for tobacco."

Rich chartered a new company in 1630 that set up Puritan colonies on the small island of Providence in the middle of the southern Caribbean and on Tortuga, off the north coast of Hispaniola. Both would become infamous in the annals of Caribbean piracy; the renegade residents of Tortuga, both English and French, cooked feral pigs and goats on grills called *boucans* and came to be called *boucaniers* by the French and *buccaneers* by the British. The Spanish ambassador in London vigorously complained of the plundering by Elfrith and Rich's other captains, but the king did not stop them. Providence in particular became a distribution point for Virginia and New England planters to buy slaves. In fact, by 1637 the Providence Island Company was becoming concerned that the number of slaves on the island endangered its existence. Many Africans had already escaped to the mountains, where they could plan an attack. The company ordered the governor to stop the purchase of slaves and to put some of the Africans already there on boats bound for London to be sold in Virginia and Bermuda on the way.

Rich's privateering reached its zenith when the parliamentarians took control of the Royal Navy during the English Civil War in 1642 and gave him command of the fleet. In one letter now held in the British Archives, he directed the captain of the *Elias*, a four-hundred-ton ship setting sail from England, not to attack any ship until he entered American or Caribbean waters—and then to have at it. Rich was to get a fifth of the proceeds of whatever loot they took, including slaves. "If you shall take any negroes by virtue of this commission, you may dispose them in some of the English plantations in the West Indies, taking care of my 5th part of them or the proceeds of them, which I specially desire may be set down at my island of Trinidad, if the same may be done without too much inconvenience to the voyage."

This was in June 1643. Within a year, Edward showed up in the employ of one of the most prominent men living in Warwick County, Colonel Walker, who represented its planters in the colonial House of Burgesses. Whether the English Earl of Warwick had any holdings or business dealings in his eponymous county is not clear. The records of Warwick County were burned in the American Civil War.

The 1640s saw a land grab that handed an elite few vast holdings along the watercourses, while pushing small planters into marginal areas next to hostile natives. While New England was populated by small farmers mostly trying to keep their families fed and clothed, Virginia had a cash crop in tobacco that bred more vigorous capitalism—and corruption. The governor granted vast amounts of land to friends and family, and an exclusive few were able to procure slaves. The planters inflated the number of servants they brought to the colony to get more land under the headright rules. The late historian of the American South Robert Spencer Cotterill noted, "A large number of the plantations of Tidewater Virginia were built up of tracts taken out in the name of immigrants who had no existence save in the fertile imagination of the planter by whom their passage was supposed to be paid. Ancestors and acquaintances long dead, and even horses and cows, lent their name to securing additional land." Virginia became a highly stratified plantation society, with a majority of have-nots and a few slave-owning have-lots.

In his position of power, Colonel Walker certainly took part in this abuse of the system. When the governor opened the north side of the York to settlers in 1649, Walker landed a patent for a thousand acres on the Ware River in Gloucester County, becoming a burgess there. By 1658 he had acquired 1,200 more acres and another 360 in the untamed wilderness across the Rappahannock in the Northern Neck. These were huge tracts for the time, impossible to farm even with the slaves and servants available. A man could cultivate only about three acres of tobacco by himself, and no one owned hundreds of servants or slaves yet.

We have a few bare details of Walker's life aside from his landholdings and political positions. He was married and had four daughters. After his first wife died, he wed Sarah Fleete, the widow of Captain Henry Fleete, who had been an explorer, sailor, trader, justice, landowner, and legislator. Presumably Colonel Walker and Captain Fleete knew each other well, as they both served as burgesses. Fleete was famous as a swashbuckling seaman who had been captured by Indians on the Potomac River and held for five years; he was said to know the Indians and their languages better than any white man. He sailed one of the Earl of Warwick's ships trading with the Indians, perhaps also attacking

Portuguese slave ships. Fleete owned thousands of acres of land in the Northern Neck, and when Colonel Walker married Fleete's widow, he inherited them and moved there, as power and land in the Tidewater continued to consolidate within an exclusive gentry.

No record is known to exist of Edward before 1672. If privateers did indeed take him from a Spanish or Portuguese ship, he was lucky. Unlike the Spanish colonies, Virginia had not yet established its system of chattel slavery. They hadn't yet worked the economics out. Slaves were more expensive and more likely to revolt than indentured servants, and mortality was so high that owning someone for life didn't mean much. Most of the tobacco plantations that existed at the time were too small to support masses of unskilled laborers. Africans landed in a gray zone. Some were treated as indentured servants, ultimately obtaining their freedom. One Angolan couple, Anthony and Mary Johnson, went on to own hundreds of acres of land, two African slaves, and several white indentured servants. They were the exception, though, as many blacks fell into permanent captivity. But even those who remained in servitude briefly enjoyed a level of freedom their descendants would never experience. They could grow their own food, sell it in the market, and mix freely. They worked alongside the poor whites, lived with them, drank and gambled and ran away with them. Black men had romantic relations with white women, and even married them. And poor white men did the same with black women.

Glimpses of this mixing are scattered about the records. In the Northern Neck, a "mulatto" woman named Elizabeth Key fell in love with one of her fellow indentured servants, William Grinstead, and had a baby boy with him. Despite his low standing and youth, Grinstead had learned the law in England and sued for the freedom of Key and their son based on the notion that her father was Thomas Key, the other burgess in Warwick County. She won the case on appeal at the General Court in Jamestown in 1656 and was freed. The irony was that Grinstead, the Englishman, had to finish *his* servitude before they could marry, which they did later that year.

In the same county, an English servant name Hester Tate married a black one named Patrick Spence. The couple had four mulatto children by 1691; three were indentured to Spence's master, and the other to Tate's. In lower Norfolk County, a Francis Stripes was ordered to pay taxes on his wife, "shee being a negro." In the newer colony of Maryland, Nell Butler, an Irish maid to Lord Baltimore, fell in love with a slave named Charles and was determined to marry him, despite Baltimore's imploring that she risked enslaving herself and their children. He realized that "she had rather marry the negro under [those] circumstances than marry his Lordship with his [land]."

Then there was the lurid case of Katherine Watkins, a white married woman in Henrico County. She filed a complaint with the sheriff, claiming she was clearing a field with other workers, black and white, when a man named Mulatto Jack took her behind a tree, held a handkerchief to her mouth, "put his yard in her and ravished her." Surprisingly, white workers at the scene exonerated the black slave, saying they were all drinking cider when Watkins, "much in drinke," started making sexual advances on three of the black men. One white man said she "turne up the taile of Negro Dirks shirt, and said he would have a good pricke." Certainly Watkins would be mortified to know this episode was preserved to be dissected by scholars three hundred years later, but it is an interesting example of blacks and whites fraternizing, notwithstanding what it says about sexism.

The elites were outwardly appalled by all this mixing, as evidenced by a general court order that Hugh Davis "be soundly whipped . . . for abusing himself to the dishonor of God and shame of Christians, by defiling his body in lying with a negro."

As the seventeenth century wore on, the elites hammered out a more codified and repressive policy on race, tightening the ropes of slavery. The first law setting apart people of African descent came in 1640, when the legislature, to defend against Indians, required masters to supply members of their household with guns and ammunition, "excepting negroes." In 1662 the legislature instituted heavy fines for interracial fornication. Five years later it stipulated that a person's conversion to Christianity did not change his bondage status, a law that would apply only to African slaves. Three years after that, the assembly classified all non-Christians arriving by sea as enslaved, again targeting Africans without saying it, and barred black freemen from having white servants. And in 1691 interracial marriage was banned to prevent "abominable mixture"; any white marrying a nonwhite was to be banished from Virginia.

The aristocrats had everything to gain from slavery and the color code that allowed it. Slaves became the instrument of wealth, the means to acquire and cultivate ever more land, while squeezing poor whites out to the edges.

The free blacks and mixed-race offspring became what historian Philip Morgan called a "pariah class." A hundred years after the racial laws went into effect, free nonwhites would represent less than 2 percent of the population in the Northern Neck, while slaves would outnumber all others, at 55 percent. Free blacks in some communities would have to constantly prove their free status or face enslavement.

Edward Mozingo was freed just before the cage came down.

Colonel Walker died in 1668 in the Northern Neck, and Edward stayed with his widow when she married Colonel John Stone, who would become a magistrate and sheriff in coming years. Edward most likely first sued for his freedom in county court, then the ruling was appealed by one side or the other to the General Court. The spelling of Edward's last name in the Jamestown court may have been arbitrary, as spelling varied greatly even among literate people's names. It would waver and drift among his descendants—Masingo, Mazingo, Massingo, Massengil, Mosingo, Muzingo, Mowzing, Montzingo, and Monzingo— but by and large remained the way it was spelled that day.

Edward lived another forty years after he was freed, settling in the Northern Neck on or next to the property of Walker's daughter Ann and her husband. He married a woman named Margaret. They had three sons and grew tobacco and raised livestock on a little creek called Pantico Run, on the border of Richmond and Westmoreland counties.

What we know about Margaret is circumstantial. A professional genealogist named Gareth Mark wrote a lineage report on the Mozingos in 1990, concluding that she was the white daughter of Richard and Elizabeth Bailey, who were people of high station. Elizabeth's father, Colonel William Pierce, was a justice of the peace and a sheriff in Westmoreland County, and had patented thousands of acres in the Northern Neck, including the plot the Mozingos lived on. The Baileys' son Samuel, a lawyer, lived next to Margaret and Edward and posted a bond to secure their appearance in a court case, something relatives commonly did. His name showed up in numerous land leases and lawsuits involving Edward and Margaret and the two of their sons who survived to adulthood. If Samuel was not Margaret's brother, he was close to the family somehow.

Debt was a way of life in Virginia, and pro forma lawsuits over payment of them were ubiquitous in the court record. Edward was as much a part of the system as anyone else. Despite the hardening of racism at the time, the court books show him standing up for himself, suing for tobacco he felt he was owed, and fighting similar suits against him. He and Margaret also filed a complaint against a Robert Withrow for assault and won a settlement (of a sum not legible in the record). They seemed to be well established in society.

"The neighbors and associates of Edward Mozingo were closely intermarried, so it must be presumed that they knew of Edward's birth status; his race must have been obvious," Mark wrote in his report. "In spite of this, they interacted with him freely." His neighbors, even Colonel Pierce, called him Ned.

Chapter 4

A Bastard Child

Edward "Ned" Mozingo was clearly the forefather of the extensive Mozingo family living in America today. Except for a few branches, the family tree was mapped out, and everyone involved in that research knew he was black. A few even heard from a historian that he likely kept his name because he was some type of African noble and soldier, a "Bantu warrior." Yet whenever a new Mozingo stumbled into one of the family web forums with a question about the origins of the name—and, as often, to offer an obscure family explanation of it—no one set the record straight. So the discussion of our origins became a surreal cycle of curiosity, willful ignorance, and amnesia. The few times that anyone dared to mention that Edward was a "negro," the statement was politely ignored, in the southern way, as if the person who uttered it had had too much to drink. Occasionally the claim was outright disputed, as when one amateur historian suggested lots of Europeans were called "negroes" back then, including Italians. (Sure, like Romeo and Juliet?) Others made slightly more sound arguments. "I believe someone made a mistake, I thought the blacks were brought over in 1617 and all were slaves with no last names," wrote Ruth Corley, one of Edward's descendants. "I thought only people from Europe were indentured or apprenticed out to pay for their passage. . . . My grandfather died young and my mother lived with her grandparents. She remembered [the Mozingos] well. She was always told they were black dutch. I understand black dutch were indians who said they were black dutch to stay off reservations." Anecdotes like this would get as much traction in the discussion as that indisputable court record.

I wondered which descendants of Edward first passed as white. They must have faced intensifying ostracism as the colonial assembly hammered out its racist code. Yet maybe their poor white brethren still felt more kinship with the blacks than with the grandees who exploited them all. Well into the eighteenth century, poor whites and blacks, even slaves, still imbibed, gambled, and danced together. (The popular Virginia jig borrowed from African dancing.) They occasionally got in trouble for jointly organizing cockfights and horse races, and black fiddlers were in high demand even at more elite dances.

People may not have asked Edward about his name because back then it was obvious that he was of African descent. But what did later generations know and tell about their origins? I suspected the quiet shuffle over the racial line happened a few generations after Edward and Margaret, when the extended family had spread out and split up. This would explain why so many different myths sprang up—that the family was of Spanish origin, or French Huguenot, Hungarian, English, Italian, Dutch, Portuguese, Native American, among others—each branch conjuring its own story in a vacuum. If Edward and Margaret's own sons had somehow passed as white in their lifetime, or if their grandsons had, they certainly would have come up with a consistent alibi, as the family was then still tightly confined to the Northern Neck. But of course they couldn't. Everyone knew who they were.

Spencer was likely the first in his line to pass as white, as he was one of the first to leave the Neck. Maybe he was able to simply walk away from his roots, a bastard runaway who came to Orange County and claimed to be Portuguese or Dutch, escaping the ruinous label of "mulatto."

I called Samie Melton to see if she knew anything else about Spencer. "We just don't know how Spencer fits in," she said, in a warm Texas drawl. "There's a Margaret Mozingo who was Edward's granddaughter. There is some thought that he was maybe her illegitimate child and got the name from her." Surnames were often passed down this way.

Samie asked if I would submit a saliva sample to the DNA project Reese had started, explaining that one other male in Spencer's line had done so, and that the results didn't match those of the rest of the Mozingos. This didn't mean the branch didn't come from Edward. DNA technology could reveal only direct paternal lines, as the Y chromosome is passed exclusively from father to son, and so a descendant of Margaret would not match.

It was amazing that this one little strand of DNA tumbled down through history with the family name, and that sequences of chemical markers, called haplogroups, were specific to parts of the world, so a scientist could determine what general region that line came from prior to European colonization of the planet: the Middle East, sub-Saharan Africa, Western Europe, East Asia.

I told her I'd be happy to have my DNA tested, hoping it would show a direct link to Edward. I wanted this mystery solved cleanly, and the more I thought about his life and his descendants' hand-wringing over his origins, the more I was beginning to feel a certain fondness for him.

Samie told me the myths about our origins she had heard over the years. "Many say they are Italian. One line out of North Carolina decided they were Spanish royalty. One line had an absolutely beautiful story about how a Native American baby was adopted by this French family of Mozingos." The story was quite elaborate: the baby was named Opinion. He was from the Wapanachki clan of Cherokee Indians. He was just two years old when his village was burned in "Indian fighting." Charles Mozingo of Culpeper, Virginia, heard the toddler crying, took him home, and eventually adopted him, calling him Robert Mozingo. Several descendant families told the same story, with minor variations. One claimed Robert descended directly from King Powhatan. But when one of Robert's living male descendants took the DNA test, the result nixed the Native American myth. He matched the rest of the Mozingos.

So with this I knew the haplogroup wasn't Native American, but Samie said she couldn't tell me what it actually was because, unlike most family DNA projects, ours was started with the promise that all results would be confidential. Instead she referred me to a couple of people, both white southerners with direct paternal lines traced through records to Edward, who were a genetic match. The two men could talk about their own results even though, by default, they would be disclosing everyone's. They were happy to show me the documentation of their haplogroup, e1b1b1a7, of sub-Saharan Africa origin.

We already knew Edward was considered "negro" in his day, but this ruled out the possibility he was the son of a white man, Walker, for instance, and a black servant. His father was African.

I reached Tom Mozingo on the phone in Florida to get his take on all this, given his admonition in the email. He told me a bit of his background. "You grow up in a little town in Indiana with a name like Mozingo and at some point you wonder where you came from. I scratched around my family for answers but never got anywhere. In 1978, when I was in the navy, I attended a conference of attachés from around the world. I had my name tag on when a giant black man came up. I saw from his patch he was from Cameroon.

"He said, 'Oh, we have people with that name in my country.'

"'A lot of people?' I asked.

"'Many, many people.'"

Years later, when Tom was in Virginia, he decided to do some real research. At the Library of Virginia in Richmond he came across the Jamestown court record. *Oh shit*, he thought, this is going to cause some heartache. But it only deepened his fascination. He traced his own line straight back to "Edward the First," as he calls him, and began looking up Mozingos during his travels and comparing notes. He started writing a Mozingo newsletter in 1991, announcing reunions, putting out inquiries about mysterious ancestors, writing articles—"Mozingo-Monzingo, is it the same family?"—and giving genealogy tips. He delved into the origins and published all manner of speculation.

But he never mentioned that Edward was a "Negro man."

"I had such a good following," he told me. "I was getting so much good information from people. I was afraid that if I published anything about Edward the First, I would get cut off."

One of his best sources was a member of the Colonial Dames of America who insisted the family descended from some kind of English royalty. When people took Tom aside at reunions and asked what he thought of the origins, he tried to brace them: "If I tell you the truth, can you handle it?" One man hissed back that he wasn't related to "no damn monkey." But most Mozingos with an interest in their ancestry had already gotten an inkling of a black forebear, whether or not they accepted the fact. The Jamestown court order was out there, and references to it could be found in several books, like the *Encyclopedia of African American History*. One man begged Tom not to write about Edward. "He had two daughters who were of marrying age," Tom said, "and he didn't want them embarrassed. It made it very personal for me to have a father ask that."

Privately he was fascinated. He had found a fellow traveler in Reese, and they started the DNA project. Born and bred in rural North Carolina, Reese did computer networking and manufactured military ammo boxes for army special forces. He was a bearish, sociable guy whom Samie's husband mistook for a homeless man when they first met at a library. He got the name bug as a child. When he started looking into it, his father told him to "stop bothering dead people." But his curiosity abided no person or prejudice. Long before the DNA project, he used to call Samie up and say slyly, "Well, it's getting darker." His friend Bennett Greenspan, the founder of the company that did the DNA testing, described him as "a chain-puller" and told me, "He loved to go up to people and say, 'Man, we're African.'"

Tom enjoyed the paradox too. "Hey, I descended from an African prince," he told me. "I left my racism in Indiana. I was in Vietnam and we all bleed red. . . . But you need to be careful with this."

I was torn between thinking he was right and thinking this caginess was ridiculous. What exactly needed to be protected: a racist myth that should have been destroyed decades ago?

To be fair to Tom, speaking openly was easier for me. The last person in my family who would have thrown a fit over this information, my grandma Helen, died long ago. Thanks to our immaculate conception, there was no extended family to pressure or guilt me into being quiet, no one beseeching me to respect my elders. My very liberation from my family history would allow me to actually tell it.

At first, I only wanted to discover where Edward came from and solve the mystery of his relation to Spencer, not map out the rest of the story of my family tree. Genealogy held no interest. In my mind, it attracted retirees who hunkered down in the local library at eleven in the morning on Tuesday and wrote self-published family histories riddled with lots of exclamation marks. I had seen how participants in family chat forums obsessed over the most tedious details: finding the baptismal record of their great-uncle Burt, or the obit of some fourth cousin thrice removed. Spouses must have passed out in their own drool as their beloved genealogist delineated his strategy for piecing together the family tree as if it were the ship-in-the-bottle kit spread over the floor of the den.

Back then, I just didn't get how the family tree became the bones of the very story that brought you forth. Once you saw the skeleton sketched out, you attached bits of flesh and personality and historical context to it, and suddenly began to feel your place among your ancestors.

Originally Americans looked at genealogy as a vestige of the Old World that was subversive to their new spirit of self-invention and egalitarianism. Colonists who traced their lines did so to establish their social standing in the British Empire, to show their connection to this baron or that duke or king. Often they made great leaps of faith and logic and fraud in these attempts, and in the hardscrabble wilderness of the colonies this all came across as a bit dandy and vain, if not vaguely treasonous. No one cared about your third cousin twice removed unless he was wrenching his back in the field.

Ironically, the revolution that liberated America from this stratified past created a new mythological era for future Americans to try to attach themselves to. Patriotic societies like the Colonial Dames of America, the Daughters of the American Revolution and Society, and the General Society of Mayflower Descendants required prospective members to prove their ancestry. George Washington served as president of the Society of the Cincinnati from 1783 until his death in 1799, yet he still recognized the elitism associated with genealogy. When he once received a sketch of the Washington family line, he remarked that he had "heretofore paid little attention to the subject."

The prescient Frenchman Alexis de Tocqueville, on his visit to America in the 1830s, repeatedly noted that our democracy came with a dogged lack of historical consciousness in comparison to the Old World he knew:

> Amongst aristocratic nations, as families remain for centuries in the same condition, often on the same spot, all generations become, as it were, contemporaneous. A man almost always knows his forefathers, and respects them; he thinks he already sees his remote descendants, and he loves them. . . .
>
> Amongst democratic nations, new families are constantly springing up, others are constantly falling away, and all that remain change their condition; the woof of time is every instant broken, and the track of past generations lost. Those who have gone before are soon forgotten, and no one gives a thought to those who follow.

Tocqueville snooted about this, claiming his own Norman ancestors fought in the Battle of Hastings in 1066. But he was right. As a society we didn't give much thought or deference to our ancestors. I hadn't even known my great-grandfather's name. I didn't have any family traditions, even a religion, and I had no idea until now where our very name had come from.

In Haiti, my friends' dead ancestors inhabited trees and streams and cemeteries and whispered in the quiet of dawn. The dead helped protect the living, and the living helped protect the dead by paying obeisance to their favorite patron spirit, a *gede*. My Mormon roommate in college knew his ancestors were living on their own planets with their families, as he would be, if he didn't screw things up. He expected his planet to have good waves to ride.

The Mormons' beliefs about ancestry and the afterlife laid the foundation for genealogy in America today. According to Mormon doctrine, the righteous live eternally in a Celestial Kingdom with their entire family of every generation. But as their religion was relatively new, the founders were confronted with a dilemma from the get-go: their ancestors could not have been baptized and confirmed by the church, which Joseph Smith did not establish until 1830. Smith was very concerned about his older brother, Alvin, who died in 1823, so he devised, or God showed him, rituals by which a kindly descendant could have his ancestor (or a famous person such as Christopher Columbus, Albert Einstein, or Elvis Presley) properly baptized by proxy. The spirit of the dead person remained in a kind of waiting room until this happened, watching on. The church claims the deceased gets to decide if he wants to accept the baptism and the gospel and live with his family forever—or not. (Still, the practice stirred up controversy when it was discovered that victims of the Holocaust had been baptized by proxy.) The Mormons' ultimate end-of-time objective was to give everyone who ever lived the choice, and to do that, they needed to know who everybody who ever existed was.

The Genealogical Society of Utah was established in 1894, and since then the church built the largest genealogical library in the world, headquartered in Salt Lake City, with 4,500 satellite family history centers in seventy countries around the world. Ancestry.com, the largest for-profit genealogy company in the world, sprouted from this Mormon hub of ancestral research. Among its six billion records, its members could search every federal census from 1790 to 1930.

The Internet created a boom in the field, the first since Alex Haley's *Roots* was published in 1976, making it phenomenally easy to find and share information and widening the demographics beyond those who were free during library hours. People were not just digging up war heroes and presidents and English barons anymore; they were searching for tenant farmers, unsung soldiers, slaves, church deacons, Chinese railroad workers, illegitimate children, housewives, prisoners, and town drunks.

And I had joined them.

One day, pursuing more on Edward and Spencer, I snuck away from the streamlined fortress of the *Los Angeles Times* building to the Mediterranean fortress of the Central Library, on the side of Bunker Hill. I crossed the tiled lobby and headed down a hallway, into its great atrium of natural light, and down the long escalators descending five stories into a deep triangular crevice. This vaulting space always gave me a flutter of anticipation. The history and genealogy section was tucked into the very bottom of the crevice. I let the escalator deliver me at its own slow pace. It felt ceremonial, as if I were shrinking into a fathomless ravine, moving back in time.

The stacks were a cave both physical and psychological. The natural light faded away. The silence was hermetic. Homeless people slouched in lounge chairs. Obscure books that must have gone decades unopened smelled like sour glue and moldy wood: *Marriage Bonds of Henrico County, Virginia, 1782–1783*; *Gravestone Inscriptions: An Inventory of Cemeteries of Wayne County, North Carolina*; *Passage to America, 1851–1869: The Records of Richard Elliott, Passenger Agent, Detroit, Michigan.*

I paged through book after book from different parts of Virginia, straining to get a sense of the era Spencer lived in. Then I came upon a little maroon book printed in 1907, *A History of Orange County, Virginia*, and took it to a table. The back had an appendix of the county census of 1782. There I found Spencer Mozingo, six whites and no blacks in his household. I already knew he should be there, but there was a truth to seeing his name in the yellowed pages of an old book. Two lines down from Spencer the census listed a name that had me leaning back in my chair in disbelief: James Madison. Six white people, eighty-eight blacks.

Spencer lived near James Madison. The list was in alphabetical order, so he may have known Madison like I knew Matt Mouton in the fourth grade: not very much. But there were only fifty-seven families in the whole census tract, and Madison himself was the census taker. Did the future architect of the Constitution ride his horse up to my great-great-great-great-great-grandfather's house, sitting on the porch smoking a pipe on an unseasonably warm day in October 1782? What would they have talked about? The weather, crops, a new baby? The underlying weakness of the Articles of Confederation?

I flipped to scan the history of the county to see if this indeed was the Founding Father, and found it was either him or his father, James Sr. This was where they had their plantation, Montpelier, where the future president lived when he wasn't working in Williamsburg or Philadelphia or Washington. He died there, and Dolley Madison eventually sold it to survive. I paged back to the census: 581 black people in their tract, 346 white. The extended Madison family owned nearly half of the slaves in the census tract, 251. Of course everyone knew that Madison had slaves, but it was somehow more troubling seen in stark numbers. The argument that "everyone was doing it" back then falls apart when you see more than half of the white families didn't own any slaves. They were the poor white bulk of American history, so often denigrated as white trash. The Madisons owned far and away the biggest lot of slaves in the county. That's how they made their money, how they could afford to send James to Princeton to develop the intellect that would create the legal framework that defined our nation.

The Madison connection handed me a minor miracle. Historians had undoubtedly preserved and pored over every letter he had written, every document he signed, his plantation ledgers and his kin's. He must have remarked somewhere about his less illustrious neighbors. Maybe they got in a dispute, or maybe Madison made a passing snipe at Spencer's "white" status.

I bought the definitive biography of Madison, by historian Ralph Ketchum, and read up on his childhood. Madison and Spencer were about the same age. Maybe they played together as children, before Madison went off to boarding school and then college and Spencer went into the tobacco fields. All that I found to help me was a mention that in 1786 the senior Madison's cousin "Francis Taylor began to keep a diary in which he recorded something of the social life in Orange County."

Francis Taylor lived in that same census tract; he must have mentioned Spencer. I searched around and learned that the only copies of his diary were in Virginia, where I was headed soon. But first came more days down in the cave, sealed in a strange state of research and imagination, so immersed that coming out on the street was a shock to my system. I felt like a hermit who had lost his ability to talk.

My DNA test came back, matching the other person on the Spencer line—but not the rest of the Mozingos. I sank into a bit of a funk, even though I knew the result only meant Edward was not my direct *paternal* ancestor.

I took out a big sketch pad and mapped out a chart of every known Mozingo alive in America at the time of Spencer's birth, likely in the 1740s. The DNA told me he did not come from the male Mozingos, so he must have gotten his name from one of the three females who appeared to be of childbearing age at the time of his birth, or, less likely, he had come into the Mozingo family as an adoptee or stepchild. It's hard to see how he would have been given that name out of nowhere. Only about a dozen Mozingo adults existed in America at the time—all Edward's grandchildren and their young kids—and in a world of Smiths, Walkers, Carters, and horrific racism, I couldn't see who would pick our bizarre name, unless as a curse.

Of the women candidates for Spencer's mother, one was Sarah. She lived in the Northern Neck with a "Mulatto" man named John Chandler, who had trouble with the law. In December 1728, the sheriff summoned him to court for being a "common and prophane swearer and drunkard." The next February he pleaded not guilty to "living in fornication" with Sarah, who must have been "mulatto" herself. If not, the court would have heaped added scorn on her for sullying her whiteness. They quickly got married, which would have been illegal by that time if she were white, and the charges were dismissed. It's possible this fornication produced Spencer, but she would have been a Chandler by then, and presumably Spencer would have been given that surname. I suspected her sister or her cousin, both named Margaret, both granddaughters of Edward, gave birth to him.

Sarah's sister Margaret never married and was about the right age, born after 1708. This was the one Samie thought was the culprit. We know nothing else about her, as she didn't get in any legal trouble, and records of women in this era were sparse. We know more about her cousin Margaret, who was married to another Chandler, Francis, but seemed to have a rocky go after the nuptials. On May 26, 1741, "Sheriff of Westmoreland summons George Hinson to be and appear at Next Court for 'Living in adultery with Margaret Chandler a Mulatto ye wife of Francis Chandler within six months past.'" This is the only known document actually noting the race of one of Edward's grandchildren, confirming they were still considered mixed. The case was dismissed upon "it being suggested to the court that the said Hinson's run away." In 1744, the court ordered Francis to be taken into custody for having a "Bastard Child . . . by force" with a Dianna Coles. Margaret seemed to have parted ways from Francis for good by then, because soon she and George were married, living on her uncle Edward Jr.'s land and paying 450 pounds of tobacco yearly in rent.

These tidbits were certainly not the truffles of history that Colonial Dames go snuffling for. The Mozingos lived in a messy, racially mixed world of drunks and profane swearers that we can only glean hints of from their court records, like a police-blotter snapshot of the eighteenth century. But even with so spotty an understanding of the rough and raucous realm of the poor at the time, it became clear how a boy could have been cut loose from his roots.

I joined Ancestry.com and wiled away countless hours trolling through old census documents, trying to learn about the people between Spencer and me. And I reached out to distant relatives, like James Dale Mozingo in Missouri, my dad's first cousin, though they had never met or heard of each other. I called him in the afternoon, and his daughter told me he would be home around at five. She answered again when I rang back and yelled out to him.

"Who is it?" I could hear him say.

She grunted, "I don't know," using only the vowels.

He jostled to the phone. "Eh?" he answered.

"Hi, J.D., my name is Joe Mozingo. Did your daughter tell you I was going to call?"

"Yih," he said, fiercely unenthused.

I told him my relation to him—his uncle was my grandfather—and that I was trying to learn a little about the family in the 1920s and 1930s. He grunted.

"Did your dad tell you anything about his childhood?" I asked.

There was a long pause and a sigh. "I only saw my *deyed* once," he said.

"Oh, where did he go?"

"He just up and left."

"Where?"

I felt like I could hear him shifting around in his chair, wincing and making a fist at his daughter for passing him the call. "I think he was all over."

"What did he do?"

"Railroad . . . or something."

"So you never heard anything about where the name came from?"

"No."

I paused for a few seconds, hoping he might fill the silence with a fresh word or two. But he didn't. "Italian or anything?"

"No."

"You never wondered?"

"No."

I thanked him and said goodbye. I hadn't expected my dad's relatives to be a spigot of family history, but I'd hoped for more than this.

I wondered if there were other white families with African names in America. The authority on the subject was Paul Heinegg, an award-winning genealogist and the author of the two-volume *Free African Americans of North Carolina, Virginia and South Carolina*. I reached out to him, and he responded that Mozingo was one of two definite African names to survive to this day. Cumbo was the other and seemed to have a similar history.

"The section of the Cumbo family in Charlotte and Halifax counties, Virginia, were considered white after about 1800 as were some of the family in their place of origin around James City County," he wrote. "However most of the families in North Carolina and South Carolina were considered Portuguese or free Mulatto. Some are considered 'Lum-bee Indians' or other Indians in South Carolina. I have come across the name Cumbo quite a number of times in lists of slaves, so it was probably a West African name."

Heinegg had suspicions about several other names associated with people of African descent in colonial America, mostly Virginia, but wasn't certain of their origin or if the names had survived. The Blango family seemed to have originated with a black man born in Kent County, Virginia, in the 1670s. Anthony Longo in Northampton County, Virginia, in 1647, was black, although the name is also Italian. Heinegg found a Henry Quando in Charles County, Maryland, in 1702, and a Philip Mongom in Northampton County, Virginia, in 1645. He couldn't trace the origin of their names or the lineage of their descendants.

I kept picking away at my own line to see how we progressed from Virginia to southern California. I found some relatives who did talk, and with records pieced together a picture of a rural people perpetually struggling to climb out of entrenched poverty. My great-great-great-grandfather Joseph was listed as a "day laborer" in Indiana in the 1860 census, as was his son, my great-great-grandfather Joe, in the 1900 census in Bloomington, Illinois. In 1920, nearing seventy, Joe walked the streets, ringing a brass bell, peddling horseradish from a cart. When he died in 1937, he was buried in an unmarked grave, having told his family to chuck him into a ditch. All he needed was Jesus.

This was a family that, by then, had been in America for 293 years.

It took the singular phenomenon of midcentury California for my line of Mozingos to break from their desultory path. Twelve years after my grandfather Joseph moved the family to Los Angeles to work as an accountant for Hughes Aircraft during World War II, he owned his home in Studio City, with its brick incinerator in back. My father went to UCLA and earned his dental degree, and I grew up in a prosperous suburb.

My wife and son and I drove an hour south one weekend to visit my parents north of San Diego, where they had retired. I couldn't wait to show them the discovery: we had ancestors! When we got there, I set a printout of the lineage on the table. My dad gave it a look and said, mildly interested, "Hmm." It was the equivalent of a dog sniffing your shin, registering the scent, and moving on.

I pointed out some of the interesting particulars. "Spencer lived in Virginia during the American Revolution. He lived right next to James Madison. He might have even met him."

"Huh," he said, in a pitch of mild interest.

He must have sensed my expectation for a deeper reaction. "I've just never been into genealogy," he said.

I suddenly felt as if we were looking at the shawl I knitted in my sewing circle. "I'm not into genealogy either. I just think this history is a fascinating mystery."

We ate lunch on their back deck. It was a brilliant winter day with a dry desert wind. Down the hill and over the freeway in the distance, the ocean was a glossy, polished blue.

I told them more about Edward, his haplogroup, and how we all likely descended from him. My mom and dad listened and showed more tentative interest. There were more arching "hmms."

"So we can't actually trace Spencer to Edward?" my dad asked.

"No, not yet anyway."

"It doesn't make sense because he's so much whiter than I am," my mom said about my dad. This was true. My dad was a freckle time bomb waiting to go off anytime he set foot in the sun. He slopped on sunscreen at the beach, underwent annual chemical peels, and constantly had skin cancers burned off.

"It wouldn't make any difference," I said. "We'd be one-one-thousand-twenty-fourth black by now after all the mixing."

I found myself making this ridiculous point more and more, as if black and white blood was actually black or white, as if I didn't know from my biology classes that every human didn't already share 99.9 percent of the same DNA, as if the fractions we bandy about—one quarter black blood—are not really fractions of a fraction of the remaining 0.1 percent. As if it mattered.

"But did you take the test?" my mom asked.

I sighed inside and gave the explanation.

"So we're not related?"

"No, it just means that there is not a straight father-son line between Spencer and Edward."

"I wonder why on Google I found Pietro Mozingo in Italy?" my mom asked.

Chapter 5

The Enigma of the Fiddler

y parents weren't intrigued, but I was hooked.

I was on my way to Virginia to see if the original records of his day would help answer any of the myriad questions I had: What African culture did Edward come from? What was his daily life like, his personality? And was he, as the hired genealogist suggested, really accepted by his neighbors at the very same time the legal framework for slavery and segregation was coming down? I hoped to ferret out a link between him and Spencer and find descendants in the area who knew anything about either of them.

Ultimately, I hoped to draw a thread from Edward in colonial Virginia or, better, Africa, to me in suburban California, summoning each person along the route.

On a damp winter morning, I crossed the mile-long breadth of Virginia's Rappahannock River as fishermen in low wooden boats hauled up lines in the gloom. The highway traversed tidal flats and pinelands and gray pastures, and then gently lifted into the low clay hills of the Northern Neck. I approached the little brick town of Warsaw, which was called Richmond Courthouse when Edward resided here, and pulled into a modern county government complex.

I had spent the previous afternoon paging through records at the courthouse across the river in Tappahannock, which held the records of old Rappahannock County before it split into Richmond and Essex counties. It was a demoralizing experience. I'd have done nearly as well trying to decipher ancient Cyrillic texts. The clerks' script was impenetrably florid, *s*'s looked like *f*'s, and the language felt as if it had been copied from *Beowulf*. The word for *surgery* was *chirurgery*. I had to blur my eyes and free-associate, or burrow in closely on each letter, transcribing them in my notebook; working at the rate I'd managed, the job would take years to finish. Dozens upon dozens of thick court-order, marriage, land, and probate books lined the shelves. And like most of his contemporaries, Edward was involved in all sorts of leases and small lawsuits over debts recorded in one-line notations in the order books. Many of the suits were dismissed or ended in fines, and the records seldom explained what they were about. In the end, I could barely check the few books that had been properly indexed, trying to find any reference to his life before 1672. In particular I had hoped to find reference to his initial freedom lawsuit against John Stone and discover the names of the people who testified for and against him and what they said. Maybe the records would mention where he came from. But nothing of these early years survived, as the courthouse had burned during Bacon's Rebellion in 1676. I found a couple of lawsuits that were already known to Mozingo researchers. In one, Edward and Margaret were ordered to court in 1685 to answer a complaint by Stone. The record didn't explain what the complaint was, but they were ordered to "keep the peace with the colonel" and to provide bail in the amount of two thousand pounds of tobacco. Samuel Bailey and Matthew Kelly signed a bail bond with the couple to pay for this.

The records here in Warsaw held more promise, as they remained largely intact. The woman at the counter directed me to a long wall of frayed canvas-bound books in a back room. I picked one out and opened it, sending brown flakes of paper swirling on the table like volcanic ash. The book smelled stale, like a trunk of newspapers in the attic. With one look at the penmanship, I cursed the peacock who had to make such a show of his artistry. It was illegible to me.

I put back the heavy book and went for the index book of 1712. In it, I managed to locate the reference to "Mozingo's will" and pulled the corresponding book to find the will written in a fairly sober script. I had never seen this before, and felt a rush of adrenaline laying eyes on it.

"In the name of God amen the thirtieth day of July 1711, I Edward Mozingo of the County of Richmond and parish of North Farnham, being sick in body but in good and perfect memory, thanks be to God do make, constitute, ordain and declare this my last Will and Testament in manner and form following." He committed his "Soul to Almighty God" and trusted to be saved by "Jesus Christ." There was as much making sure Jesus knew where he stood as there was actual willing of his possessions. These old wills were written as if God had an attorney scanning for any loopholes to condemn the terrified petitioner to Hell.

Mozingo divided his "land and housing" between his "loving wife," Margaret, and his two surviving sons, Edward and John. His third son, Michael, had died as a child. Edward had been in America sixty-eight years. If he was eleven at the time of his indenture, he would have been seventy-nine at his death, beyond the normal life expectancy of the time but not abnormal once someone reached adulthood.

I paged forward and found the inventory of his possessions when he died: two guns, two feather beds, two chests, a trunk, three couches, a couple of tables, seven cider casks, a spinning wheel, four clay jugs, all sorts of kitchen necessities. He seemed to have done quite well for his family, better than most people at the time. Many items suggested a certain refinement of the upwardly mobile: cloth napkins, tablecloths, ceramic dishes instead of wooden, candlesticks, pewter salt containers, a chamber pot, and a looking glass. His fields boasted five sheep, a young horse, a mare and a colt, a heifer, two cows and two calves. He had a "parcel of old carpentry tools," which may have come from his apprenticeship with Walker. The second to last entry was "a fiddle." That must have been the Mozingo fiddle Tom had mentioned in the *Wired* interview—a sure sign that there was more to Edward's life than mere survival. I wondered if he played it at local festivities.

A historian of the era would later help me put this in the context of those times. She said that Edward appeared to be a middling farmer, aspiring to a higher station. Given the general dearth of possessions at the time, the things people owned spoke directly to their skills and interests. If Edward owned a fiddle, he was a fiddler. If he owned carpentry tools, he was a carpenter.

I saw little sign that he was part of a pariah class. He had business deals with all types and seems even to have made peace with John Stone; one lawsuit had Edward, Stone, and Bailey all dragged into court together for concealing "divers Titheables."

Edward's sons Edward Jr. and John leased a hundred-acre parcel on Pantico Run from Sir Marmaduke Beckwith, a big planter and a baronet who owned one of the tobacco warehouses on the river and seemed to lord over the Mozingos' lives. John leased an adjacent gristmill and small house from Beckwith for seven years for an annual rent of thirty barrels of "good Shelld Indian Corne," three and a half barrels of wheat, and a hog of at least "fifty weight." John fell on hard times and was in constant debt to Beckwith, finally getting kicked off his land and having to sell his household goods and carpentry tools. Edward Jr. seemed to do better, dying with possessions similar to those of his father, presumably some of which he inherited. He also had a parcel of books (the first sure evidence of literacy in the family) and a parcel of shoemaker tools.

Two remarkable records gave a glimpse of how Edward's sons may have fit into the increasingly binary society of free white and black slave. On May 4, 1726, Edward Jr. "was sworn into court and his claim of taking up a runaway negro belonging to John Shelton of Westmoreland County was certified." "Taking up" was the term for apprehending a runaway slave and returning him or her to the sheriff or owner, usually for a reward. On October 16, 1738, John Mozingo reported doing the same, having "taken up a Negro woman slave Named Pegg."

I wondered if these slaves thought they could find refuge with the mixed-race Mozingos, and if Edward and John had any empathy for them, any sense of solidarity or connection. Of course, even if they did, what could they realistically do? If they had harbored the fugitives or helped them flee the county, and were caught doing so, they would have been imprisoned—if not worse, given their own color. Their families would have fallen into destitution, possibly even slavery.

Perhaps the two brothers felt no kinship to the rapidly growing population of African and American-born slaves, or even resented them for reminding society and themselves of their own origins. Maybe they actively lured or pursued the runaways as a way to ingratiate themselves with white society.

Yet another interesting case suggested the Mozingos were connected to some type of network of mixed-race free families. In 1708, Edward Jr.'s sister-in-law married Thomas Grinstead. He was thought to be a descendant of Elizabeth Key, the mulatto woman who won her freedom in court in 1656 and married her white English attorney, William Grinstead. The parallels between Elizabeth Key and Edward Mozingo made me suspect the families were close. Edward and Elizabeth were likely about the same age. They both started in America as slaves or servants owned by the two burgesses of Warwick County and moved to the Northern Neck as land opened up there. And they waged two of the earliest known cases of people of African descent suing for their freedom and winning. Such bonds between mixed-race people might have buoyed the families in the early days, before the racial stigmatization grew so fierce that their only hope for prospering was to pass as white.

By the third generation of Mozingos in America, as the clouds of bigotry gathered and the Tidewater's soil grew ever more depleted, the lineage became more marginalized and dysfunctional. Of Edward's ten grandchildren, only two seemed to have done well, both outside of the Northern Neck. Edward Jr.'s son John had purchased 175 acres in Richmond County, but perhaps the land was sour or the bigotry became too much to bear, because he sold this land in 1744, migrated south, and patented two hundred acres in North Carolina, where the soil was fresh and the racial code was not quite as harsh. A hundred years after his grandfather landed in Virginia, he was the first known Mozingo to leave it behind. Then sometime around 1766, John's son Charles moved from Richmond County about eighty miles west to Culpeper County, where he purchased or patented 390 acres. The rest of the grandchildren seemed to wallow in the Northern Neck. John's son Gerrard became an indentured servant to pay off a debt owed to Marmaduke Beckwith. A court record from 1740 showed Gerrard, age unclear, agreeing to "serve after his contract time expired" until he satisfied the debt, or his father or brother did. Another of John's sons, Edward, was taken to jail for breaking into someone's tobacco house. And John's daughter Margaret (possibly Spencer's mother) was living in adultery and called a "mulatto" in the court record, a word growing in usage and pointedly aimed at putting anyone with any "black blood" into a lower category of humanity. Of Edward Jr.'s children, his sons Edward and George became tenant farmers to a local grandee, Landon Carter, and his daughter Sarah was accused of "living in fornication with John Chandler," the mulatto alleged to be "a common and prophane swearer and drunkard."

The lines that stayed in the Tidewater didn't have any chance for reinvention, and by the look of it, seemed to be squeezed into narrowing tunnels of a pariah class.

Reading all this in the court record, I suddenly felt a need to walk on the land where these lives rose and fell, to see if it spoke anything. I put the books away, left the courthouse, and drove north on Menokin Road under a heavy gray sky. The low hills looked neglected and bleak, as if humanity were in retreat. The detritus of last year's corn stubbled the red soil, which faded to purple in the recesses of the forest. Boxy little homes and weatherworn trailers gave way to abandoned farmhouses and islands of gray woods, unmoving skeletons of locust, oak, maple, dogwood, poplar, sycamore, and holly. I saw no people. The road was empty. A fetid old millpond lay suffocated with algae, and fallen barns shot through with trees and dead vines tilted this way or that. This was a place that had once flourished, but where at some point long ago the clock started running backward.

When Edward won his freedom in 1672, the settlers were again at war with Indians from the north and stayed mostly to the shoreline of the Rappahannock River, where log-raft ferries shuttled them across to the safer southern bank. Anger that the governor did not drive the Indians out of treaty-protected land sparked an uprising of thousands of frontiersmen, led by a young planter named Nathaniel Bacon. White and black farmers and servants took part, although we do not know if Edward did. Bacon's Rebellion pushed the Indians west and allowed the settlers to move into the Neck, where they widened the Indian roads and cleared the timber to grow tobacco. Most of the poor farmers lived in windowless log lean-tos with dirt floors, and life was prone to deadly disease and starvation. Wolves regularly killed the livestock, and children died so often that no parent could count on any child's survival. Settlers were squeezed to the margins by a corrupt governor who bestowed the best land on his friends, and their profits suffered severe fluctuations as the price of tobacco rose and fell on the English and Dutch markets. In the 1680s, rebellious workers and poor farmers rampaged through the country, burning crops to ease the glut of their product.

Plagued by drought, hornworm, flea beetles, and moths, tobacco needed to be nurtured. The plant grew best on virgin soil and sucked up nutrients so fast that a parcel could produce only three or four crops before new fields had to be cleared. Farmers were constantly cutting into the forest, letting old fields go back to a "sourland" of pines and sedges behind them. The endless hours they spent on tobacco left them little time to cultivate anything else or raise livestock to replenish the sandy loam with manure. In March they planted the seeds in beds and covered them with brush, until the shoots were strong enough to be transplanted in the open. In spring and summer, they pruned the sucker branches and topped the upper branches to keep the plant from flowering. In autumn, they cut the leaves and skewered them on long stakes to dry and wither, properly hung in a shed or mold would grow. Then they removed the stems and twigs, sorted the leaves by size, and loaded them into giant wooden casks called hogsheads. Weighing up to twelve hundred pounds apiece, the casks were rolled by oxen to the four warehouses along the river. Settlers had to keep the "rolling roads" thirty feet wide, maintain the bridges, and keep wagons and coaches off to prevent ruts.

The road I was barreling along grew out of one of these rolling roads, itself grown out of a Chickacoan Indian path. As forest and pasture flickered by, I slowed down when passing a boarded-up blacksmith shop at Farmers Fork, the crossroads where Edward and his sons sold their goods, and then accelerated back into the woods. Down in a deep hollow, I glanced over my shoulder at a ranch-style house on a hill to the left. Through the bare trees, a homemade sign next to the driveway said "Pantico Run."

Pulling to a stop on the shoulder, I felt my heart beat faster. My research had told me that Colonel John Walker had purchased land just south of this road before he died in 1668. William Pierce had owned the land to the north. In his will of 1702, he gave his grandson Samuel Bailey "all my land on the south side of Pantico runn next adjoyning unto Ned Messingo." This was where Edward settled. A stagnant green mill pond lay to the right of the road, probably a relic of the gristmill his son John leased.

I got out and walked up the swooping driveway to the house. A woman named Lisa answered the door, her children peering out from behind her. As I told her my story and said I'd like to walk along the creek, she showed a surprising lack of suspicion about a lone man showing up on a winter day. She said it shouldn't be a problem, but the land down by the creek was not her property.

"Well, no one's going to shoot at me or anything, right?" I asked.

"I don't *think* so," she said.

I chuckled and thanked her, and she said, "You know, there is a Mozingo Road in Oak Grove."

"Really?" I hadn't heard of the road or seen it on a map. She gave me directions.

As I picked my way down the hillside to the creek, the pallid winter air gave the scene an eerie cast. I slipped on the slope and caught my balance. The ground was a decaying mat of moss and fallen leaves and rotten stumps crumpled underfoot. The creek pooled into a swamp, then sluiced back into a clear channel. Geese honked somewhere downstream.

I dug a hand into the cold, sandy soil and contemplated it. This was the earth Edward worked every day, the grit he must have scraped from under his fingernails at night, as Margaret cooked in their cabin. The area had all gone back to forest. Dogs barked in the distance. I hiked deeper into the woods, looking for a clearing, hoping some hunter or bootlegger wouldn't draw a bead on me. People still made moonshine in these hills.

Where could Edward's cabin have been? In 337 years this land could have cycled between forest and farmland and sourland many times over. The terrain presented no hint, just a forlorn, lonely maze of wood.

The heavy silence and the repetition of the timber were disorienting, and I was getting anxious, the way you can at high altitude. What was I doing?

I wanted to feel something, to get a glimpse of Edward out in a field or on a porch playing his fiddle. I wanted to see a ghost.

I suddenly felt that this was not a rational endeavor. I was walking alone in cold woods when I should have been reporting a news story, working, as it were, or at least playing with my son in the backyard, being a dad. These were the aspects of our lives that neatly defined us, our jobs and roles. I wasn't going to find the ruins of Edward's cabin or stumble upon his diary lying among the rotted logs. This research had already consumed weeks and weeks of my professional life at a time when journalists were getting laid off in reams.

I couldn't conjure any sense of Edward's presence, maybe because when I summoned my deepest instinct, Mozingo was still an Italian name to me. I couldn't connect to what I now knew intellectually. Reality had the ring of a joke: my Bantu roots.

Would I have such a hard time conjuring Edward if he were European? Being Basque or Italian was easy to accept because Europe was familiar, but the Congo was a hazy, exotic phantasm.

I walked back to my car, feeling a bit depressed, frustrated with my stubborn mind.

Turning on some music and reading the directions Lisa gave me, I headed across the valley of Cat Point Creek, and off Oak Grove Road I found a modern green street sign with my very name in reflective lettering: Mozingo Road. I stopped to take a picture for my family and then drove down through the trees. A rural mailbox on the right read "Mozingo," and then another in front of a trailer, and then a third. *This is it*, I thought, *the Mozingo motherland*. Everyone here is a Mozingo. This must be the old homestead. Excitement overtook my melancholy, and I jumped out and knocked on the door of a trailer with faux-wood siding. As I waited for an answer, I studied the machine-painted grain and pondered the Dodge Ram 1500 in the dirt drive, with a "Size Matters" sticker on the back window.

No one appeared. I wrote a note on my business card, saying I was a fellow Mozingo and to please call me, and wedged it in the door.

Starting off on foot to the next trailer, I could hear Mexican ranchero music inside. This confused me; no backwoods redneck was going to be listening to this. Then I saw several young Latino men in the back. Maybe farmworkers were renting these trailers. But why would a landlord keep his name on the mailbox? At which point it hit me: the mailboxes simply registered the street name and house number. As many Mozingos lived here as Mains lived on Main Street.

I got back in the car, clucking at my gaffe. The paved road ended at a gate just a quarter mile down, with a nice brick house on the left. A middle-aged couple was working in the garden outside, and I introduced myself and asked them if they knew anything about how the road got its name.

"There was a family that lived down there, where the road is still dirt past the gate," said the wife, Barbara. "There's an old barn falling down and a cemetery."

A cemetery sounded promising. The couple generously put on jackets and walked me there as a light rain started. A two-track dirt road continued past the gate through a pasture that sloped down to Cat Point Creek, and continued on to where it joined with Pantico Run. This was the other side of Walker's old property in the 1600s.

"The hunting club owns this," said the husband, Steve. Amazing that one of the first settled areas in America remained rural enough to have hunting grounds.

We got to a pile of rotten timber that was once the barn, I figured, and some heaps of bricks. "The cemetery is over there," Steve said. "You can't get to it most of the year because of all the briar." He pointed to a stand of trees twenty feet wide. I'd never seen a cemetery like it, an abandoned, snaggletooth cluster of headstones draped in dead vines. All but sprinting to it, I was sure I'd found Edward's grave site—only to find that the Bowens were buried there, circa 1913.

Lying on the high bed of my bed-and-breakfast room that night, I was struck by what an unbelievable fluke of history it was that there was any record of Edward's African origins. If the clerk at Jamestown hadn't written "a Negro man"—and many did not make such notations at the time—we would have had no clue, really, as he could have just been a white indentured servant fighting for his freedom. And that document survived by the purest happenstance.

The colonial records were first kept in disarray in a damp ground-floor room of the secretary's office in Jamestown. Many were lost when the statehouse burned to the ground in 1676 during Bacon's Rebellion. The rebuilt statehouse burned in 1698, and the records were hustled out and thrown into heaps on the ground, then moved to the new capitol building in Williamsburg, where, in 1746, one visitor reported they were "mangled by moths and worms," lying in a "confused and jumbled state . . . being huddled together in single leaves and sheets in books out of binding." A year later, that building caught fire, and the records were again tossed outside into piles. During the Revolutionary War, they were carried in haphazard loads to the new capitol, in Richmond, only to be decimated during the British advance in 1781. Many more perished with age, as the paper grew brittle, cracked, and fell apart. Somehow the document attesting to Edward's suit made it through all of this. By 1829, the 157-year-old papers lay safely in the state courthouse in Richmond.

Then came the Civil War, with Richmond serving as the Confederacy's capital, less than a hundred miles from Washington. By sheer proximity, northern Virginia suffered far more than any other region during the war. In April 1865, the Confederate government abandoned Richmond as the Union Army advanced, and retreating soldiers and angry rioters set fire to an armory and a number of warehouses. Soon the flames engulfed the entire commercial district, and the state courthouse burned to the ground, fueled in minuscule part by the records of the colonial General Court.

Miraculously, the court records from 1670 to 1676 happened to be somewhere else that day, the lone volume that had gone missing. Another volume, containing the cases from the years 1622 to 1632, had vanished decades earlier, ending up in the hands of Thomas Jefferson, and by the time of the fire, it resided safely in the Library of Congress. How our volume happened to be absent from its shelf during the fire remains a mystery. A catalogue of the Virginia Historical Society in 1901 first noted its existence. No one knows how it got there or what condition it was in. The society was little more than a gentlemen's club with a mishmash of books and records. If the volume looked anything like the one in the Library of Congress, it was a mess, with mutilated and missing pages, thoroughly out of sequence, with most of the dates on the edges worn off. Sheer luck kept the notation from that Saturday afternoon in 1672 fully intact.

In the 1920s, the diligent state librarian Henry Reed McIlwaine undertook the daunting task of putting the records in order and transcribing them into a book, the *Minutes of the Council and General Court of Colonial Virginia: 1622–1632, 1670–1676*, where our family's roots appeared on page 316. The book made its way into a few big libraries across the country and is now immortalized in digital form on the Internet.

Still, it was a shame that the notation didn't offer more about Edward, or the conditions of his servitude under Colonel John Walker, or how he had come to sue for his freedom from his deceased master's widow and her new husband, or how he won.

I felt dejected that the records in Edward's vicinity didn't disclose anything else on these matters, but the court clerk knew of some Mozingos in the area, and I called one, Junior, who agreed to meet me the next day. The innkeeper had a friend, Hannah, who also gave me a lead. She knew about Mozingos—"They're mostly rednecks," she said—and about an old Walker plantation twenty-five miles south, in a hamlet called Walkerton. A quick bit of research on my laptop showed that the plantation had been owned by Colonel John Walker's brother and was a repository of Walker family history. I hadn't been able to learn much about Walker because his name was so common. Maybe this was where his personal records ended up, in some old trunk in the attic. My imagination reeled with the possibilities: a diary, accounts of Edward's work for him, the contract of his indenture.

Chapter 6

Living with Ghosts

In Walkerton, a white sign marked a dirt road into the fields: "Locust Grove, 1665." Colonel John Walker's brother Thomas had patented 2,350 acres here on a high bank of the Mattaponi River. The family still owned six hundred of them, growing corn, soybeans, wheat, and sod. I drove a half mile down the dirt road through bare fields as the periodic crack of a rifle broke the silence. Turning down a lane of locust trees, I arrived at a white-columned mansion with gabled dormers, small-paned windows, weatherboard siding—the very vision of the antebellum South.

The driveway circled in front of the home, under canopy of pecan, walnut, and ash. Jerry Walker came out to greet me. We had talked briefly on the phone in the morning, and he had invited me over to talk about the plantation and its history. He was a fifty-seven-year-old architect with a neatly trimmed gray beard, cool blue eyes, and a mellifluous southern drawl. I asked him about the gunfire. "They're shooting groundhogs," he said. "A single groundhog will eat an acre and a half of beans. We have to get them before the planting, while you can still see them."

I glanced about at several decrepit shacks under the trees.

"Let me show you around," he said. He pointed to an old gray out-building. "That was the cooking house. They cooked out there in summer. In winter they cooked in the main house to keep it warm. Next to it there is the last of the old slave houses." It had the same splintered gray planks as the cooking house, on two floors, narrowly built. We walked around back just as the setting sun was dipping below the ceiling of clouds, blood orange, showing itself for the first time in days. Peeper frogs cried from the banks in rapture. The river below cut through the ocher-lit landscape, its water deep and black with the tannins of leaves decaying in the bogs. A small rapid broke in the middle of the current, and a storm-battered pier lay half-sunk on the bank, where Jerry said their crops were once loaded on barges. "They sold all their goods in Baltimore. They thought the merchants in Norfolk were pirates."

Much of the family history was recorded by Jerry's great-great-grandfather, John Walker, a diarist who inherited the plantation in the mid-nineteenth century and owned fifty slaves at the outset of the Civil War.

"This house was built in 1773, after the original burned, with additions in 1868, and then my dad added that wing in 1951," Jerry said. Oddly, the newest addition looked the most colonial, with its gabled dormer windows. "My great-grandmother Virginia Henley Walker removed the colonial detailing and tried to give it a Victorian look. She did the additions in 1868."

Up close, the house did not look nearly as opulent as when I first glimpsed it from the lane. The paint was peeling, and some of the planks were rotting. Even its size was deceptive; its broad side faced the road, but it was very narrow front-to-back. To call it a mansion would be a stretch now, although it certainly was one in its time. We walked in through a back porch with torn black screens and patio furniture, through a creaky door, and onto the worn floorboards of a cramped dining room. "This was built by the slaves around 1850," Jerry said, resting his hand on a mahogany china cabinet. "John Walker had his slaves do different industries."

Jerry seemed to enjoy the role of steward of the family home and history. I mentioned the home itself looked like it required a colossal amount of work. "You could put a hundred thousand dollars into this place and not even notice a difference," he said. "It's not built for modern people. The rooms are very small. The kitchen is tiny. There are no hallways. To leave the upper back bedroom, you have to walk through two other bedrooms to get to the stairway. People ask us if we'd turn it into a B&B. It would have to be for people seeking an alternative lifestyle."

I peeked through the door to the kitchen: old linoleum floor, drab Formica counters. The sight conjured something Hannah had said, that many of these old planting families were "land rich, cash poor."

From a cabinet he pulled out a black poster-size paper with the heading "Chart of the Walker Family," a vast circuitry connecting a thousand or so names with microscopic writing in postage-stamp-size boxes. This was the type of family tree of yore, made so every distant relative could claim his or her pedigree. Three corners of the chart featured a written passage about prominent forebears on the tree and the last had a history of the plantation itself. Major Thomas Walker served as a commander at Fort Mattaponi when he got the patent for the land from a former governor named Edward Digges, who had given himself the original patent but never settled on the property. Digges stayed on his Bellfield plantation near Yorktown, where he brought in two Armenian men to build up a silk industry in Virginia. I recognized that name, Edward Digges. He was on the panel of judges on the General Court that freed Edward Mozingo. I wondered if his connection to the Walkers factored into the court order. Strange how the threads of history intertwined. An action by Digges played a role in Jerry Walker's living where he did today, and another action by him played a role in my being a Mozingo. And neither of us knew anything about him.

I skimmed the passages for any information about Edward's owner, John. It mentioned only that Thomas had a brother, "a very prominent man known as Col. John Walker." There is a reason more is known about Thomas than his brother: Major Thomas Walker had a daughter and two sons, who passed the name to more sons, and so on down the line, so that his plantation is still owned by a Walker and the family has meticulously documented the Walker family tree. Colonel John Walker had six daughters, who took their husbands' names into new family trees.

Jerry said this was all he knew of John Walker. I groaned inside. So went my vision of trunks of dusty records in the attic.

I swallowed my disappointment and asked him what it was like to live in the place where his fifth great-grandfather had lived, where his father was born and died, to be constantly confronted with the chain of life and death. "I grew up with it," he answered. "It's second nature to me."

The more I learned, the more it was clear his very station in life was set by that grant of land 345 years ago. Not to discount his success, but the Walkers were all born of a landed, educated class. His grandfather went to engineering school in Pennsylvania; his father was an architect. They went through low times, even deeply impoverished times during Reconstruction, but the land and history anchored them to a certain status that was theirs to lose.

He could not avoid their history, he told me. His was one of those families that Tocqueville described, in which "all generations become contemporaneous." As a child, he worked in the fields in summer alongside the descendants of slaves who had worked for his great-great-grandfather. He knew which dead relatives added which rooms and walls, made which repairs, bought which cabinets, sold which parcels of land, and he talked about them like he knew them well. The house literally creaked with his ancestors, mainly big Uncle William, who moved to Ohio, lost his family, and returned alone to live in the attic in the 1870s. He apparently didn't leave after he died and was suspected of making most of the noise Jerry and his wife, Cecky, heard up there all the time. There were other ghosts too. Jerry saw his first as a child while learning to type in the basement, when a little girl appeared with an annoyed look, as if to say, "Haven't you figured that out yet?" Another evening, he was doing homework in the living room when he heard a cavalry regiment clop and jangle up to their home, stop, and then continue on back out the lane. He figures this was one of the foraging parties, either Union or Confederate, that came to the house during the Civil War.

When workers were doing his father's remodel in 1953, they reported seeing a man sitting in a wing chair watching them. They could see him only from the corners of their eyes. That was Humphrey, the father of John the diarist. Later, as an adult, Jerry said he was having a party in the backyard when he came inside to see a deceased female relative carrying drinks on a tray.

He talked about these sightings in a strikingly matter-of-fact way, with no fear of my reaction.

He was right to have none. I was envious. There were no ghosts in Dana Point.

In the morning, I crossed the river again into Richmond County to see the Mozingos who lived in the area now and learn what, if anything, they knew about Edward. By now I had the clawing feeling that this trip was a frivolous waste of time. This is what hit me on Pantico Run: I was in the Way Back, rekindling that child who wanted only to be lost in imagination.

But I couldn't give up yet. I told myself I'd give the endeavor a couple more weeks. If nothing panned out, I'd go back and find real news to report.

I got a McDonald's coffee in Warsaw and went looking for Junior Mozingo's house to the south in Farnham. A light fog had settled overnight and still hung in the trees. State Route 3 swooped through hills and dipped down Totuskey Creek by some rusted grain elevators, and rose up again. Here and there the woodland gave way to sandy patches of scraggly pines that looked almost like stretches of high desert. The road passed horses in mist-shrouded pastures, a general store, squat brick homes, taller plank ones, decrepit trailers, and white church steeples. I wished my destination was farther away, because I enjoyed driving rural roads alone.

I was starting to feel a longing to be back with my flesh-and-blood family, those whose lives I knew in every daily detail. Funny what you miss: I laughed at how my wife slapped snore strips over my nose at night, and how one end would always come undone around two in the morning so that, when I woke up, the strip was always sticking straight up like a mailbox flag. Noses had become big comedy in our house of late. Just before I left, I was lying on the floor with Blake, almost three years old, when he looked up my nostrils and earnestly asked, "Are there spiders in your nose, Daddy?" Another day in the backyard, he was trying to see if rocks could fit into his own nose. I told him not to put rocks in his nose, which turned out to be an overly narrow admonition. The next afternoon my wife had to pull him out of day care and take him to the doctor. On the admission form, she wrote, "Lima bean in nose." The doctor tried to get the bean out with tiny forceps, but Blake kept asserting that he wanted to keep it in there. Then he sneezed, and it flew out.

Did Edward's family have such light moments, I wondered. Or was life too severe? If your children had a poor chance of surviving, wouldn't you hold a part of your heart back for self-preservation? In the poorest parts of Haiti, I had seen how mortality permeated everything, as it no doubt did throughout most of human history. I'd try so often to get a mother to describe her young child who had died of malnutrition or cholera or stray gunfire. "Did he do anything funny? What was his personality like?" I'd almost always get a flat "He was a good boy."

Continuing on through mist-shrouded pastures, I arrived at the little crossroads of Farnham, nothing more than a post office and the worn redbrick North Farnham Episcopal Church, built in 1737. I turned up Cedar Grove Road and parked in the driveway of Junior's brick colonial-era house. *This is nice*, I thought. But it looked empty. And honestly, it didn't seem like the home of a man whose actual birth certificate name was Junior and who named his son Elvis. Then I saw someone across the street, waving in front of an old wood-framed farmhouse and a scattering of old trucks and eviscerated appliances. "Over here!"

I crossed over and parked next to a rusted tractor collapsed in the dirt. In some rickety kennels along a great stand of trees, half a dozen hunting dogs clamored to be let out. Junior had stepped back inside and now came down the steps of the back stoop. "They think they're going hunting," he said. "How you doing?"

We shook hands. "Good, good. Thanks for meeting me."

"It's good to meet another Mozingo."

We looked about awkwardly, keenly realizing a name wasn't much to have in common. Junior was a short, solid, pale-skinned man of sixty-six with sharp hazel eyes and a broken-veined burl of a nose. He wore a blue flannel shirt with a crinkled pack of Southern Pride tobacco in the pocket, and a stiff camouflage trucker's cap perched high on his head, as if the wind had discreetly dropped it there and might soon reclaim it.

"Well, come on in."

We sat down at a worn maple table in the kitchen, and I told him I was looking into our ancestry. I started by asking about his family.

"We grew up by Farmers Fork," he answered. "All them ones that I knew were around there."

"That's interesting, because we have a common ancestor who lived right by Farmers Fork in the 1670s. Edward. So Mozingos have been there since then."

"I guess so." He said he knew only as far back as his "dad's grand-daddy." "He used to run that Menokin mill. It was a big mill that turned your feed."

His father Rhoda and uncle Milton were born out of wedlock, he said, and got the Mozingo name from their mother. She went on to marry a Hinson who they always suspected was their father, but no one would ever say. Strange how similar this was to my suspicions about Spencer's parentage, with another Hinson no less. He said he ran across other Mozingos now and then, mainly "Socks" Mozingo, who sold socks at the swap meet and lived up by Mozingo Road. "I think Socks is supposed to be kin to us. Him and I were talking and we don't know we're kin or not." He also knew of a clan of Buck Mozingos down the road, but had never met them.

I asked him if he ever talked to his father or uncle about their background. "They didn't talk about it and we didn't ask," he said. "We knew not to ask about our old people back then." His tone suggested an aggressive lack of interest.

Did he wonder about the name?

"It's Italian, isn't it?" he asked, shrugging.

"I've heard that, yeah," I said.

He went upstairs to get something. "Show him my dead heads, Mama," he called out.

Mama was his wife, who called me into the sweltering living room, which had a big oil heater in the center. A half-dozen deer heads were mounted on the paneled wall. I must have heard "deer" as "dead," but couldn't be sure, as the heads were both. "He and Elvis shot these," she said.

"Is Elvis around?" I asked.

"Nah, he's out."

"That one's a ten," Junior said, coming back down. "He's got two little kickers." Eight branches and two little nubs.

"So you eat the meat?" I asked.

"We give to the church for the hungry."

He had brought down an old Remington shotgun he'd inherited. "It's all I got from my granddaddy." I gave it a feel and admired the craftsmanship, thinking of the Winchester .32 caliber on my parents' mantel, the only thing passed down to my father.

He opened up a phone directory on the kitchen table. There were twelve listings for Mozingos in the area, and I wrote them all down, including his uncle Milton's. Junior thought the Charles Mozingo listed was probably Socks.

We stepped back outside. The fields were gray and brittle with broken stalks of corn. Junior was just renting this house. For all their time here, the family had not amassed any land. They had only their hands to survive by, working in mills or tilling the depleted red soil on rented patches of land. His dad was a tenant farmer and never learned to read. He lost his thumb in a mill and signed his name with an X. Junior worked for forty-four years at an elastic plant and still mowed lawns to help pay the rent.

Was this the invisible legacy of the pariah class, working generation after generation, rarely getting more than a step or two above subsistence?

I later found that in the late 1700s, Junior's ancestors were still considered mixed race. The three brothers of his fourth great-grandfather John appeared on a court registry of "Free Mulattoes," which, along with registries of "Free Negros," were kept so authorities knew which people of color were not enslaved.

I had read through these registries before, and nothing spoke to the marginalization of the free people of color more powerfully. One that I glanced through in nearby York County catalogued them like jail inmates: "Mary Wilson is a dark girl about 20 years of age, five feet four inches high, has a scar on the right side of the nose and one on each big toe, has a mole on the breast, long hair which she wears tucked with comb, rough face, high forehead, born free." Elizabeth Alors was twenty-five, tawny, with a scar on her right breast, a long face, "pouting lips and long hair which she wears plaited." Thomas Combs was twenty-two and probably mixed race, "a man of whitish complexion . . . no scars . . . good teeth, small eyes, with a cast in his left eye and long straight hair."

Status was fixed in these parts at the end of the seventeenth century, and the stigma of mixed race must have imprinted itself on the Mozingo family and been passed on in the collective consciousness for generations. The Walkers are still landed gentry, with a good name. The Mozingos are rednecks, with a crazy name. My own line was probably much like Junior's until my grandfather got an accounting degree in Bloomington and launched his family into the middle class in California.

Junior and I walked to the end of the drive, a virtual scrapyard of pickups and Blazers in varying degrees of dismantlement, with dried-up cobs piled next to an old rusty hand-crank corn sheller. He showed me how the tracking device on his truck monitored the whereabouts of his hunting dogs. He had seven hounds and four beagles in the kennels.

"What do the beagles go after?" I asked.

"They run rabbits."

I was stalling, trying to think of how to raise the race question. I had envisioned myself making some dramatic proclamation of the truth, no matter how unwelcome it might be. But I suddenly felt that would be a gimmick, and not particularly wise. Who was I to show up and bother this man with something he didn't want to hear?

We chatted more about Mozingos. His nephew was a minor league baseball player famous around these parts. He mentioned that the Buck Mozingos all had one green eye, one blue eye, and a white streak of hair.

His mention of appearances gave me a lame way in. "What about black Mozingos?"

"Never heard that," he shot back.

"Really, none?" Long pause. "I heard there were some in North Carolina."

"I never heard of that."

"Had you ever heard anyone say the name might be African?"

His look, with those sharp pupils, was the puzzled stare you might give to someone who, after an hour of conversation, you suddenly realize is insane. It was as if I'd asked if he thought we were descended from a tribe of potted ferns.

He said nothing. I let it go, thanked him for his time, and drove off.

I had believed that, by sheer proximity, some shred of truth, some piece of oral or written history from Edward's immediate descendants, would have survived in the land where he had lived. As if that truth were soil or a creek or a bend in the river, not just a memory that could be blinked away.

Later that day I met Socks Mozingo. He was older than Junior and lived in a trailer on Newland Road. "I do sell socks, but that ain't how I got my nickname," he said. "I can't remember exactly how, but think I was shaped like a sock when I was born." I tried to picture this.

Socks said he grew up on the homestead that Mozingo Road was named for, and we drove over to it. The pile of bricks I had seen earlier was the remains of three chimneys of the house they started building in the 1920s. The cemetery was already there when they moved in. "I used to keep it real cleaned up," he said. The timber I had seen was from a shed he built in 1957. It had all looked so ancient.

We drove to a church graveyard to look at his own family's plots, Hinsons and Mozingos. They were all "mixed up with Hinsons one way or another." I could only imagine what that part of the family tree looked like, with the two families marrying each other for 250 years, so many branches and recessive genes reunited.

I asked him what he knew about the name. "It's probably Italian, I think," he said. "We're part Indian and Italian. That's what I've been told."

I didn't linger with Socks. I got the gist.

The Northern Neck wasn't letting go of any secrets. I'd have to follow Spencer west for more answers.

Chapter 7

Setting Out for the Piedmont

B y the time of Edward's death in 1712, tobacco had exhausted the Tidewater's thin layer of soil, and property was consolidated ever more into the hands of the great planters. Most poor farmers were stuck in tenancy, but some who had enough means to buy a small piece of land looked west. A number of these were the luckless second and third sons of the big landowners, who often bequeathed their plantations whole to their first sons to keep their estates intact, according to the tradition of primogeniture.

The migrants moved up the peninsulas first, and then over the fall line into the rolling country of the Piedmont. Virgin timber bespoke the ground's fertility—great chestnuts, sweet gum, oaks, poplars, pines, ash, walnut, and red cedars. A saying had it that if you were looking for good land, you should ride until you could tie your horse to a walnut tree because those always grew in the best soil.

The elite had already snapped up vast acreage, but much still lay unclaimed. The government was trying to reform the land laws to rein in speculation and promote the actual settling of the Piedmont, and already Quakers and Mennonites from Pennsylvania were moving into the Shenandoah Valley on the other side of the Blue Ridge. The English needed to push west before the Spanish crept up the Mississippi Valley from New Orleans or French settlers followed the trappers down from

Canada and hemmed the colony in. Fredericksburg grew into the gateway and commercial hub of the northern Piedmont, sitting right on the fall line, at the highest point of navigation on the Rappahannock River.

The historian Robert Spencer Cotterill wrote this of the Virginians: "The principle of primogeniture and the prevalence of indentured servants filled the land with 'poor white trash' whom the very slaves despised. The descendants of this class, whom conscience or the lack of opportunity prevented from acquiring land, were as distinguished for their shiftlessness as for their poverty. They sank lower and lower with each generation; by 1750 they had lost all initiative and were living in such misery as to attract the attention of contemporary writers. They were separated from the aristocracy by caste distinctions and joined to them by a mutual depravity."

Reading this, I couldn't help but wonder about Edward's grandchildren and their children.

The first Mozingo recorded in the Piedmont was Edward's grandson Charles Mozingo, the son of John. He was the intrepid pioneer of family myth who rescued the crying Indian baby named Opinion. In reality, like the rest of John's children, he seemed to be under the yoke of the baronet Marmaduke Beckwith in the Northern Neck, having signed a lease deal with him in 1741 for ninety acres of land at an annual rent of 530 pounds of tobacco.

Charles first showed up in the records in Culpeper in 1766. His unrecorded trek marked the beginning of the Mozingos' westward migration, chasing cheap land and, no doubt, a place where they could be Portuguese or French or whatever else without anyone knowing the better. No one knows exactly when they started clinging to myths. The earliest reference to our origins I could find was in a newspaper article about a reunion of Charles's descendants in 1918: "Charles Mozingo (originally written Montzingo), of French Huguenot stock, came to Virginia to gain religious freedom about 1750."

This third generation fascinated me. Edward was long dead now, and even the ones remaining in the Neck probably were starting to brush a layer of dust over his origins, if only by leaving what they knew unsaid. Their children were undoubtedly taunted sometimes, or heard whispers, or felt some unarticulated impulse, but as time passed and many moved west, the truth existed only in a heap of decaying papers at the capitol.

I drove out of Fredericksburg on Route 3, hoping to learn more about Spencer, my fifth great-grandfather, who'd shown up in the Orange County census taken by James Madison. I had a rendezvous at noon at a local historical society to see if a diary kept by Madison's cousin Francis Taylor mentioned anything about Spencer or his origins.

The thin winter sun cast a malted light. Strip-mall suburbia—Home Depots, Subways, KFCs, and Targets—clung to the highway well past the Interstate, finally giving way to rolling hay country. Signs for Civil War points of interest dotted the road: "Salem Baptist Church," "Wounding of Jackson," "First Day of Chancellorsville." This area around Fredericksburg saw the worst fighting ever on America's soil, with more than fifteen thousand men killed. The consequences of a system that started with a few hundred Africans like Edward in the seventeenth century came to a bloody full circle here two centuries later.

I had spent the day before scanning through microfilm at the Library of Virginia trying to determine who Spencer's parents were, but walked out with only a headache and the theory I had before: he was the illegitimate son of one of Edward's granddaughters, Margaret. Spencer might have moved out here with his uncle Charles, or followed him later, and ended up in Orange, the county neighboring Culpeper.

At a crossroads called the Wilderness, where an astounding 160,000 men once clashed and 3,741 died in a single battle, I turned onto Route 20 heading southwest into Orange County. As the terrain rose, gaps in the trees offered fleeting vistas that stretched to the Blue Ridge Mountains. My mood lifted. The sun was out, and I was flying home that night. I felt a certain release to be out of the Neck, where the atmosphere felt airless and morose, like one of those fallen barns strangled in vines.

I pulled into the lot of the modern courthouse to spend some time while I waited for the historical society to open and sifted through the old court files and marriage records. The eighteenth-century script was easier to decipher, although the spelling was still arbitrary. In one document the clerk had spelled Spencer's last name numerous ways—Mersiangon, Mossiangon, and Morsingon—and then at the end, next to

Spencer's seal, a perfect "Spencer Mozingo." I pictured the clerk telling him in frustration, "Okay, say it one more time." A little while later, I found the marriage license of his son Joseph, my fourth great-grandfather, to Polly Clemmons, signed on March 31, 1800, by Joseph and her father, Henry.

I still had some time to kill, so I decided to page through some old history books of Orange County and the Madisons. It turns out the great family came up from the Mattaponi River, just a few bends downstream from the Walkers at Locust Grove. Ambrose Madison, the president's grandfather, settled in Orange County in the winter of 1732. When he fell ill in June or July of that year, and then died on August 27, three slaves—Pompey, Turk, and Dido—were arrested and accused of poisoning him. Charges were filed in the capital, Williamsburg, a hundred miles away, and within two weeks of their arrest, they were tried and convicted. Pompey was hanged the next day. His value was appraised at £30, which the county paid to his owner. The judges determined Turk and Dido had played a lesser role in the murder, and they were sentenced to twenty-nine lashes each. It would be nice to think of this as leniency and not merely a financial decision, but slaves were expensive. I wondered how they even knew Ambrose was poisoned, given that they had no blood analysis and his illness lasted over a month, at a time when having "a good vomit" was considered sound medical advice.

The fear of murderous slaves ran rampant throughout Virginia at this time, as more enslaved Africans poured in and began to outnumber whites. Orange County had suffered throes of violence and paranoia at its inception. A man named Peter was convicted in 1737 for killing his owner with an ax, and his head "put on a pole to deter others from doing the like." A woman named Letty was accused of poisoning two people in 1748 but was acquitted, while a woman named Eve was convicted of poisoning her master and was burned at the stake. Back in Richmond County, I found a case from 1730 in which a slave named James was accused of murder and taken to jail. He was found dead one morning, and the court ordered his body to be cut into quarters, each displayed at a specific spot, such as the ferry dock and crossroads, and his head put on a pole at the courthouse so that no one, not even children, would be spared the putrescent, fly-ridden sight and smell of a dead bogeyman.

When Spencer showed up in Orange County sometime before 1782, life was still austere and tenuous. Wolves still howled in the night and devoured livestock. Poor farmers lived in "puncheon cabins" made of bark-covered scraps from the sawpit, with dirt floors and light from a wick stuck in a ladle of grease. People regularly starved to death, and children died of fevers, colds, cholera, and typhoid. Of James Madison's eleven siblings, only six lived to adulthood. Even the big planters ate squirrels and trapped meat. By the end of autumn, however, they rolled their hogsheads of tobacco to Fredericksburg and returned with oysters, brandy, and whatever they could find and afford from the larger world.

I grabbed a sandwich at Subway and ate in the parking lot of the historical society, waiting for it to open. It had been difficult to locate Francis Taylor's diary, as it was never published, but I had finally tracked down a copy here.

An elderly volunteer let me in, sat me at a folding table in the middle of the room, and handed me a three-ring binder with the Taylor diary transcript, about five hundred pages of small type. I had an hour before I needed to leave for the airport, and given my luck with records so far, my expectations of finding mention of Spencer Mozingo were low. My mind was already flying home.

Taylor's words were spare. He made simple observations of the natural world and accounts of his day. On the first page, dated January 11, 1786, he noted that he sent to a Mr. Thomas for a gallon of cider and heard that "a negro of Capt. C. Conways yesterday wounded his overseer with an ax, in a dangerous manner, and was sent to jail for the crime." That week Taylor went to a dance with "young people," dined with James Madison's father and other notables, and got a violent headache and fever.

The people and atmosphere of Spencer's world came to life in these small details not captured in the courthouse records. Taylor noted the arrival of young bluebirds in March, and spring beginning "to show by the trees looking green in the mountains." He planted "white speck'd" melon seed in the garden one dry afternoon, and he took an evening stroll in Mr. Ingram's "old cherry orchard," registering that the cherries were ripe. He went to court now and then to catch up on gossip or see a trial or a slave auction. "Negro boy 9 years old sold for £20.2.0." Many of Taylor's notes were about his own family's slaves. "Negro George who went rolling [hogsheads] Monday got home about two o'clock—says the horse K Herod won the race at Fredericksburg yesterday," he wrote on June 7.

Taylor was a bachelor who fought in the Revolutionary War. His father, George, was Madison's great-uncle and one of the area's big planters and slaveholders. Francis was in the midst of overseeing the building of a new house for his father. Slaves had dug the cellar in May and put the stone walls up. He noted that their overseer, Joe Clark, stockpiled boards, bricks, and sand at his house.

On June 26, a cousin named Hubbard Taylor sent for some bricks with lime, Charles Porter sent fifteen rafters, and "Spence Mozingo came to J Clarks to get boards for covering tobacco house."

"Oh shit," I whispered.

The volunteer looked up from behind the counter.

"I found my ancestor," I said.

She smiled politely.

Seeing his name in a diary was far more visceral than seeing it in census and court records. Those excerpts were like dusty bone fragments. This was him walking up with his tools on a warm summer day ready to get to work on the tobacco house. I felt as if I suddenly noticed my own face among the Founding Fathers on the back of the two-dollar bill. Just a few pages back Taylor ate breakfast with James Madison. Now he was talking about my forebear.

I began skimming frantically, looking for Spencer's name.

"Went down the run to Mozingos to fish . . . caught only two," Francis wrote in May 1787. "Spence Mozingo came to work," he wrote on October 9.

Time was closing in on me. I was going to miss my plane if I didn't put the diary down. I knew I could pay someone to copy it and mail it to me, but I couldn't wait for that, so I furiously scrawled out notes.

"S. Mozingo came here in Evening & expects his wife to [give birth] soon, Let him have . . . Brandy & 2 lb. bro. Sugar." This was the first known reference to his wife, who never showed up in a record, despite having six children by him.

Taylor made notes of Spencer cutting logs, raising another roof, putting up a stable, and training with the local militia on Saturdays. I thought of how Edward had those carpenter tools and the tradition of trades being passed down through family lines.

Then I hit a peculiar entry. On March 23, 1790, "George Taylor sold Mozingo to Hub Taylor for £60."

What was this? *Sold?*

Then this on March 31: "Mozingo (whom G Taylor sold Hd Taylor) set off down to his new master."

My great-great-great-great-great-grandfather, who was listed in the 1782 census as white and paying taxes, was a slave?

I whipped through pages but could find only one more entry: "Had some Spanish Potatoes planted. S Daniel said they were all that were sound belonging to Mozingo." He was gone.

I quickly copied a few of the pages and jumped in my car, my head spinning. I could grasp having a black ancestor way back in the seventeenth century, but having a direct paternal line to a slave in the nineteenth? This could not have been kept a secret so easily. And if Spencer had actually been a slave, first owned by George Taylor and then sold to Hubbard, wouldn't his descendants all be Taylors? Wouldn't I?

This was unfathomable.

But the words were clear. *Mozingo. Sold. Master.*

I spent days at home trying to make sense of this and began to track down the story of Hubbard Taylor, Spencer's new master. Before the purchase, he had bought big plots of land in the frontier of Kentucky, and he'd returned to Virginia in 1789 to settle his affairs. He wrote a brief first-person account of his life near his death: "A party of Indians followed us all the way home through the wilderness. A party of whites that would not keep along with us was attacked, some were killed, others wounded. In April 1790, I set out with my family to the new settlement, now the State of Kentucky and reached it the 13th of May safely."

I consulted a local historian in Orange County, Ann Miller, with whom I'd discussed Spencer and who was growing ever more intrigued by him and the Mozingo clan. "Curiouser and curiouser, as Alice said," she emailed. She was convinced Spencer was a craftsman working for George Taylor as a free man, and the fact that Francis mentioned Spencer's wife certainly suggested that my ancestor was free. "Then bang! The 1789 and 1790 entries which seem to be describing another situation altogether."

She vowed to investigate.

Anyone who dabbles in genealogy at some point finds himself entertaining whimsical fantasies about his ancestors and trying to chase them down. I didn't see how Spencer could have been a slave, but I allowed myself to flow with it for a few days, to the point that I briefly convinced myself he was an illegitimate son of James Madison's father with a slave. I found the African-American Roots Project run by a doctor at the University of Massachusetts, who was testing the DNA of descendants of Madison's slaves to see if any had been fathered by the president or his father. I ordered my test kit. Maybe my Y chromosome was Madison's.

I looked for records of Madison's life in Orange County in which Spencer might show up, just to see if they even crossed paths. Many of the fourth president's personal letters were burned by overprotective and stunningly myopic relatives after his death. But many can still be found in the Library of Congress.

Madison wrote in a tight-knit hand that fit his restrained demeanor. In 1786, he had come home to Montpelier after serving on the Continental Congress and worked on his plan for the Constitution. At the time, Spence Mozingo was working for George Taylor, building the house about six miles away. Ever the introvert and scholar, Madison holed up in his room in his family's Georgian mansion, where his cousin Francis visited one day in March. Francis wrote in his diary that young Madison "came to breakfast of which he ate sparingly, then would go to his room till a little before dinner, after dinner play at Whist for half bits till bed time."

On May 12, Madison wrote to his friend Thomas Jefferson, then U.S. Minister to France. It is thought by some historians that Madison mostly wrote at a small desk in the second-floor library, looking over a green where they raced horses, then beyond over stands of tulip poplar and oak that sloped down to the Rapidan River, to a distant horizon of the Blue Ridge Mountains. This was a warm day, with some clouds but no rain. Madison had just received Jefferson's letter of February 8. The two men of voracious intellect were using Jefferson's ambassadorship to acquire books and trappings of cosmopolitan Europe that were difficult for even the great planters to find in America.

"I can get for you the original Paris edition in folio of the Encyclopedie for 620 livres," Jefferson wrote, in loose, slanting script. "The new one will be superior in far the greater number of articles: but not in all and the possession of the ancient one has moreover the advantage of supplying present use. I have bought one for myself, but wait your orders as to you.

"I remember your purchase of a watch in Philadelphia. If it should not have proved good, you can probably sell her. In that case I can get for you here, one made as perfect as human art can make it."

Madison dipped his pen in the inkwell and wrote back. "A copy of the old edition of the Encyclopedia is desirable for the reasons you mention, but as I should gratify my desire in this particular at the expense of something else which I can less dispense with, I must content myself with the new edition for present."

He did take Jefferson's offer of the watch, though, then went on to update his friend on the falling price of tobacco and local elections— using one of his famous ciphers at one point to tell him something confidential—and then continued an ongoing discourse they had on the wildlife native to the area. Jefferson had a famously wide array of interests and was trying to classify the Piedmont's quadrupeds. Madison, eight years younger than Jefferson and not nearly as illustrious, was a student of the land himself and eager to help.

"You have I believe justly considered the [groundhog] as the Marmotte of Europe. I have lately had an opportunity of examining a female one with great attention. Its weight, after it had lost a great deal of blood, was 5½ pounds. Its dimensions, shape, teeth, and structure within, as far as I could [judge], corresponded in substance with the description given by the [French naturalist] D'Aubenton. . . . The principal variations were in the face, which was shorter in the [groundhog] than in the proportions of the Marmotte, and was less arched about the root of the nose. In the feet, each of the forefeet having a fifth nail about ⅓ of an inch long growing out of the inward side of the heel."

He went on for two more pages on the matter before signing off.

That same day, Francis Taylor paid Spencer Mozingo three shillings for work, according to his diary. (Two lines down, he recorded buying a "Guinea" for £20, 10 shillings, about the same price as the nine-year-old boy sold at the courthouse, but just a third of the price that Mozingo would fetch four years later.)

That day, May 12, 1786, was as close as I could tie Spencer to Madison in space and time: six miles apart, one man writing to Thomas Jefferson, the other getting paid for some rough carpentry. I doubted their worlds intersected much, unless Spencer was the worker bringing Madison his dead groundhogs to measure. When the mail brought the DNA test kit to determine if they had the same father, in which case I'd have the same Y chromosome as Madison, I put it in a drawer that usually gets emptied in the trash every couple of years. The fantasy had run its course.

Madison and Hubbard Taylor were close, and when Hubbard moved to Kentucky with his slave Mozingo, Madison regularly wrote him. Madison was speculating on land there, and his cousin managed his holdings. A librarian in Clark County, Kentucky, told me she would look through Hubbard Taylor's papers for any mention of his slaves or the name Mozingo.

But before she got back to me, Ann Miller, the Virginia historian helping me with Spencer, sent me a note: "My checking of the 1782 Personal Property tax lists for Orange County indicates there were indeed two Mozingos." Spencer Mozingo had his own household, no slaves, one horse, four cattle. George Taylor owned eighteen slaves, including one named Mozingo.

By now my copy of the diary had arrived and I could see the difference. In some instances, it mentioned an S. Mozingo or Spence Mozingo who was clearly a free man: "Spence Mozingo was here, settled his account with George Taylor, balance due Mozingo $^{16}/_{10}$," or "S. Mozingo stayed two nights past, went home." In others, it mentions only a Mozingo, as when "Mozingo says a mad cow died today and if it should be skinned, which I directed to be done."

"Pretty amazing," Miller wrote. "You have two individuals named Mozingo, both with some sort of association with the Taylor family—what are the odds?"

That same night I heard back from the researcher in Kentucky. The only entry in Hubbard Taylor's ledger in 1790 about slaves was this: "Bought two negro men of Mr. Taylor's, James and Austin. £60 each—120." One of those had to be Mozingo renamed, as the transaction occurred at the same time, at the same price, with the same seller.

On the next page, Taylor wrote, "Austin died in Kentucky."

Sometimes you wish you could ask the dead a few questions.

Who was this slave Mozingo? Maybe he was Spencer's son by a female slave. Maybe George Taylor named a slave after Spencer as a poke at his murky racial status. Maybe Mozingo was a "saltwater slave," as they called those born in Africa, and kept his name, as Edward had done 146 years before. Or maybe he was one of Edward's descendants who didn't cross the color line; free people of color were in constant risk of enslavement, and maybe that's what befell this Mozingo. A family could diverge to the extreme in just a few generations when their blood was mixed, such were the vagaries of race in America at the time.

Chapter 8

White in Bourbon County

The next trace of Spencer was a reference in the tax records of Bourbon County, Kentucky, from 1808. Spencer, listed as a "white male," paid taxes that year for himself, his horse, and another white male between sixteen and twenty-one years old, presumably one of his younger sons. Remarkably, the record also shows that he was living only about twelve miles from Hubbard Taylor and Mozingo the slave, if he was still alive. Spencer must have moved there only recently, many years after Taylor, who had made the journey in 1790. As different as the two men's backgrounds were, they both found themselves in this booming frontier territory, following the call of the rich limestone soils and sweeping savannahs of bluegrass.

Kentucky had become the new American Eden. As early as the 1750s, word had trickled back to the eastern colonies of a Great Meadow beyond the wall of mountains. Kanta-Kee's shale hills and gentle valleys coursed with streams teeming with beaver, otter, and mink. A trapper could take as many pelts as he could carry, and food abounded: buffalo, bear, elk, and turkeys converged in great droves on the region's muddy salt licks and could be hunted down with little effort. While Shawnee, Mingo, Cherokee, Delaware, and Iroquois used the region as their hunting grounds, none called it home, and pioneers saw it as free for the taking. Painters would later depict Daniel Boone gazing down into the Great Meadow from Pilots Knob in 1769 as if he were Moses looking into Canaan. Much like the earlier accounts of Tidewater Virginia, the depiction of Kentucky as an Eden proved to be a bit overstated. But it did have rich soil, some of the oldest and richest in America, and abundant meadows, which made settlement exponentially easier.

Though Boone was not the first white man to set foot there, he did more than anyone to explore the forests of Kentucky and settle the "Bluegrass Island" at its core. The Shawnee from the north and Cherokee from the south dogged his expeditions, and his ability to escape harm at dire moments turned him into a towering figure in American lore. But the real Boone, who never wore a coonskin cap, also suffered terrible losses from tribes who resented his incursions. His son James was tortured and murdered, his daughter Jemima was kidnapped and held for three days before Boone rescued her, Boone himself was shot in the ankle and taken hostage for months, and his brother was killed in an ambush meant for Boone. But all the tales of his exploits mask his true lasting legacy: unleashing a human stampede on the place he loved, and would soon deplore. In 1775, Boone was commissioned to hack a path from Virginia through the Cumberland Gap and northward to the Great Meadow. It was known as "Boone's Trace" and later the "Wilderness Road." With the Revolution, the Americans saw the populating of Kentucky, still a county of Virginia, as a means of staking their claim on the Ohio Valley before the British loyalists in the north or the Spanish on the lower Mississippi moved in.

But with more whites streaming in and poaching their buffalo reserves, native hostility grew fiercer. As the war ground along in the east, the British played on old Indian alliances to incite the Shawnee against the new Kentuckians, who were vulnerable out there in the bush. Supply lines for the frontiersmen became woefully overextended, with the nearest stores and militias over two hundred miles away. Misery, starvation, and violence sent many settlers huffing back on the narrow trails across the Appalachians. By 1777 only two settlements were occupied, and they were desperately undersupplied, enduring constant attack and showing a grim likeness to early Jamestown. A settler named

Sarah Graham later wrote of this period, "14 persons, that I knew their faces, committed suicide." Indians ambushed them when they left the cramped forts to hunt and tend crops or venture to distant springs to boil salt to preserve their food. Their predicament grew even worse when Americans at Point Pleasant murdered one of the more conciliatory Shawnee chiefs, Cornstalk, who had come to talk peace. He and his son were thrown in jail and executed, and after that the tribe resolved to drive the settlers out of the region for good.

But the forts were able to survive a terrible winter and repel several sieges. More settlers and Virginia militiamen arrived, and by 1782 the heavy fighting was over. The Great Meadow was open for business. Surveyors poured in as the Virginia legislature offered cheap land to anyone who would clear a few acres and build a cabin. A man just needed to get a warrant from the newly established Land Office and a survey of the property he wanted to claim. Boone found himself in high demand as a "jobber," looking for land for new arrivals.

Grandees like Madison tripped over themselves speculating on rich Kentucky soil, and hardscrabble pioneer families streamed in from the Shenandoah Valley, Pennsylvania, Maryland, and the Carolinas. Fewer settlers came from old Tidewater Virginia, according to the historian Cotterill in his book *History of Pioneer Kentucky*, because the "low ridges of the Blue Ridge had formed an impenetrable barrier to the shiftless peasantry and effete aristocracy of the Tidewater."

Kentucky surveys were done with little skill and in much haste, using trees, rocks, and shifting stream bends as reference points, which after the fact proved impossible to delineate. Many claims overlapped one another, and as the place got more crowded this "shingling" erupted in scandal and a flood of lawsuits.

Hubbard Taylor managed the Kentucky ventures of his relatives in the Taylor and Madison clans. He was one of those younger sons of a great family forced to set out on his own. Starting in 1780, he embarked on several long expeditions, locating lands for his family and friends, including his lucky firstborn cousin, James Madison. Many of the speculative ventures ended in failure. Madison sold his Kentucky lands at a loss, and Hubbard seemed to have found himself entangled in many a man's misfortunes there.

But the settlers kept coming, subduing the wilderness of Kentucky in a shockingly short amount of time. In 1780 only several hundred white people lived there; twelve years later more than a hundred thousand did. The last buffalo in the Bluegrass was killed just two decades after Boone first peered down on the virgin terrain from Pilots Knob. Disheartened by the loss of game that drew him to Kentucky, and beset by lawsuits from his surveys, Boone zagged back to the wilds in western Virginia and eventually trekked far west, into Spanish Missouri.

The year after Boone left, Taylor traveled back to Virginia to retrieve his family and settle in Kentucky for good. With the two slaves he bought for £120 in tow, Mozingo presumably being one of them, the family trekked up the Potomac River Valley to Fort Redstone, on the Monongahela River in southern Pennsylvania, then floated north to Fort Pitt, joining the Ohio and on down to the Kentucky port of Limestone, where a wide buffalo trace ran to the salt licks in the heart of the Bluegrass. They settled at Springhill in what was then Bourbon County. Hubbard became a magistrate and important figure, living to the age of eighty.

Spencer's life in Kentucky played out very differently. He must have known of the slave Mozingo who had been sold to Hubbard. One can't help but imagine the different dramas that might have ensued when he arrived in Kentucky, so close to Taylor's homestead, if there was any relation between them: Spencer sneaking around to the slave quarters at Springhill to see his son, a tense, awkward interaction, words never spoken, a showdown with Hubbard. Or, of course, the two Mozingos may never have met. So many aspects of the lives of the poor of any color went unrecorded, it is impossible to know.

We can certainly speculate that back in Virginia, Spencer must have talked with his friends about the cheap rich land to be had in Kentucky, the waning Indian battles, the more egalitarian society. Perhaps he had saved his money from carpentry to get a parcel of his own. The 1810 federal census gives little more information. It says that Spencer Mesinger was living with his wife and three of his children in the township of Stoner, Bourbon County. His son James lived nearby with his wife and young son and daughter. Joseph, my fourth great-grandfather, lived in neighboring Scott County with his wife and five children under the age of ten.

Spencer had six children we know of—Joseph, James, Benjamin, Nelly, Thomas, and Polly—and four of them married into the Clemmons clan, who, like the Mozingos, spelled their name every which way. By 1817 they were all living in adjacent Harrison County, and they owned land. Spencer had a hundred acres on Mill Creek, which flowed into the Licking River just north of the township of Cynthiana. Joseph owned sixty acres on Raven Creek, which met the Licking just downstream. Spencer appears to have sold or lost his land within two years and moved in with Joseph's family.

Joseph acquired forty-four more acres there in 1819 and kept his land until the whole lot of them moved to Indiana in the 1830s. For about fifteen years, there in that drainage of Raven Creek lived all sorts of Mozingos and Clemmonses. I headed there to take in the scene and look for any remnant of their lives.

Harrison County used to be part of Bourbon County, so naturally the first thing I did when I arrived that afternoon was stop at the state liquor store outside of Cynthiana to buy a bottle of Jack Daniel's. The man at the counter told me lustily that if he bought that bottle, 750 milliliters, he would drink it dry in one sitting; he'd have no choice. "Yep, it's good stuff," I said. "I'm pretty sure I'll get at least two nights out of it." When I saw where I was staying, I wasn't so confident. The Evergreen Motel consisted of a low row of derelict rooms about twenty feet from the truck traffic going to and from Ohio on Highway 27. The louvered windows in the back faced a pretty swath of forest, but for some reason the owners had glued the curtains to the glass so you could not look out. The faux-wood paneling made the room yellowish and claustrophobic. Workers had plugged sprawling gaps and holes in the paneling with white spackle. I wouldn't bother to note that it reminded me of the Bates Motel if I didn't soon find out that's what the locals actually called it.

I headed out to see if I could find Raven Creek before dark, driving north along the Licking River. Forest and pasture shutter-framed by. The sluggish river coiled in and out of sight. Spores and gnats and dragonflies caught the late afternoon sun, drowsily drifting about like embers.

The rolling shale country was about as populated now as it was in Spencer's time. The 1830 census counted about 6,500 people living on the west side of the river. About 1,200 of those were slaves. Joseph Mozingo, my fourth great-grandfather, owned one, a girl between ten and twenty. His sister Polly and her husband, Thomas, owned two. Such small-time slave owners were usually only a step or two above basic subsistence themselves, but could afford to have an extra hand in the fields or a girl to help with housework. In the case of Joseph, the girl probably lived in the house, as it would have been too costly to build separate quarters for a single person.

I wondered how he treated her.

Forty-one "free people of color" lived on the west side of the river back then, most of them with white families, presumably working as servants. The free black and mixed-race families of the pariah class generally had so little to provide for their children that they had no choice but to bond them out as indentured servants so the kids could eat and have decent clothes and perhaps learn a trade.

I had found only three or four free colored households. Cyrus Vena lived with his young wife and three children under ten next to a white family who owned eight slaves. George Davis, who was over fifty-five, headed a family of nine. Rebekah Penny was hard to figure out. She appeared to be a "white" woman over forty in a household with two colored males and two colored females between the ages of ten and twenty-four, and a colored boy under ten. Perhaps she was a widow whose children were mixed race. Or maybe she was just light-skinned enough to pass for white. In the next sixteen years, Penny would go to court asserting that her children were all freeborn. It's not clear whether they had gotten pulled into slavery or were simply making sure they wouldn't be. Free blacks lived in perpetual fear of this. In April 1839 "Allen and Joseph Penny came into court and from the oath of William Gray, it appears they were freeborn. It is ordered that emancipation be prepared for them. Allen is about 5'9" tall, yellow complexion, aged about 20 years. Joseph is about 5'11" tall, aged 18 years, bright yellow, no marks."

The number of slaves in Kentucky paled in comparison to Virginia, where a good 40 percent of the population was enslaved by this time. In Richmond County, where Edward had settled, black slaves made up 56 percent of the populace. And Kentucky was slightly more clement than Virginia and the Deep South in its treatment of people of color. The law allowed slaves to learn to read and write, even to attend one of the few schools taught by free men of color. Poring through the records of Harrison County, I read of numerous slaves emancipated by their owners. While one can only guess whether that happened for economic or compassionate reasons, there was no doubt some slave owners developed more empathetic connections to their slaves than did others. Still, the system was relentlessly cruel at its heart: slaves had to be absolutely servile or risk beatings or death, their marriages meant nothing in the eyes of the law, and even their children were legally their master's, who could abuse them and sell them off at will. In Kentucky, the slaves' lot ironically grew worse after 1807, when the U.S. Congress followed England in banning the transatlantic slave trade. To supply labor to the sprawling cotton plantations of Alabama, Louisiana, and Mississippi, Kentucky and Virginia became "slave-breeding" states. The great fear among slaves in the breeding states was to have their children "sold south," never to be seen again. I could only hope Joe Mozingo was a man to emancipate his slave, not sell her off.

I came around a bend into the shade where the map indicated Raven Creek crossed the road, and saw a deep clear stream running through a culvert. Up the hill sat a big stone house, with a historical landmark sign. This was Stony Castle, built in 1807 by a John Smith on the stage road between Cincinnati and Lexington. Smith became postmaster in

1829, and the castle became the first post office between the two cities, anointed the Mouth of Raven Creek Post Office. My ancestors lived around here somewhere. Daniel Boone conducted the original surveys of Raven Creek, and Boones still resided here in Spencer's time. I doubled back to the stream. Down on the right, a peeling old home sat under a few big hickories in a field. I pulled down the gravel embankment and knocked on the door. The shade was moist and cool and smelled rich and mossy. A dog barked from a kennel in a wedge of sun at the deep end of the property. No one answered, but a car was parked there in the drive. I knocked again, but again got no answer. I'd come back tomorrow.

Walking back to my rental car, I noticed the silhouetted figure of a man in the field. He stood still, looking straight at me. I called out, "Hello." He didn't move or say anything, then silently sidestepped behind a tree. My neck hairs went up. I paced hard to my car, fumbled with the key, and winced as I accidentally spun the front wheels going back up the embankment to the highway. Glancing over my shoulder into the field, I couldn't see the man. He must have still been standing behind the tree.

I wasn't going back tomorrow.

I headed back to Cynthiana, had some dinner, and then tucked in with that bottle of Jack Daniel's at the Bates Motel. I was kind of hoping someone would be sitting in the patio chairs out front enjoying the warm evening, but the place was mostly empty. I got some ice and my disposable bathroom cup and lay down on the bed with my book and a drink.

I had brought Faulkner's *Light in August*, the great southern writer's exploration of racial hatred and the entwined obsession with ancestry, figuring he could help me envision my own forebears struggling with their low station and mysterious origins. Faulkner knew the "bleak heritage of bloodpride" among the poor whites who'd had everything else sweated out of them. He described the violent restlessness of a rural people pressed down by the long arm of the past and the North. I envisioned Spencer as his character Joe Christmas, abandoned to an orphanage as a baby, restive and tortured by the suspicion of mixed-race ancestry that floated about him.

Christmas, who looked white, showed up one Friday morning at a planing mill in Faulkner's mythic Yoknapatawpha County, Mississippi. No one had ever seen him before, and a worker named Byron Bunch sized him up:

He looked like a tramp, yet not like a tramp either. His shoes were dusty and his trousers were soiled too. But they were of decent serge, sharply creased, and his shirt was soiled but it was a white shirt, and he wore a tie and a stiffbrim straw hat that was quite new, cocked at an angle arrogant and baleful above his still face. He did not look like a professional hobo in his professional rags, but there was something definitely rootless about him, as though no town nor city was his, no street, no walls, no square of earth his home. And that he carried that knowledge with him always as though it were a banner, with a quality ruthless, lonely, and almost proud. . . .

"Put this man on," the superintendent said to the foreman. "He says he can handle a scoop, anyhow. You can put him on the sawdust pile."

The others had not stopped work, yet there was not a man in the shed who was not again watching the stranger in his soiled city clothes, with his dark, insufferable face and his whole air of cold and quiet contempt. . . .

The newcomer turned without a word. The others watched him go down to the sawdust pile and vanish and reappear with a shovel and go to work. The foreman and the superintendent were talking at the door. They parted and the foreman returned. "His name is Christmas," he said.

"His name is what?"

"Christmas."

"Is he a foreigner?"

"Did you ever hear of a white man named Christmas?" the foreman said.

"I never heard of nobody a-tall named it," the other said.

I sat up and took a good draw of bourbon. "His name is what?" I muttered, the liquor giving speech to my thoughts.

Mozingo.

WHITE IN BOURBON COUNTY

Is he a foreigner?
Did you ever hear of a white man named Mozingo?
I never heard of nobody a-tall named it.

That was the first time Byron remembered that he had ever thought how a man's name, which is supposed to be just the sound for who he is, can be somehow an augur of what he will do, if other men can only read the meaning in time. It seemed to him that none of them had looked especially at the stranger until they heard his name. But as soon as they heard it, it was as though there was something in the sound of it that was trying to tell them what to expect; that he carried with him his own inescapable warning, like a flower its scent or a rattlesnake its rattle.

Faulkner flashed back to when Christmas was a child in the orphanage and was brought to the matron's office one day. Two strangers were there with her, and she informed him he was going to live with them in the country.

Then it came: "Christmas. A heathenish name. Sacrilege. I will change that. . . .

"From now on his name will be McEachern."

"That will be suitable," the matron said. "To give him your name."

"He will eat my bread and he will observe my religion," the stranger said. "Why should he not bear my name?"

The child was not listening. He was not bothered. He did not especially care, anymore than if the man had said the day was hot when it was not hot. He didn't even bother to say to himself, *My name aint McEachern. My name is Christmas.* There was no need to bother about that yet.

I imagined Edward saying, "My name is not Walker. My name is Mozingo."

I dozed off in a smooth whiskey descent and later woke up with a jolt to a strange sound from the minifridge. I inspected and found it wasn't even plugged in, that the sound was coming through the wall. I lay back down, anxious, and listened to the trucks rumbling down Highway 27 as if right through my brain.

How did I get here? I asked myself. I had told myself in Virginia that I wouldn't go too far with this search, and here I was alone in a cheap motel in northern Kentucky feeling completely lost. *What the hell was I doing?*

I had become obsessed. I dreamed day and night of finding out exactly how Edward got to Virginia, which Caribbean island he must have stopped in, how his neighbors treated him, where in Africa he came from, how he was related to Spencer. I thought of both of them constantly, and down in the stacks of the library or in some county courthouse when I felt I was coming upon the tiniest revelation, a fibrillating excitement sent me pacing around the room. Understanding my origins had become more existential than just solving a mystery or resolving a racial conundrum. It was like reading my own blueprint, seeing how I came together. But the plans were still too hazy to read clearly.

I couldn't give up now. This was just a predawn crisis of confidence a little sleep would wipe away.

I hadn't felt that connection to Edward I had sought on Pantico Run, but I was determined to find some palpable trace of Spencer to cross that divide of time and space, and race.

In the courthouse the next day, with a hangover like a light-duty staple rusting in my cranium, I gleaned some more details of Spencer's life. By 1825, nearly forty years after he had shown up on a warm summer day to build a tobacco house for James Madison's great-uncle, he was "a poor person in the care of John Smith," the postmaster in the stone building. The county paid people to look after their impoverished neighbors. In 1827 an Asbury Broadwell was watching out for him. Spencer's wife must have died by then, her name lost to history. His two oldest sons owned land, and Joseph had his slave, but they weren't caring for their father. Did the dysfunction in our family line go back that far? Was he truly like Joe Christmas, a person so tormented over his identity that he reacted violently toward anyone he got close to? Maybe Spencer, suffering the demons delivered to him by a racist society, drove everyone away in the same way.

Just before his death, Spencer apparently moved in with his daughter Polly, whose husband, Thomas Clemmons, had died. The census of 1830 showed her living with six children and a man between eighty and ninety. Her aging in-laws, Henry and Mary Clemmons, lived nearby. Henry was in his nineties by then. They too had been listed as "poor people" in the care of others.

I spent a couple of hours trying to locate where Joseph Mozingo's land would have been, but the surveys gave few clues. When he sold his hundred acres to Solomon Perrin for $250, the property was described as "on the waters of Raven Creek, and bounded as follows to wit: beginning at a sugar tree and buckeye, on the bank of Raven Creek, corner to Jacob Huffman, thence North, 80 degrees east, 154 poles to a buckeye, thence North, 27 degrees West, 125 poles to a buckeye and hickory on the bank of said creek, thence binding on the several meanders of the creek to the beginning."

I wasn't going to find that spot. My only hope was to track down whom he sold it to, and whom that person sold it to, and so on, until the current owner or modern address popped up. Unfortunately, Perrin sold the land in five separate parcels in 1846. I managed to track James Mozingo's land a little further, to 1896, before the trail vanished into the thicket of probate actions and subdivisions.

Leaving that morass for some fresh air, I headed over to the Battle Grove Cemetery to see if I could find Spencer's grave. The lawn draped like a soft green towel over a big round hill with giant maples overlooking the city and valley below. A little morning gray hadn't burned off yet, while a team of lawn mowers sawed through the peace. I walked around studying graves, lichen coated, some so eroded I could barely read the inscriptions. The span of a whole life boiled down to a few words and dates, and even that didn't survive in the end.

I found Spencer's caretaker, Asbury Broadwell, buried in Section F. He died at fifty-two in 1843. The office had a registry of the graves, but no Mozingo, which I figured would be the case.

Spencer didn't even get words on a stone. It's hard to imagine he once lived in the same neighborhood with a man who changed the course of human events, a man with cities, counties, colleges, a state capital, avenues and boulevards, and naval ships named after him. Spencer's hard life was of no distinction in the end. He lived, worked, had children, and died, a soldier ant of American history. His family probably buried him on their property with a pine cross, and a few years later, when they moved west, left the cross to rot in the briar and vines.

At the local library, I found a map of the Raven Creek area in the late 1800s and suddenly drew a bead on where my family had lived. Thomas Clemmons Jr., the son of Spencer's daughter Polly, still lived there at the time this map was made. And three families who had bought the land once owned by Joseph Mozingo resided right nearby. My hangover lifted in a great mania as I barreled down a ridge toward their nook of Raven Creek, blazing into my fatherland in the bright, white, lovely, lonely light. Wild irises lined the road ditches. I braked for a moment by a weatherboard house half-consumed by nature, choked in vines and spiderwebs, speared from floor to roof with maple shoots. This could have been the old Clemmons house where Spencer lived his final days, but I couldn't tell exactly from the crude map, so I kept driving. The pavement meandered down and gave way to two dirt tire tracks, swooping down into a red-dirt valley and up a little bluff. It ended at a huge abandoned barn, its lower planks long picked away, the upper boards hanging, warped and splintered, like gray scabs. I parked and locked up. Down the hill I could hear the gurgling of water through the trees. Loose gray shale cliffs loomed on the other side. I didn't see any "No Trespassing" signs, but a couple of blue shotgun shells in the weeds made a similar point.

I put some gas-station cigars in my shirt pocket and strode down to the creek. At the bottom, the ground grew soft and moist as I pushed through waist-high clump grass and stepped over rusted barbed wire strung between trees and stumps, half buried in the flood detritus. And there I came upon the creek, braiding serenely through the riparian trees. I took a deep breath and looked around. A tremendous euphoria rose in my chest. Crickets and cicadas sputtered and buzzed and revved their engines. Amber butterflies and electric-blue dragonflies dipped down for sips of water. The creek divided around a stand of alders and fell over some sticks into a broad pond, a few feet deep. The water was silty but clear enough to see the bottom. Ghostlike fish, with black spots on their sides, flitted out from under submerged branches.

I sat on a little saddle of grass next to the creek and lit one of my cheap cigars, and lay back in the soft grass, staring up at the mottled white limbs of a sycamore reaching into the deep blue. It felt like my chest was expanding into the sky.

The new spring foliage was so green and lithe it shimmered and set the whole world in motion, a swimming vibration that drew in the warblers and sparrows and larks, the riffle of the stream and the insect engines and grasshoppers clicking like misaligned fans and the falling twigs and branches landing with a crack in the bramble, and me now sending up puffs of blue smoke, curling and swirling, as if conducting the show all around.

A Mozingo is smoking tobacco on this creek again.

Spencer Mozingo lived here once. His son Joe Mozingo must have smoked his pipe at this creek, tilled the red soil of this bottomland, and grown tobacco, corn, hemp, and wheat. I hadn't discovered exactly where Spencer had lived in Virginia or uncovered the truth of his connection to Edward. But here, I could feel him.

I am here, Spencer.

The fish hit every little twig and leaf that landed on the surface, hungry. I wished I had a pole. I took off my shoes and dangled my feet in the water as a fitful breeze pushed leaves up the stream.

I could not see what separated Spencer and me on this day. Time, yes, but sitting there I felt like the creek coursed outside of time. It had flowed along in its quietude as Shawnee Indians hunted buffalo, as the Twin Towers fell, as Union and Confederate soldiers fought twenty miles away, as we fought a war that spanned the world, as the economy collapsed and boomed and collapsed, as settlers came and moved farther west, as Daniel Boone hiked along it in a buckskin coat with his surveyor string, and as a newspaper reporter in a plaid shirt and jeans hiked along it smoking a cigar.

Spencer's great-grandson lived long enough to know my grandfather.

I picked a thick stalk of grass, put it between my molars, and felt the stiff husk give way to the sour pulp juice. I felt I could have been in any time, watching the water striders dart about my toes.

Eventually I noticed the gnats were coming up for the evening in little dervishes. A big brown and yellow butterfly bobbed along, heading up the valley. It struck me that I hadn't had a moment like this since I ended my lateral drift in life with journalism school, a career, family, adult responsibilities—this sense of being interwoven with something deep and yawning wide, of a dimension opening up, just sitting alone in a field. I didn't want to let it go. But the light was falling and the cascade of sensation was ebbing, as it always had.

What time was it?

It was getting dark, and the eeriness was coming on.

Spencer's descendants moved on from Raven Creek to Indiana, and all evidence shows they were forever after seen as white. I could never know what Spencer knew about his roots. That slave Mozingo made me think he must have known something, and it's certainly possible his mother told him that his great-grandfather was African. But Africa was a long way away by the time Spencer was born more than a hundred years after Edward landed. It seemed unlikely that Spencer would have any feeling for Africa or, if they were trying to bury that history, that any lore had been passed down. I had no strong sense of Sweden from my mother's grandparents, who emigrated a century before my birth, and that side was a tightly intact family proud of its heritage. If awareness of the mere fact that Mozingos came from Africa had endured as far in space and time as Raven Creek in the 1830s, I suspect it died there. Spencer's children's migration to super-white Indiana must have washed away any speck of that knowledge for the generations that followed.

Chapter 9

A Tortured Netherworld

The majority of Edward's descendants had sailed into whiteness by the nineteenth century, more than eighty of them fighting for the Confederacy in the Civil War. But I learned that a branch out of North Carolina had drifted the other way on the color scale and suffered through terrible poverty and isolation in the antebellum and Jim Crow South. I wondered if the black side had any more awareness of their family's heritage than my father and grandfather had. Perhaps the bonds of memory and tradition held stronger in their ranks. Might any lore of Edward have survived in them?

When I called Wiley Mozingo in North Carolina to arrange to visit him and his relatives, he mentioned that his sister, Shirlyn, lived in Los Angeles. I called her and we agreed to meet for lunch at a deli in Studio City. I got there first and was seated for a few minutes when I noticed a woman standing up near the hostess. She didn't look like the person I expected. My mom was as dark. But she looked around as if she was waiting for someone, so I went up and asked, "Shirlyn?"

"Yes," she said, with a sweet smile.

She was forty-eight but looked and dressed much younger, with tight sweatpants and a Sinful hoodie. We went to our table and I suddenly felt very awkward, not knowing whether or not she was black. I couldn't just ask, "What are you?" But I did need to know, or our conversation was going to be awkward and constrained. She brought out family pictures and told me about her upbringing in the tobacco fields of Wayne County, North Carolina. The first photo showed her and her brother, Rickie, who looked whiter than she did. Then a snapshot of the larger family cleared things up a little. Her siblings, all born of the same two parents, ranged from easily passing as white to definitely black. "We had every shade in our family, and we were all the same race, the same family," she said.

She described how they had occupied a tortured netherworld of Jim Crow. Her father, Fred Sebastan Mozingo, was mixed race but could sit at the lunch counter without a problem. Her darker mother could never do that, even though she was mixed race too, the product of a black housekeeper and the white man of the house.

In Shirlyn's early years, she was sheltered from the tangled skein of the racial code she would have to abide. But as they grew up, each child faced his or her own torment. Wiley, her oldest brother, had dark skin and coarse hair. He was a star football player and the first "colored" boy to integrate his high school in 1965. Fans of opposing teams screamed "Kill the nigger!" during games, and white classmates with cars tried to run him off the road when he rode his bike home from school. Rickie, the lightest of the siblings, fought black kids so often that he dreaded leaving the house. And Shirlyn endured abuse from both sides. When they moved from sharecropper shacks into a black neighborhood in the city of Goldsboro, a little kid came up to her and asked, "Are you all white niggers?" White students would taunt her in the cafeteria, "Pass the vin-nigger."

She made her first real friend in grade school, a white girl named Ronda Holland. They ate lunch together every day and talked on the phone every night, coordinating what clothes they would wear the next day. Ronda talked about riding horses and Shirlyn imagined what that would be like. But Shirlyn's mother didn't let her visit Ronda's house, and Shirlyn didn't understand why until much later, when she got hints about what her mother went through in her own life.

One day in sixth grade, a group of black girls came up to Shirlyn and

Ronda in the hall. "Ronda said her mom didn't want her being friends with you because you're a nigger."

Ronda didn't say anything. Shirlyn doesn't remember much about what happened next, but that evening she told her mom, who called Ronda's mother and got in a heated argument that ended with something akin to "Fuck you." Shirlyn and Ronda found they were not friends after that, and she had never had any good friends since. "I didn't know where to fit. I'm a total loner and have been my entire life," she told me.

Looking at her now in her Sinful hoodie, I was amazed at how recently all of this had occurred. It felt like an old woman should be telling these tales.

I asked her how she came to Los Angeles. She said it was an escape. She was at North Carolina Central University, a historic black college, when she met the actor Thalmus Rasulala, who was doing theater there as an artist in residence. They fell in love. "That was my first husband," she said, and showed me a photo. "He died of leukemia in 1991."

Rasulala had been an original cast member of the soap opera *One Life to Live* and had success in the 1970s in Los Angeles in blaxploitation films like *Blacula* and *Willie Dynamite* and as a frequent guest on the sitcom *Good Times*, the show that pretty much introduced me to black people. (At age ten, I somehow idolized J.J. and even thought of going by that name when I happily realized my own initials were the same.)

"He was Kunta Kinte's father in *Roots*," she said. "He was the one who held up the baby to the stars and said, 'I name you Kunta Kinte.'"

"Really?" I said, almost in a gasp. I marveled at the irony; in a sense, of course, I was looking for my own Kunta Kinte.

She said he couldn't get enough work in Hollywood when the blaxploitation films dried up, so he took the teaching post in North Carolina. When he and Shirlyn got together, she desperately wanted to leave North Carolina and its festering obsession with race. They moved to the Sherman Oaks section of Los Angeles, about three miles from where my grandfather bought the house. My brother and I would have been climbing the sycamore in the front yard when she was making her new life.

Shirlyn found theater work and did some commercials. She got a role in a touring production of Eugene O'Neill's play *The Emperor Jones*, about an African American man who goes to prison for murder, escapes, and makes it to a Caribbean island, where he becomes emperor. She played a Carib Indian woman and did all manner of stage production. John Amos, who played the father in *Good Times* and the adult Kunta Kinte in *Roots*, played the emperor.

After her husband died, Shirlyn met her current partner, John Arthur, a retired professional fighter who once engaged in "sudden death" mixed martial arts matches overseas. Today she and Arthur were managing the career of the heavyweight fighter James "Lights Out" Toney. Much of the job entailed her husband preventing Toney from beating the brains out of anyone who'd irked him.

I pictured Edward in the afterlife looking down at this conversation between two of his descendants. What disparate lives we had led. Such different trajectories brought us to this same part of California, and the only thing that brought us together today was this name he had managed to keep.

"I've found that all Mozingos are loners," she said. I knew she was talking about her family only, but it had a ring of truth to my experience.

I started telling her about Edward and showed her a copy of the ruling. She had never heard of him.

"Let me ask you," I said. "What does your family think the name is?"

"We heard it's from Milan."

"Really? How'd you hear that?" I asked.

"My brother went to one of those Internet sites that does your family heritage, and they said it was from Milan."

"I think those sites are scams, I hate to say. The name is from Africa, probably the Congo. He was one of the few to keep his actual name."

She looked a little stunned. The presumptuous white guy in me had thought this might be transcendent for her, learning hers was one of the few African names to survive slavery in America.

She took a bite of her sandwich. I sipped my Diet Coke.

"I like Milan more," she said.

"Why?" I asked.

She glanced around, grasping for what she was trying to say. "Africa is like, uh, I don't know, like bones in the nose."

Wiley had hinted on the phone that he suspected some of his older cousins and uncles might know something about their history that they weren't telling. Either way, I had to visit them in North Carolina and see how their stories of racial fluidity might illuminate the era in which the other Mozingos had become white.

As I drove down the Interstate one afternoon, the soft, leafy forest of Virginia turned drier and pinier. Lone clouds drifted in the pale sky, dragging trails of rain the sun burned away. I was traveling with a photographer this time, Luis Sinco, as the newspaper stories I was working on had started to coalesce. We went west on Highway 70, then south on Route 117 into an undulating coastal plain of pineland and sandy red fields of tobacco and soy.

The first of Wiley's ancestors to come to North Carolina was a mixed-race man named Christopher Mozingo, born around 1800. Like my line, no one is sure of his exact connection to Edward; the family tree mavens believe he, like Spencer, was also the illegitimate son of one of Edward's female descendants. He first showed up as white on a tax list in Greene County, North Carolina, in 1816, then in a census as a free person of color in 1830, with a woman who presumably was his wife and was listed as white. He undoubtedly came from Virginia, where the free black population was growing rapidly. The Virginia legislature in 1782 had made it legal for slaveholders to free their slaves, and a good number did. By that year, some historians have concluded, there were fewer than three thousand free people of color in Virginia. At the time, Thomas Jefferson estimated the state had 297,000 free people, total, and 271,000 slaves, so only 1 percent of black people would have been free. Then the first federal census of 1790 shows 12,254 free blacks, a fourfold increase, living among 391,000 whites and 300,000 slaves. By 1810 the number of free blacks had risen to 30,269, accounting for about 8 percent of the black population, and by 1860 at the outset of the Civil War, 55,269 free blacks resided in the state, 12 percent of all people of known African descent.

The more free people of color there were, the more the landed class considered them a threat and cracked down with more racist laws and harsher sentencing. Black people convicted of committing small crimes for which a white person would be fined often received lashes on the public whipping post. One law, which was not uniformly enforced, mandated that all manumitted slaves be banished from the state.

Some moved west into Appalachia, where in the high hollows around the Cumberland Gap they lived in mixed-race isolation long enough that when they were later "discovered" they were a mystery. Were they a new race altogether? Were they descendants of the long lost Phoenicians, or shipwrecked Portuguese sailors, or Indians and the lost settlers of Roanoke? Whites and blacks who came later to the region feared them, and told tales of how these "Melungeons"—as they came to be called, although no one knows exactly why—came in the night to steal children to eat.

Other free people of color in Virginia, including Edward's grandson John, crossed south into North Carolina, where they evoked fear in the whites' fervid imaginations, as they had in Virginia. Slaveholders accused them of fomenting slave plots and, by their very existence, giving cover to runaways. The aristocrats, policymakers, and newspaper editors claimed that more repressive laws in Virginia were pushing them into their state. In response, the North Carolina legislature passed a law in 1795 requiring any free person of color entering the state to register with the local sheriff and place a bond of £200 to guarantee "his, her, or their good behavior." Those who didn't would be put in jail and dragged into court. If they still refused, the court would "order such person to be sold, for the benefit of the state, at public auction."

That's how fragile a free person's freedom was. But this didn't satisfy the slaveholders, who pushed for a tighter and tighter grip on the pariah class. In 1826, the Grand Assembly passed a law requiring many free children of color to be bound to white families in indentured servitude "to teach them an honest and industrious occupation." The next year the Assembly made it flat-out illegal for "any negro or mulatto to migrate into this state." Violators who didn't leave in twenty days had to pay $500, a colossal sum at the time for most Americans. If they couldn't afford that, they were put into servitude for up to ten years.

The *Carolina Observer* commended the passage of the law, even though the vote was far from unanimous: "The laws of our sister states, Virginia on the one hand and South Carolina on the other, are such as to drive considerable numbers of this refuse species of population from both those states into this. They are as unwelcome here as there."

Refuse species.

Colonial-era laws in North Carolina had long made it illegal for white and black people to marry and fined anyone who did so £50. But those who ignored the law and married anyway remained married. In 1830, though, the legislature declared all mixed-race marriages null and void. It is in this very year that we find Christopher Mozingo in a census, living with a white woman his age—his wife, no doubt—and their child. The new law must have pushed their marriage or relationship underground, because in the next census no woman is living with him, yet he has two more children.

Despite the laws, plenty of cases came to light of white women marrying or having children with free men of color. "The records seem to indicate that more free Negro children of white mothers were born after 1830 than before," wrote the historian John Hope Franklin in *The Free Negro of North Carolina, 1790–1860*. He cites numerous cases of white men seeking divorce when their wives delivered children, as one jilted husband put it, "bearing the most certain marks of a colored father." One white mother went to court to compel a black man to support their child. Another fought to keep her two mixed-race children out of indentured servitude on the grounds that she was white.

By 1860, nearly 70 percent of the 30,463 free people of color in North Carolina were mixed race. They lived in clawing fear of being pulled into the slave population, ten times as large. "It was by no means enough to have been born free," Franklin wrote. "The free person of color had to maintain a strict vigil over his status lest it be reduced to that of a slave."

Some went to the courthouse to have their status officially recognized. Others fought the suggestion that they had African ancestry and were compelled to trace their lineage and refute contravening witnesses. Anyone with a "full Negro" ancestor within five generations was "colored," so that one black great-great-great-grandparent outweighed thirty-one white ones. That's how culturally poisonous black blood was. People on the dividing line learned the hard way to keep matters of ancestry to themselves; secrecy became endemic. For a short spell in some cities, free men and women of color were required to wear badges that said "Free" on their left shoulder. Traveling outside of their own area proved particularly dangerous, as they could be targeted as runaway slaves if they didn't have their papers with them. And often those papers were kept at the courthouse. Even at home, when the records went missing or the court burned down, which happened often enough, they had nothing but their word, which was worth very little. Perhaps most appalling, many free people of color were simply stolen and sold into slavery. This one offense outraged even white society, and the sentence for anyone who committed such a crime was death. Franklin found an 1801 case detailed in the *Raleigh Reader*: "On the 29th Instant, about Midnight, four men came to the house of Valentine Locust, an aged free negro, who resides on Leek Creek, in Wake County, and calling at the door to gain admittance, as soon as the door was opened, two of them entered with clubs and instantaneously knocked down the old man and his wife and beat them to such a degree as scarcely to leave life, and whilst they were in that situation the robbers carried off two of their children."

A few years later, a woman named Nancy Valentine placed a newspaper ad looking for her kidnapped children. "Stolen from the subscriber in Wake County on Friday 21st Inst, three Girl children, of Colour, Free Born," she wrote. "It is supposed that some dishonest person has taken them off for the purpose of selling them as slaves. Any person that can give any information to the Printer hereof so that I can get my children again will be thankfully received, besides making any satisfaction I am able to do."

Reading all this, one wonders how any free people of color made it through the gauntlet, when even children were a commodity to be stolen. But they did. Some even became respected members of the community. In 1829, white neighbors came to the aid of a Thomas Day, a black cabinetmaker in Caswell County, when he threatened to leave the state if his new wife, from Virginia, was not allowed to live with him. Sixty people sent petitions to the Assembly, according to Franklin. One noted that Day was "a first-rate workman, a remarkably sober, steady and industrious man, a high-minded, good and valuable citizen, possessing a handsome property." Another asserted that he trusted that Day, who owned two slaves himself, would alert his fellow slaveholders to any disturbances among the blacks. The Assembly passed a bill allowing his wife to stay. Twenty years later, the census showed them owning more real estate than all but five households in their township.

He was the exception. Free people of color were mostly limited to working on other people's farms, logging, mining, fishing, turpentining, building railroads. Skilled black workers faced violent hostility from the whites pushed to the same margins by the planters. Unskilled black workers faced cheap competition from slaves, whose owners often rented them out; many freedmen worked alongside the slaves. This was the world Wiley's ancestors had to find a way to survive in.

The 1850 census shows Christopher Mozingo living in Sampson County, with no job, no wife listed. His race was marked "M" for mulatto, as was that of his three sons. His oldest son, Wiley Mozingo, was eighteen and also had no work. They were probably temporary farmhands or bootleggers. That year in Sampson County, the free people of color included two blacksmiths, two carpenters, three common laborers, six coopers, one ditcher, two masons, nine farmers, and sixty-eight farmhands.

The Mozingos moved around a bit, as did their racial categorization. The census listed them as "M" until 1890, when they became "B," which lasted until 1920, when they returned to "M." They were in Cumberland County in 1860, the year before the Civil War erupted. Christopher's son Wiley (the living Wiley's great-grandfather) still had no job but had $50 worth of real estate and $10 worth of possessions. The census noted that his two daughters had red hair. It's unclear what they did during the war. While some black people found refuge in Union-held areas along the coast, the repression generally grew worse under the Confederacy, with freemen evicted and forced into hard labor or the army. There is no record of Wiley or his relatives being drawn into the fighting.

They eventually settled in Wayne County in the 1870s. From then on, Wiley and then his son James worked as farm laborers or tenant farmers.

History meets up with the living family's recollection around 1930, when Shirlyn's father, Freddie, was seventeen and his grandfather James was already seventy. James had married Betsy Johnson, who was said to be half white and half Croatan Indian. She had two sisters with light hair and blue eyes. James told his three sons that if they didn't marry light-skinned women, he'd disown them. Under the weight of Jim Crow, slight differences in skin tone and hair texture held outlandishly inflated import in the mixed-race community. When Freddie married the darker-skinned Naomi Hobbs, his dad never set foot in his son's home again.

But Freddie could pass as white to people who didn't know him, with light skin, straight dark hair, and high cheekbones framing a broad face. He did well for himself. He was a savant of sorts, a carpenter, farmer, and mechanic who kept the boilers working at Wayne Memorial Hospital, then at Seymour Johnson Air Force Base. He and Naomi bought a home in the city of Goldsboro, and he soon acquired three adjacent properties, which he turned into a self-sustaining farm. Their first daughter, Ruth, recalled that they grew butter beans, corn, peas, tomatoes, okra, brussels sprouts, cauliflower, sweet potatoes, and broccoli. The orchard hung heavy with figs, cherries, apples, and grapes. They plowed with a mule, had a cow for milk, and raised pigs, ducks, geese, chickens, pigeons, and hunting dogs. The hunting dogs in particular fetched a high price. Freddie built a smokehouse and made his own ham, while Naomi handled the fowl. He bought a car and a work truck and started framing a new family home on the fourth lot. After Ruth was born, Freddie and Naomi had six more children, between 1950 and 1960: Wiley, Stephen, Edward, Dwight, Rickie, and Shirlyn.

Fred pedaled his bicycle to work and then attached a small motor to it. He loved to read and quoted the Bible. He subscribed to *Life* and *Look* magazines, and he followed politics closely. Ruth remembered her dad saying that soon there would be so many Chinese they'd be able to "win any war with just sticks."

For a brief moment, race didn't intrude into their lives as it had before and would later. Their neighbors, mostly kin of some sort, lived in similar circumstances. "If you went there, you'd see children with blue eyes and blond hair," Ruth said. "But everyone was mixed."

Freddie's driver's license said he was white. He could eat at white lunch counters, go to white movie theaters, and get jobs meant for white people. His wife and children only heard about this side of him, they couldn't accompany him. But even Freddie's grasp on the white world was tenuous. Reputation and old records, birth certificates in particular, kept even the lightest people of color in their box. Maybe if Freddie had moved out of the South, he might have shed the burden of the "colored" label if he had wanted to, but not where he was born and raised. Freddie worked in a quarry for a spell, and lined up with the white workers on payday to get his check. The black workers lined up separately to get paid less for the same job. One day, his niece's husband spotted him from the black line and, resentful of his "passing," called him out as colored. Freddie fumed inside as supervisors ordered him to the black line.

This was one of Ruth's fragments of family lore. Another was that Freddie's uncle on his mom's side was white-looking like him. He found himself in court once for a car accident, the details of which are forgotten, and the judge ruled he was not at fault. Then a man stood up and said, "Judge, are you *away-yare* that Mr. Johnson is a *cullered* man?"

The judge did not say, "But he doesn't look black to me." He may not even have thought it. In this era, whites could nimbly perform the psychic contortions necessary to winnow down and spot inherent blackness when there were no physical signs of it.

"He don't look any more like a nigger than I do," the townfolks said about Joe Christmas. "But it must have been the nigger blood in him."

According to Ruth's family lore, the judge promptly reversed his ruling.

Freddie never completed the two-story house he was building. Heart disease struck him when Ruth was about ten, forcing him to quit his job at the air force base and sell their properties. He cashed out a life insurance policy meant for his children's college education, and the family of seven moved into the rural southern reaches of the county where Naomi had grown up. They had Rickie and Shirlyn before Freddie died. He wanted even more children, as if he could extend his own mortality with them. But raising seven alone would be enough for Naomi, who learned to make herself scarce when he called her into the bedroom.

Freddie spent his final months rocking baby Shirlyn on his lap for hours and hours.

After his death, the family sank into poverty and moved between old bare-board sharecropper houses, working on different farms. Ruth graduated high school at sixteen and escaped, going to New York to work as a nanny. She had long wavy black hair that she now calls Kardashian hair.

As a young woman in New York, she was constantly asked what she was: Are you Spanish? Are you Greek? Are you Italian? Are you Hawaiian? Are you Yemeni? She mostly just answered no. "If I said I was black it would just change the dynamic." It didn't matter that she looked like all those other groups. Black was set apart in the American mind. If she answered "black," her inquisitors would mentally inject her with some biological quality imperceptible on the surface but infused throughout, as if deciding she were made of different proteins.

Ruth had this happen many times. She remembered having an intelligent conversation with a coworker about a novel or news event, until he found out she was black and began asking her, with no apparent ill intention, if New York was a good welfare state. "Everyone turned stupid," she told me. For a while she was living in the home of a Jewish biochemist whose sister she was a nanny for. One night, her host beckoned her to come downstairs during a party and announced to her guests that Ruth was actually black. One woman studied her and then marveled, "I can't believe it. I didn't know you looked like *that*."

Outside of Goldsboro, in the rural community of Dudley, Luis and I pulled into the Rollingwood Estates, a black subdivision with a white twin, Foxfire Estates, next door. The neighborhood sat under high pines on a clean mat of needles, with only a few chain-link fences and no hedges or landscaping separating the little rectangular homes, so that they looked like they had just fallen from the sky.

Wiley Mozingo lived in one of the nicer brick homes, on Brentwood Drive; his gray Buick LeSabre was parked in the drive.

I knocked and Wiley, a stoutish black man in an undershirt, opened the door. "Hey, how ya doing?" he said quietly.

He invited us into the wood-paneled den where his two-year-old grandson, Christopher, was toddling around in a Lightning McQueen outfit. Grandpa was watching him for the afternoon.

Wiley eased back into his lounger. He told us he suffered from a painful autoimmune disease called sarcoidosis, which forced him to retire after eighteen years as a prison guard. At fifty-nine, he was soft-spoken, with high cheekbones and plaintive eyes. He was much darker than Shirlyn, with almost a reddish cast to his skin, and had a thin mustache and close-cropped silver hair.

Christopher waddled over and handed him a sippy cup with great satisfaction, then demanded it back with grunts. The boy was named after his mysterious fourth great-grandfather who arrived from Virginia.

"Yeah, I never heard anything about the family," Wiley said. "I always assumed we came from slaves. Then Reese came by one day and knew something about our roots. . . . He looked like one of my uncles, actually, kind of shaped like him . . . round head."

Before he was shot, the bearded oracle of our heritage, Reese Mozingo, visited Wiley and gave him the family tree and the lowdown on Edward Mozingo. "I'll be," Wiley had responded. It struck him that his father might have known about Edward; a relative once said Wiley's brother Edward was named after the first Mozingo in America, just as Wiley had been named after his great-grandfather.

Wiley had been curious about the family name since he was a child. But his interest didn't derive from its strangeness, as it had with me; there were dozens of Mozingo families in Wayne and surrounding counties. It came from a classmate in high school, a white boy named Larry Mozingo, who used to taunt Wiley in front of other students, saying, "You used to be my slave." Reese's news brought a certain sense of comeuppance, knowing it would irk the hell out of Larry to find out his name was African. If only Wiley had known earlier. He vowed to carry a copy of the Jamestown ruling with him whenever he went into town, in case he came across Larry or any other white Mozingos.

But events in the present overshadowed any grievance he had with the past. On October 15, 2004, a marijuana dealer named Billy Joe Gregory was shot and killed on his own porch near Dudley. Wiley heard about the killing, but didn't think too much of it. Two weeks later, police arrested his youngest son, Michael, seventeen, and two other teenagers and charged them with first-degree murder. Michael was a senior at Southern Wayne High School; his cohorts were a sophomore there and a freshman in community college. Wiley didn't know how his son got involved with those two. He'd never known Michael to use drugs or get in fights, and he had no criminal record. Short and overweight, he got picked on a lot and often lay about the house.

The more Wiley learned, the more he thought Michael had a chance to beat the charges because of evidence that he was in the car when the two others went to the house with a gun. (Gregory apparently reached for the gun, and was shot.) In the long months before the trial, Wiley complained that the public defender never even visited Michael and called him only once. He grew desperate and tried to raise $50,000 for a private attorney, refinancing his house and borrowing money from family. He sucked up his pride and asked for loans from acquaintances, even other Mozingos he met through Reese. But he couldn't get enough, and Michael's public defender recommended he take a plea deal. Michael pleaded guilty to second-degree murder and attempted armed robbery and was sentenced to eight to ten years in prison.

Wiley knew what prison did to young men and couldn't bear to see Michael there. He visited once a week, no matter how bad the attacks of his sarcoidosis. He saw his boy getting harder and leaner and more distant. Michael was getting in trouble, smoking marijuana, dealing in cigarettes. He had a bad temper and got in fights. Wiley feared he'd rack up violations and wouldn't get out, or he'd come out as a different person altogether.

"I've been depressed ever since," he said. It showed. He had a way of talking almost in sighs, and seemed to retreat back into his head between every statement. He said he was curious about what I knew about our history, but just gazed off when I told him our family name was one of two African names known to survive slavery in America, with a few other possible candidates. Still, he seemed to appreciate the diversion and wanted to tell his story.

Wiley's wife arrived and warmly greeted us. Now that she could watch Christopher, Wiley offered to take a drive to show us where he used to live. He put on a red polo shirt over his undershirt and a denim baseball cap. We got in his Buick and headed off into the fields. The sere midday light had softened now, and the passing landscape seemed to tease out bits of his memory.

"The first place we lived was around back there," he said. "It was an old farmhouse." His recollections of his early years were composite and scattered. He didn't remember too much about his father. Freddie died when Wiley was ten, and it was hard to separate what he experienced and what he heard from his mother, older sister, and cousins. He remembered that his dad used to eat at white lunch counters, and he couldn't understand why, when he went to the Woolworth's with his mother, they were told to eat outside.

He remembered moving into the sharecropper houses and working in the fields all summer and on weekends, picking tobacco leaves with other black families. His hands turned so dark with tobacco gum that he dared not touch his eyes for the sting. At night the family scrubbed down with the lye soap his grandmother made. He remembered his mother growing furious at the farmer, Mr. Britt, who wanted the children to miss school to tend the crops. They moved on to the next farm, and stayed there until that farmer demanded the same. After the corn harvests every summer, Naomi made the rounds working out deals with farmers: for 50 percent of the take, she and her children would pick up the corn left by the machine harvesters and put it in piles for the farmers to sell at market.

Wiley pulled down several one-lane farm roads but couldn't seem to find the houses they had lived in. Many had been razed. But he remembered them well enough: no plumbing, no insulation, a bare lightbulb, heat coming from the single wood stove. "You'd be burning up front, freezing in back," he said. The winter wind blew right under the floorboards and whistled up through the cracks. At one place they sealed off the crawl space beneath them with plastic. In another, the electricity didn't work, and they used kerosene lamps.

We walked out into the fields to inspect an abandoned house. "I think we lived in this one. It wasn't like this then." Today it sat in waist-high weeds in the middle of a cornfield. Vines grew out of the cracks between the boards and along the roof. One wall was covered in oxidized aluminum roofing sheets. "It's hard to tell," he said.

Down Old Mount Olive Highway we came to Southern Wayne High, a long building with a swoop roof and vertical rows of windows, in the 1960s style of public school architecture. Here, his memory came into piercingly sharp focus.

He was in the eighth grade at the black school, Carver Heights, living in a sharecropper shack just north of the town of Mount Olive, when he and his friends heard about the new high school and decided to enroll, hoping the football team would be better and that they might get a better education. The books at Carver were all hand-me-downs from the white schools. "The first day of school at Southern Wayne I showed up and my friends didn't," he said. "It was the most stress I've ever been in in my life." It was 1965; only five or six other black students had enrolled in the entire school.

Wiley caught the bus running up from Mount Olive. Students threw trash at him and spit on him and didn't let him sit down. He started riding his bike, looking back and swerving as drivers tried to run him into the ditch weeds. Within a few weeks, he went to the principal and said he had made a mistake and wanted to go back to Carver. "I think you just got a chip on your shoulder," the principal said. "Why don't you think about that and head back to class?"

Wiley wanted to drop out, but his mother wouldn't let him. He had no choice but to endure the abuse, running when he was outnumbered, fighting when he had a shot. When a group of white boys threatened to jump him in the bathroom, he put his hand in his pocket like he had a knife. They stayed back and he slipped away. An hour later, he was pulled out of class and searched for the nonexistent weapon.

Football practice became his one refuge during the day. His team-mates didn't cause him much grief, and he got along well with a few of them. The coach tried to keep his spirits up, and Wiley became the Saints' star middle linebacker. Opposing fans were not as accepting, screaming "Kill the nigger!" when Wiley had the ball. Coach told him to ignore them. Wiley came and left the games through a side gate.

The harassment never ended. The family kept finding their tin mail-boxes blown to shards with blasting caps, and one of his black classmates found a cross burning in front of her home. The Klan operated openly in Wayne County. There was even a billboard on Highway 70 for Wayne Auto Salvage upon which Klan meetings were advertised. Wiley remembered seeing men in white hoods gathering in the back of the salvage yard, visible from the road.

His mother was renting a sharecropper house from a farmer named Bud Wolf. The deal was that she pay a little rent and she and her children take care of the crops. One evening around dusk, Wolf came with two men in a truck and ordered her off the property. Naomi went into the house and came back out with a shotgun. "We ain't leaving until we find somewhere else to go." The farmer called the sheriff, and a deputy came out and talked to her. She explained that she had a deal with Wolf and could not leave until she found a new place. The deputy said Wolf had to give her thirty days to do so.

The family had seen Wolf as a decent man and didn't understand his sudden problem. Soon they got word that Wolf had been at a Klan meeting, where the leaders began inveighing against a wave of black children entering white schools. Wiley's name was mentioned, then Wolf's, who was chastised for letting this happen.

I asked Wiley if he hated white people after going through all of this. The question seemed only natural, but felt tiny and feckless when I heard myself asking it.

"Yeah, I was mad," he said. He paused and looked off. "You know, I used to work as an apprentice electrician for a white man named Norwood Mozingo. We had a team of us, but he always made me do the dirty work, if a hole had to be dug, or we had to punch through wall, or crawl under a house. I found out that the owner of the company was the Grand Dragon of the Klan. I didn't work there too long."

We drove up to Wayne Memorial Park outside the county seat of

Goldsboro to see his mother's grave and meet Wiley's younger brother Dwight, who stepped out of a white Ford F-150 pickup and heartily shook our hands. He was no darker than I was, and at fifty-four was balding with a salt-and-pepper goatee. Dwight immediately got to bonding over our common name, which he had tattooed on his arm. "There's just always been something mysterious about it," he said. "It always meant something to me."

We walked into the graveyard. The sun was low and cast a honey light over the withered grass and the dry-buzzing trees down the hill.

"You know, I was getting my car fixed at Sears and the woman there looks at my driver's license and says, 'What is this name? I've always wondered.' You know, we got a lot of Mozingos around here, so she's known a few before. She says, 'I notice all them Mozingos stay to themselves, and it's like they know something other people don't know.' You ever notice that?"

"Kind of, I guess," I said. "Staying to themselves, yes."

Wiley and Luis had stayed back and were beyond earshot now.

"My mother said my dad's uncle came down once from the mountains, and he was a great big man with red hair and a red beard, and she asked him a question, and he'd just look at her. He wouldn't talk. She thought he couldn't even talk, until she heard him talk to my dad."

Dwight said he kept to himself from a very young age. Children who didn't fit in box A or B of the binary racial code were outcasts, mocked as "half-breeds." His mother told him to be peaceful, but Wiley told him, "If you don't fight you're going to get your ass kicked."

Wiley was so soft-spoken and polite, I had a hard time picturing him using the term "ass kicked."

"Wiley was badass when he was younger," Dwight said. "He used to protect all of us. They used to call him Gator. No one would mess with him. He didn't take nothing from nobody. He wasn't scared of anyone. You know, playing football once he hit a guy so hard they had to cut his arm out of the guy's helmet. . . . I was once playing sandlot football. There was a guy called Doc Brewington that we was all terrified of, everyone. He was about Wiley's age. Well, playing football I tackled this kid and he broke his leg. He was Doc Brewington's friend. Doc came up and had me by the collar and I thought I was dead, when he glanced back and looked as if he'd seen a ghost. 'What's up, Gator?' he said. He put me down and kind of dusted me off. Wiley never said a word to him."

Dwight had to get to work, cleaning floors at a local community college, and we agreed to meet the next day. Back in the car, we talked about Wiley's mother. She was not a warm woman, but she was a protective one, always with a gun in the house, and her children always had the sense that she went through unspeakable assaults in her youth. Wiley said she never knew her father, but she assumed he was the white man her mother was working for. Her mother didn't really want her and, when Naomi was thirteen, basically sold her into indentured servitude. She worked as a live-in caretaker for a sickly widower, Mr. Jackson, and his four children, and stayed with them well into her twenties, when she was abruptly let go. She never let on to what happened, but it was clear to her children something had. There was a whisper that a group of white women thought she was too close to one or more of the Jackson men and beat her up one day. Wiley had a vague memory of hearing that she shot the leg off a Klansman who came to their door when she was home alone. "I heard she was in jail down in Duplin County, but I could never get to the bottom of it," he said. "Yeah, I always wondered about that."

Naomi died in 2009 without saying a word about the story. Wiley asked some cousins who knew what happened, but they refused to speak. "Just let the past alone," they would say.

Even from the battened-down secrecy of their history, terrible shards of it slipped out now and then. Wiley's next youngest brother, Steve, was taking their mother to Baltimore to visit some relatives in the 1970s. She started talking about her uncle, who delivered babies and did other unlicensed medical procedures for the black community. Steve could not remember his name, but he would never forget what his mom recalled, whether it was true or apocryphal or somewhere in between.

One night, a horse and buggy pulled up to her uncle's home. A group of armed whites came to the door, put a bag over his head, tied

him up, and took him off. He was terrified, thinking they were going
to lynch him in the woods, but they carried him into a house and up a
flight of stairs. When they pulled the bag off, he realized he was in the
bedroom of a big planter in the county. There was a roaring fireplace and
a young woman lying in the bed. The men who had taken him stood
by with their guns. The planter said his daughter was pregnant and that
he wanted Naomi's uncle to deliver the baby. Okay, he said, wondering
why they didn't call the town doctor instead of kidnapping him. As the
baby came out, he understood. He swaddled the brown infant, then felt
a gun to his head. The old man said, "Throw it in the fire."

He was aghast.

"No, I cannot do that, sir."

"Do it or we'll kill you."

"You can kill me, but I am not throwing that baby in the fire."

They went back and forth, until the old man grabbed the baby himself and threw it in the fire.

"It's the Lord God's abomination, and I am the instrument of His will,"
hissed the grandfather, leaning over the baby Joe Christmas.

The crackling and screaming haunted Naomi's uncle for the rest of
his life. He told her the story just to try to relieve some of the burden
he kept inside.

Steve never doubted the horrific tale. As the darkest of the siblings,
albeit with straight hair, he had his own chilling experiences with white
supremacy. When he was about ten and living in a house in the fields, he
went down to the road to get the mail. The path was about forty yards
long and well worn by children's feet. It was a warm afternoon in early
fall, with a deep blue Carolina sky. The corn had already been harvested,
so their house stood out, naked on the red dirt.

He got to the mailbox and was looking at the mail when he heard a
car pass, then the squeak of brakes as it came to a stop. Steve looked up.
The car idled about forty yards down the road. A man and a boy stepped
out in the unwashed light. They stood facing him but didn't say anything
as the boy, holding something in his right hand, raised it up as if he were
pointing it at Steve. *Pap! Pap!* Steve didn't move. *He's shooting at me,*

he thought, paralyzed. The boy shot five more times. They got back in the car and drove away.

Steve walked back to the house with the mail and told his mom. They went to Goldsboro and flagged down an officer. He asked Steve what type of car it was. He didn't know. Did he see the license plate? No. The officer said, "Okay, I'll look into it."

Steve still thought about the surreal episode now and then. "It was as if a southern dad was taking his son out to teach him the ways of the South," he said. All of the racism Steve grew up with felt like a waking dream. It never really got to him, he said, he just walked through it, looking around, puzzled by these people and their nonsensical behavior.

In eighth grade Steve got a scholarship to a boarding school, the North Carolina Advancement School in Winston-Salem, where he did so well that he got another scholarship, to study in England for four years. His mom turned it down for reasons that were never clear, and when he graduated high school, he joined the Marine Corps and went to Okinawa on his way to Vietnam. Nixon pulled back the troops before he got to the fighting, and Steve came back, worked as a prison guard, went back to college, and finally got his degree in international studies at the University of North Carolina at Chapel Hill. He became a manager at Mitsubishi, then IBM, and then at a company that builds the diodes for LED lights. His wife is a school administrator with a PhD. They have a daughter who graduated from Appalachian State University and a son at the University of North Carolina.

They lived for a while in a country club neighborhood that, until they arrived, was exclusively white. Steve was jogging there one day when the police pulled up next to him. "Do you need any help?" the officer asked.

"No," he said.

"Well, what are you doing?"

"I'm jogging."

"Uh-huh."

"I live here," Steve added.

"Oh, all right," the officer said, and pulled away.

Steve wasn't angry. Wiley would have been furious. He visited Steve and couldn't understand why he would want to live there, and Steve didn't understand Wiley's concerns. He bought the house because the area had good schools and he thought the property values would go up.

But Steve didn't see himself as black in the way Wiley saw himself. He never did. He never saw himself as white either. "I don't fit into any group," he told me. "You could put me in Iraq, Egypt, Somalia, Mexico, or Polynesia, and no one would look twice at me. I always mark 'other' on my census forms. That's the way the world is going. There isn't going to be black and white anymore."

I asked him if he could see how this might offend black people, in that he's distancing himself from them; historically, mixed-race people "passing" as something other than black have often been seen as cowards, snobs, or traitors, servile to a white society. He said he wasn't distancing himself from black society at all. It was a part of him. He just saw himself as "other," always had.

Chapter 10

A Covenant Between God and Mozingos

The next morning, Wiley, Luis, and I pulled up to the Rexall in the little downtown of Mount Olive, North Carolina. When Wiley was about eleven or so, in about 1961, his mother handed him some money and sent him to town to pay a couple of her bills, including one here. It was a three-mile walk on a sweltering summer day. He went to a furniture store first, then paid her electric bill, and was burning up by the time he got to the Rexall. He went to the back to pay the pharmacist, then ordered an orangeade and sat down at a table in front.

"Son, you can't sit there," the pharmacist said.

Wiley was sweating profusely and wasn't ready to step back out in the heat. He just looked at the man.

"We just can't have you sit there. If you need to sit, you can come sit behind the counter where no one can see you."

Wiley knew society was unjust, but this was the first time it hit him in the gut that the color of his skin marked him in America's eyes as a refuse species—his "baptism of racial emotion," in Richard Wright's words. The pharmacist would allow Wiley to drink behind the counter where no one would be disturbed by the very sight of an eleven-year-old boy sipping an orangeade. *Fuck this*, he said to himself, and stormed out, cussing all the way home.

We opened the glass door to the jingle of bells. The drugstore looked like a snapshot from that era: plastic tables in front, Formica counter to the left, with a coffeepot and stainless steel orange juicer. Above the pharmacy window in back, two men in horn-rimmed glasses looked down from a black-and-white photo on the wall.

"May I help you?" asked a blond woman behind the old soda-fountain counter. She glared at us, hyperalert.

I muttered, "Nuh-uh." I turned toward the items in the aisle as if I were looking for something. We really had no objective here. I just wanted to see the place and Luis wanted to get a photo of Wiley there.

"May I help you?" she demanded.

"Yeah," I said, drawing the word out, trying to buy time. "You guys want some coffee?"

"Sure," Luis said.

She was looking at us as if we were going to rob the place. Admittedly, Luis and I were a bit scruffy, but Wiley was wearing a dark blue polo knit tucked into khaki pants, with crisp white tennis shoes. His Buick LeSabre was parked in front. Not exactly a gangster car.

The three of us sat at the table. Luis set his camera on it, trying to discreetly get a couple of frames, but the woman stared at us as if her eyes were blue lasers. She all but slammed down our coffee. Normally, I would expect a "So, where are y'all from?" but she clearly just wanted us out of there. When she turned back to the counter, Luis snapped his frames. I paid and we left.

"They were sure watching me closely in there," Wiley said outside, in his soft-spoken way. "They always have."

Wiley's youngest brother, Rickie, eight years younger, joined us for dinner that night at Wilber's Barbecue. They had told me that Rickie was the whitest looking, but his appearance still surprised me. He was as light as me, tall and broad-shouldered, with a lean face and a thick gray goatee. He wore a camouflage Best Sand & Gravel cap and greeted me with a "howdy." He looked like a good ol' boy.

We ordered chicken and ribs, and Rickie got to telling me how he was tormented more by black kids as a child than white ones, and his resentment skewed that way. But Wiley's wife and their grandchildren were with us, so we kept the conversation light. By the end of dinner, Rickie seemed to want to tell me something important in a quieter atmosphere, so we agreed to meet at the bar downtown.

I ordered a Jack Daniel's on ice and he had a Corona.

"My childhood was hell on earth," Rickie said. "I learned early the wrath people can feel just from the color of your skin. . . . Wiley was just dark enough that white people hated him. I was light enough that dark people hated me."

A few years after Freddie died and Wiley was finishing high school, Naomi remarried and moved back into a black neighborhood in Goldsboro. Rickie was about nine years old. "It felt like I got dropped off in the wrong neighborhood. I kind of felt like a mistake for a long time. They just saw us as a strange enemy, both sides."

I recalled Shirlyn telling me that Rickie dreaded even going outside because he had to fight somebody nearly every time he did.

"You know, one of my first cousins was telling me once, 'Oh my, your granddaddy and your daddy were prejudiced.' They probably had good reason to be. If black people approached them as the enemy, what were they supposed to do but defend themselves?

"You know, if a person does not like white people, they're not going to like me neither.

"In high school, I tried to look and talk black." He described how he put his head under the dome of his mom's big bonnet hair dryer on a moisture setting to get some extra frizz. He grew a little pencil mustache that was popular at the time. Still, he had no good friends and put up an emotional guard against everyone. When he went to the black North Carolina Central University, he gave up trying to be any one race. "I realized God doesn't make mistakes," he said.

He sought answers for his alienation in the Bible and began to see a spiritual import to his life, and his name, Mozingo. "I'd always been proud of that name."

"Why?"

"I haven't a clue why. I just felt, if nothing else, I had that to be proud of. But then I started reading and I felt it was something transmitted to us for a purpose."

I feared this was heading toward a Jesus sermon and took a good draw on my whiskey.

"I believe there is a blood covenant between God and Mozingos."

"What is that?" I asked.

"A promise God made to us that runs in our blood."

He had an unwavering gaze and a slow, icy southern way of talking that reminded me of Robert De Niro in *Cape Fear*. He looked like a man who had some dark recesses in his mind.

"You know, when Reese came, I had some specific questions I wanted to ask him about, based on some experiences I had."

"Like what?"

"Like did he know of any connection with the Jewish race? Because I had some Hebrew-like experiences. He told me that he thought we descended from Moses' brother Aaron. He kind of blew my mind when he said that. But he said not to tell anyone because nobody'd believe it."

"Why did he think that about Aaron?"

"You know, I'm not really sure. I wish I would have asked him more."

"So what were your Hebrew experiences?" I asked.

Rickie explained that in 1987, just after he got out of the navy, he was visiting Shirlyn in Los Angeles, when one afternoon, as he was sitting on the edge of his bed in their guest room, he saw particles swirling before him. "I didn't know where they came from, whether through the wall or what. It's like in *Star Trek* when the person is transported. I would learn later that this was called 'the Silence.' The particles came together and I realized it was the Lord Jesus Christ. He was sitting with his legs folded and arms out, suspended in the air.

"I put my hands on my knees and put my head on the ground. A heavy grief came over me over his crucifixion. I returned to the edge of the bed and I was looking in the face of Jesus.

"He began speaking to me telepathically. Never opened his mouth. He said, 'Tell people I'm real. Tell people I love them. And wherever you go, I will be with you.' Then the image turned to smoke and flowed into me. The last words I heard were, 'Be not afraid to enter the Holy place and open the Ark.' 'Why me?' I asked. What have I done to deserve this? Nothing. I was a sinner, always was. It came to me that it was a long-standing thing, a privilege, that someone in my bloodline did me this favor."

That night, in his sleep, he had a different vision, of a translucent Jesus standing up, and the next morning he found the same image on a book in his brother-in-law's room, *The Aquarian Gospel of Jesus the Christ,* in which he learned about "the Silence."

"My life has never been the same since. My dreams and visions just escalated. When I came back to Goldsboro, I could read people's minds and see right through them. He kind of commissioned me at that point. Wherever I go, I have a ministry. Like John the Baptist or Jesus."

"So do you actually preach, then?" I asked.

"In my way," he said, then paused. "Just my presence. When Jesus commissioned me, he said, 'I'll be with you.'"

I was well beyond having anything to say.

"I know a lot of people think I'm crazy. I don't care."

If I had lived in isolation most of my life, with no checks and balances on my thinking, who knows what I might have been bending people's ears about? In the right circumstances, perhaps anyone could drive himself to a point of consciousness that many would call mental illness and others, or at least the person himself, would call visionary.

He looked up at the TV above the bar. "You ever see this show, *Jon and Kate Plus Eight?*"

"No. I've heard a lot about it."

"I watch it sometimes."

"Hmm," I said.

We talked a bit more, and I got the check.

"I like to stay in the higher part of myself. He'll warn me. If there is someone I'm dating and it's going to interfere with my gift, I don't need it. . . . The sons of God fell from the highest realm to mingle with human women."

"So I still don't get the connection to all this with Mozingo."

He thought for a moment, looking off. I knew I was asking him to put an inchoate feeling into hard linear thought.

"My dad, that's what he left me, his heritage. God makes certain people promises that would be passed through their seed forever, to this very day."

"What was the promise?"

"An inner circle to secret, spiritual stuff," he said. "It goes way back. I think Mozingos might be a Lost Tribe of Israel."

He wanted to show me his mom's house just around the block, so I signed the bill and drove over to meet him there on West Mulberry Street.

The night was warm and chattering with crickets. The home was over a century old, with a big porch and gables. All the windows were dark and no porch light was on.

He was now wondering if the Lost Tribe may have wandered across Africa and settled on the coast where Edward was taken from.

"You want to come in?" he asked.

I didn't really want to. His intensity over a strange vision felt safe out in public. He gave me something to ponder, and I figured I'd leave it at that. "I gotta get going," I said.

Driving to my hotel, I recalled how Shirlyn, Dwight, and Rickie had said that all the Mozingos they knew were loners and outsiders. My family was very genial, in a midwestern way, but we certainly had no social butterflies. We avoided clubs, teams, movements, fads, organizations, cliques, and religions. We found no comfort in them. A strain of this came from my Swedish relatives. The question was whether this trait had also been beaten into our ancestry as a mixed-race pariah class, a refuse people, even if in our case it happened so long ago.

I felt it somehow depended on whether Faulkner's vision of a fiercely overbearing past was true. He had an immediate eye on a time and place consumed by race and ancestry, while I was looking at it distorted through the California sunlight. He saw a world where the people in the present drifted in a rickety boat on a roiling sea of the dead and gone. They were held captive and plagued by their forebears, and strained feebly to atone for ancient acts of cowardice and sin as if they were committed yesterday. The Reverend Hightower grew so obsessed with the day his grandfather was shot off a horse in the Civil War that it was "the only day he seemed to ever have lived in." It was a place where black blood represented the ultimate sin of the past, at times literally fighting the white blood inside Joe Christmas—a place where people "learned it beyond all forgetting and then forgot the words."

Perhaps we had learned beyond forgetting and then forgotten the words, and the original sin of our family in America, "the abominable mixture," was still knotted up somewhere inside us all. The immaculate conception of my immediate family in Los Angeles might have been a deliberate effort to get past it.

It was hard for me to accept the authority of the past. I was raised in a place that tacitly taught family history was something you avoided wallowing in and whining about, and the future had nothing to do with it. But it was intriguing that this new middle class on the new edge of the continent felt that way. Maybe their pasts were embarrassing because they didn't follow the American Dream, even as California became the world's most potent distillation of it. They were full of hard, stoic characters who didn't pick themselves up by the bootstraps, who trudged along on the bottom, just getting by, generation after generation, with no war heroes, mayors, or newspaper editors, no great artists or entrepreneurs or astronauts or even notable criminals. On my dad's side, at least, I got the sense that a squalid languor resided in the past, a migrating Yoknapatawpha County of poverty, dirt, boredom, petty fractiousness, and blown opportunities—of prejudice and bellicose religion. That's what my more recent forebears had to escape.

But I couldn't accept that this weary, individualist trait came down from Edward, based only on this abstract, literary view. It didn't seem enough. There had to be a sociobiological mechanism for this one psychic knot to get passed along all the way from Edward, reinforcing an outsider's view, while not getting drowned out by opposite traits coming down from my other lines of ancestors. The only way I could envision it was this: men had children with like-minded women, keeping their own traits from diluting out in their children. My father was a go-it-alone type of person who clicked with my mother, who struggled with shyness. Neither would have functioned well with a socialite. Nor would my wife or I.

Not to mention that our society was clearly patriarchal for much of its history. In that context, my line back to Edward was not just one out of 1,024, but a kind of lead paternal thread, weaving in the complementary threads of the women they emotionally bonded with and self-replicating like the twin strands of DNA. Now, if the traits I were looking at were a sense of entitlement and nobility, this wouldn't add up, because my paternal link was broken somewhere between Edward and Spencer. But if the trait was feeling like a perpetual outsider, being the illegitimate son of an outcast "mulatto" woman would only tighten that knot, and that feeling would certainly continue down the line.

This sense of a biological-emotional chain was just a theory in my case; I was trying to decipher fossils to see if they had any effect on my soul today. In stark contrast, Rickie's link to the pariah class was as real as the blood beating through his heart. There was no need to speculate where his alienation came from. Society kept that knot alive and visible in every generation.

It astounded me that his personality had a direct connection to Edward's. This was a revelation. It was as if I had met someone far back in my own lineage, as if I had just had drinks with Margaret or Spencer. Rickie had personally crossed the racial barrier that my ancestors crossed three hundred years before. He was the living legacy of that boy who landed on the banks of the James River in 1644.

On my flight out the next day, I thought about what Wiley and Rickie had gone through and why we develop our prejudices. Mine were not about race so much. I certainly had accepted racial and ethnic stereotypes in my youth, but they were mostly worn away by meeting enough people who defied them. My prejudices were aimed at different personalities, better ones mostly, by which I mean threatening ones. When I was younger, I denigrated people (in my mind) to protect my own sense of uniqueness. If someone did better in school, then he had to be worse at something else. If someone was funnier or more outgoing or more athletic, he was shallow. I was an "introvert," as I learned from my fifth-grade teacher who scolded me constantly for it, and I imbued that with "deep" qualities extroverts could never have. This defensive scorn was aimed mostly at individuals, but stereotypes coalesced. By college, my hardest prejudice was toward frat boys, which said a lot more about my defects than theirs. We start arranging these mental hierarchies so early and innocuously—with four-and-a-half-year-olds finding a sense of superiority over mere four-year-olds—it becomes a deep-rooted habit.

I could see now that racism fed partly off the same basic inclination to diminish others to buoy your own status. Yet instead of flickering in solitude, its fire ran wild, fueled by family, friends and coworkers, by Christianity, demagoguery, economics, and bloody history. My hatreds were weak and ephemeral, but a society's hatred engulfed the whole house.

As I got older, married, and had my son, longheld illusions about myself fell away; so did the compulsion to lessen the value of the "other." Looking into my ancestry only made it seem all the more absurd. Seeing the generations that have come and gone with barely a trace, running my hand over gravestones and studying birth records and yellowed marriage certificates, imagining all the struggles in each of those lost lives, stripped me of conceits about my significance.

The personas we create for the wider world are just shadows in the end. Unless we're Michelangelo or Winston Churchill or Jonas Salk, all we really leave is our posterity.

I hoped against my innate skepticism that Rickie was right about that "blood covenant," which now signified to me a connection to immortality, to our ancestors, to an African man who found himself in America so long ago. That was the part of my family's story that had been swiped from our memory, the missing piece of my identity. It was there, echoed in our name, but lost to our consciousness, because my ancestors buried it somewhere along the way. I just needed to learn how to feel it.

Chapter 11

A Deep-seated Fear

How can one idea like segregation become so hypnotic a thing that it binds a whole people together, good, bad, strong, weak, ignorant or learned, sensitive, obtuse, psychotic and sane, making them one as only a common worship or a deeply shared fear can do? . . . We know it has woven itself around fantasies at levels difficult for the mind to touch, until it is a part of each man's internal defense system, embedded like steel in his psychic fortifications. And, like the little dirty rag or doll that an unhappy child sleeps with, it has acquired inflated values that extend far beyond the rational concerns of economics and government, or the obvious profits and losses accruing from the white-supremacy system, into childhood memories long repressed.

Lillian Smith, *Killers of the Dream*

Spencer might have slipped the bonds of racial pariah status that Wiley's ancestors had to endure, but doing so didn't secure his descendants' future prosperity. Most struggled to gain a foothold to rise above basic subsistence, owning next to nothing while working as tenant farmers or day laborers. The country was falling into a great crisis of identity as it expanded west. The South feared its "peculiar institution" would be pushed into extinction unless new states and their representatives in Washington were pro-slavery. The North, which had abolished slavery by the early nineteenth century, did not want to expand the institution further. But a series of compromises in Washington put off the final reckoning.

Following Spencer's death in 1831, most of his descendants decamped from Raven Creek and moved to the frontier of Indiana. The end of the War of 1812 and the defeat of a confederacy of Indians under Tecumseh cleared the way for pioneers to move into the expanses of forest northwest of Kentucky. Spencer's old neighbor, President Madison, signed the law ratifying the Indiana territory as a new state in 1816 and established a federal land office in Vincennes on the Ohio River. Two years later St. Mary's Treaty opened up the untracked wilderness of central Indiana at $2 an acre. Unlike Kentucky a generation before, few white people had ever traversed these lands. The federal government sent out squads of surveyors, cutting their way with axes, fording rivers and swamps. They laid their lines for new counties, including Decatur County in southeastern Indiana, named after a hero of the recent Barbary Wars, in the southeast corner.

According to Lewis Albert Harding's 1,326-page *History of Decatur County, Indiana*, published in 1915, Henry Mozingo, the twenty-two-year-old son of my great-great-great-great-grandfather Joseph, walked the roughly 110 miles from Raven Creek to Decatur County. Based on the routes of the era, he likely would have hiked up the pike from Colemansville to Covington on the Ohio River, made his way west, crossing the river at some point, to the Indiana port of Lawrenceburg or Madison. Rough wagon trails started inland from there, degenerating quickly into a mess of mud holes and roots. At a place called Jericho the trails merged into the Wilson Trace to Decatur County. This was still rough frontier in 1832, an endless span of beech, walnut, oak, elm, and maple, filled with bear, turkey, and deer. Newcomers hunted their food and built rough shelters called "half-faced camps," closed on three sides, with the fire at the open end. Many just squatted on the land. If they found a piece they liked and had the money, they trekked twenty miles to the federal Land Office in Brookville to buy it, then marked their property lines by pushing brush up against the edges and blazing perimeter trees with hatchet marks.

Charles Dickens took a steamboat down the Ohio in 1842 and offered a beautifully bleak description of the poor settlers in the region:

> The banks are for the most part deep solitudes, overgrown with trees, which, hereabouts, are already in leaf and very green. For miles, and miles, and miles, these solitudes are unbroken by any sign of human life or trace of human footstep; nor is anything seen to move about them but the blue jay, whose colour is so bright, and yet so delicate, that it looks like a flying flower. At lengthened intervals a log cabin, with its little space of cleared land about it, nestles under a rising ground, and sends its thread of blue smoke curling up into the sky. It stands in the corner of the poor field of wheat, which is full of great unsightly stumps, like earthy butchers'-blocks. Sometimes the ground is only just now cleared: the felled trees lying yet upon the soil: and the log-house only this morning begun. As we pass this clearing, the settler leans upon his axe or hammer, and looks wistfully at the people from the world. The children creep out of the temporary hut, which is like a gipsy tent upon the ground, and clap their hands and shout. The dog only glances round at us, and then looks up into his master's face again, as if he were rendered uneasy by any suspension of the common business, and had nothing more to do with pleasurers. And still there is the same, eternal foreground.

Henry Mozingo found farmwork with a pioneer to the area named John Hillis and returned to his parents' home on Raven Creek with good news of the prospects in south central Indiana, according to Harding's history. His father, Joseph I, sold their land on Raven Creek for $250 on October 5, 1832. He must have sold or freed his slave girl, for Indiana was an abolitionist state. The following spring, the family—Joseph I and his wife Polly, and their children Henry, thirteen-year-old Mary Ann, and ten-year-old Joe (my third great-grandfather)—set off for their new home in Decatur. Two of Joseph's adult sons, Tandy and John, either accompanied them or followed shortly thereafter, as did his brothers James and Thomas and sister Nellie and their families.

As soon as they arrived, Joseph bought eighty acres of land from

Isaac and Catherine Ricketts for $150, near Sand Creek, about four miles south of the town of Greensburg. The Rickettses hadn't lived on the land, and the Mozingos set about clearing it and building a log cabin. This was brutal and relentless work. Fever disease ran rampant, and the winters swept off the northern plains, viciously cold and snowbound. Many immigrants returned to where they came from. Those who stayed engaged in an all-out assault on the dense, unbroken forest, hacking, burning, ring-barking, and uprooting the timber every way they could. Resinous smoke hung over stump-ridden clearings as if they were battlefields.

Then they had to cope with the soil. Decatur County had wonderfully fertile soil and terribly poor soil, all decomposed glacial waste spun and deposited haphazardly by the end of the last Ice Age. Some valleys and hollows boasted rich black ground good for corn; others were layered in clay loam that would not drain and could grow only wheat and grasses. The higher benchlands were usually good, as the limestone underlayer resisted erosion and held deep soils with enough sand to break up the clay. Farmers had to buy their land wisely.

Decatur was sparsely populated in those early days. While each township featured several whiskey stills, children would walk miles to school, if there was one at all, usually held in a vacant log cabin for a fee. And there were no churches, so services took place in people's homes. The Baptist Mozingos worshipped in a log cabin on a hill above Sand Creek until it burned in the 1850s.

William H. Herndon, a friend of Abraham Lincoln's in Indiana, recounted how families would walk up to ten miles to go to church, the women carrying their shoes to preserve them, the men coming with their rifles and wearing buckskin pants. He described the poor whites of early Indiana as a superstitious lot:

> They believed in the baneful influence of witches, pinned their
> faith to the curative power of wizards in dealing with sick animals,
> and shot the image of a witch with a silver ball to break the spell she
> was supposed to have over human beings. They followed with reli-

gious minuteness the directions of the water-wizard, with his magic divining rod, and the faith doctor who wrought miraculous cures by strange sounds and signals to some mysterious agency.

The flight of a bird in at the window, the breath of a horse on a child's head, the crossing by a dog of a hunter's path, all betokened evil luck in store for some one. The moon exercised greater influence on the actions of people and the growth of vegetation than the sun and all the planetary system combined. Fence rails could only be cut in the light of the moon, and potatoes planted in the dark of the moon. Trees and plants which bore their fruit above ground could be planted when the moon shone full.

In those early days, farmers took their products—corn, flour, pork— to the Ohio River at Madison or Lawrenceburg and loaded them onto flatboats for the long serpentine journey to New Orleans. Often the farm boys made the trips, glimpsing the world outside of their stump clearings for the first time and disembarking in the bawdy, multihued, multilingual city. They sold the goods and traded for coffee, sugar, rum, and molasses. The flatboats were taken apart and sold for scrap, and the boys usually walked back home. A nineteen-year-old Abraham Lincoln did this in 1828. Mozingo boys undoubtedly did too, perhaps including my great-great-great-grandfather Joseph. What would have been their reaction to the great Creole city, I wondered? Dirt-poor farm boys from the frontier, they probably didn't know about the threads of history that stitched the racially blended city together—the events that made it a portal to the Caribbean and infused it with mixed-race refugees of the Haitian Revolution in the late 1700s and vexed a young nation that wanted to see only white and black, free and slave. It seems implausible that the Mozingos knew on a conscious level that these strands had been threaded together with their own lines, with Edward's marriage to Margaret in the Northern Neck. This was little over a century after Edward died. But maybe soundings of him and his African origin still echoed out of the limbic depths of these descendants. Children do not form lasting memories until grade school, but that does not mean parents and siblings, even those who die before the child's memory of them is fixed, do not inhabit some part of their consciousness. Maybe in such a layer some impulse of this African lineage took root, inexplicable, like déjà vu.

On a more conscious level, they may have had suspicions for another reason. People who didn't know about their lineage didn't know for a reason. Joe Christmas never truly knew his origin, but he knew why he didn't, which amounted to the same. The forgetting spoke as much about one's status as what one actually forgot. But the farther Spencer's children and grandchildren pushed into the wilderness and mixed with other poor refugees with other destitute pasts, the fainter any soundings of their forgotten or repudiated ancestor must certainly have grown.

Unlike Kentucky, Indiana was a free state, but racial stigmatization in all its caprice and contradiction didn't just disappear on the northern bank of the Ohio River. I found a telling anecdote in Harding's history of Decatur County. In 1853, county leaders decided to set up free public schools for "all white children." One day soon thereafter, an angry father protested to a school trustee named Dr. Moody that a "little negro girl was attending the school. He said he would take his own daughter out unless the colored pupil was removed. The colored girl was very light in color, while the protesting citizen's daughter was a very dark brunette. 'Very well,' said Dr. Moody. 'We will send a man around tomorrow to pick out the negro. If he picks out the negro, she goes out, and if he picks out your child, she goes out.' The irate citizen was content to drop the matter."

Whether or not this irate citizen was a Mozingo we will never know. But given his daughter's dark hair and perhaps his own, an unease or uncertainty about his own racial admixture must have given him pause to proceed. Poor white trash had to watch out. The momentarily benevolent and smug Dr. Moody, who was no doubt involved in the original decision to ban blacks from the schools, had no such worries. In that vaunted book I grew up on, Atticus Finch had the leisure to be noble within the boundaries that white society allowed him, while the terrible white trash Bob Ewell did not.

My great-great-great-grandfather Joe had more in common with Ewell, I suspect, living a short, rough life with little to show for it. In 1844, at age twenty-one, he married nineteen-year-old Lucy Jane Barter.

By the time of the 1850 census, they had three children and no real estate, and his occupation was listed as "none." Ten years later, he was listed as a "day laborer." They had six children by then, the fourth being my great-great-grandfather Joe, age nine at that time. Again, they had no real estate, and the value of their "personal estate" was $50, making them perhaps the poorest family in the township.

The 1850s saw the nation rapidly sectionalized over slavery. Harriet Beecher Stowe's *Uncle Tom's Cabin*, published in 1852, became wildly popular in the North, pouring fuel on the abolitionist fire. Congress then passed the Kansas-Nebraska Act in 1854, which allowed settlers to decide whether they would allow slavery in those territories. This ignited a sporadic guerrilla war in Kansas, as pro-slave "border ruffians" poured in from Missouri and abolitionists such as John Brown came from the Northeast. The Kansas-Nebraska Act also sparked the formation of the antislavery Republican Party, which quickly won majorities in most northern states. When the party landed in the White House with the election of Abraham Lincoln, southern leaders saw slavery and their cotton economy under grave threat, and seceded, drawing America into the bloodiest war in its history. An estimated 620,000 soldiers would die between the firing on Fort Sumter, South Carolina, in 1861 and the surrender of Robert E. Lee at Appomattox Court House in 1865.

Before the war, Decatur drew people from north and south alike, with all manner of views on slavery and race, though the abolitionists seemed to be more organized and in the open. The Decatur County Anti-Slavery Society and the Decatur County Colonization Society fought each other over the best way to end slavery, whether to send slaves back to Africa or just set them free. A branch of the Underground Railroad ran up the east side of the county from Madison, with a safe house at McCoy's Station. A white farmer with substantial real estate, Luther A. Donnell, was indicted for helping a black woman and her four children escape from slave hunters trying to take her back to Kentucky. When he was convicted of that, the escaped woman's aggrieved owner sued him and won a $1,500 judgment. Donnell paid but stood by his principles, as many did. When the Fugitive Slave Act passed in 1850, requiring that runaways turning up in free states be returned to their masters, a county preacher told his congregants, "To law framed of such iniquity, I owe no allegiance. Humanity, Christianity, manhood revolt against it. For myself, I say it solemnly, I will shelter, I will help, I will defend the fugitive with all my humble means and power." Yet the area maintained strong links to the South, and some families who had come from there were rumored to have brought their slaves with them while other residents hunted escaped Kentucky slaves for bounties.

During the Civil War, Decatur County furnished the Union with twenty-six infantry and cavalry companies (of up to eighty-four men each) and one battery, according to Harding. Seventy-nine men died. It's unrecorded how many other men went south and enlisted in the Confederate Army. An unknown number joined the southern-sympathizing secret Knights of the Golden Circle, just as they would join the Ku Klux Klan in the twentieth century.

In June 1863, at age forty, my great-great-great-grandfather Joseph appeared on a draft registry of men subject to military duty in the Civil War. There is no record that he ever was drafted, but he died before the war ended, with no documentation of the cause.

By the end of 1865, his widow, Lucy, had remarried, to a, middle-aged, Kentucky-born farm laborer named Michael Hockersmith. They owned no land, listed no value to their estate, and would get a divorce in short order. After the divorce my great-great-grandfather Joe stayed with his adult first cousin William, the son of Spencer's son Tandy. In the 1870 census, Joe was eighteen and enrolled in one of the county's free schools that didn't accept blacks. William was forty-two, owned no land, and valued his estate at $200.

Joe married Nancy Wren, and they moved with their two-year-old son, my great-grandfather Ira, and Joe's mother, Lucy, to the prairies of central Illinois, where he was listed as a white tenant farmer in 1880. The two hundred miles from Decatur County, Indiana, to DeWitt County, Illinois, marked a pronounced change of landscape. The forests and broken limestone hills leveled into a great treeless prairie, with some of the deepest, richest topsoil in the nation. Farmers here produced more corn than in any other region of the Midwest. Their biggest problem was drainage, so they underlaid the fields with thousands of miles of clay drainage pipes. Joe arrived too late to get in on the game. The frontier had receded way over the Rocky Mountains by then, railroads had reached California, and the land here was long spoken for. Many farmers owned such big swaths they could not cultivate them themselves, so the type of poor tenant farmers whom we normally associate with the South filled in the labor gap. This is the seldom-mentioned counterpoint to our notion of the small family-owned farm of the Midwest, that nostalgic icon of American identity.

Sure enough, tenant farming didn't give Joe the step up he wanted. In fact, he stepped down and moved to Bloomington as a day laborer. Bloomington was a thriving market city of 23,000, with department stores and banks and manufacturing. The largest employer, the Chicago & Alton Railroad shops, comprised its own little village on the west side of town. The Mozingos managed to rent a home at 407 Jackson Street, with the help of their sixteen-year-old daughter, Ada, who dropped out of school and worked full time as a laundress.

My great-grandfather Ira, twenty-three by then, had moved out and married a local girl from DeWitt County, Josie Longberry. They had a one-year-old boy, John (father of the vigorously uncooperative James Dale, whom I called in Missouri), and lived just outside of Bloomington, where Ira labored on other people's farms. Family lore my uncle heard has it that the Longberrys had gone to Colorado in a wagon train, but that Josie's mother took one look at the arid plains and said then and there, "We're going back." Such were my intrepid ancestors. This is the earliest bit of oral history to survive in my family's consciousness today, aside from that vague whisper that we had come from Virginia. And it came with a physical piece of history: the rifle they brought for the journey, a Winchester '73, which now rests by my parents' fireplace.

By 1910 Ira had moved the family west to Marion County, Missouri, renting a farm near the Mississippi River. My grandfather Joe was born there in 1913. The family looked to be on the same path to nowhere, with the Great Depression not too far off. But out of the blue—at least from my opaque vantage—Ira and Josie started a small grocery store nearby in downtown Hannibal. Mozingo Grocery. They must have come upon some money, perhaps a bank loan or an inheritance from the Long-berrys. I suspect the latter because the city directory of 1916 lists "Mrs. Ira Mozingo" as the grocer and "Harry (Ira) Mozingo" as her salesman. Their teenage son, John, was a clerk. Two years later, Ira had taken title of the store, and John had started out on his own, working as a black-smith at the cement plant.

This is where our history going forward officially meets memory going backward: Hannibal. The tarantula in the banana delivery, the caves a young Samuel Clemens explored more than half a century before. The family lived in an apartment above the store, and their clerk and deliv-ery driver lived next door. Goods were delivered by horse and buggy. The municipal directory at the time listed exactly one hundred of these little markets, in a city of just eighteen thousand people.

Hannibal had thrived as a milling town in the nineteenth century, when lumber companies sent rafts of logs, sometimes a mile long, down the Mississippi to be sawed into boards and loaded onto freight cars. As the forests thinned out, Hannibal sagged until it drew manufacturers by first convincing the Roberts, Johnson & Rand shoe company to build a factory there. With that seed the city hit a new peak, sporting three flour mills, two breweries, four grain elevators, and one of the largest Portland cement companies in the country. Five train lines kept the town alive and healthy for a spell, fifty-four passenger trains rumbling through Hannibal on various lines every day. But a long era of stagna-tion would soon follow.

Ira registered for service in World War I but was never drafted. His registration card said he had black hair, brown eyes, and a stout build. Since no photos of him survive, thanks to my uncle's indiscriminate use of a trash bin when he sold and moved out of the family home in 1998, this is all I will ever know of his appearance.

The family was on the move for the next four years. Ira and Josie relocated back to Bloomington in 1920. Ira cleaned trains' water tanks at the railroad shops, then opened a new grocery on the west side of town. His dad, Joseph, was sixty-eight and living nearby, having divorced Nancy and married a woman named Molly. He walked the streets, ring-ing a brass bell, peddling horseradish from a wagon.

Ira died at the age of forty-six in 1923 and Josie died four years later. My grandfather was an orphan at thirteen. He moved in with his sister Cecel and her husband, Orville. Their mother left the siblings a small inheritance to be split, and probate records show that my grandfather had $113.84 left of it in 1930. That was spent over the next couple of years on school supplies, clothes, and dental appointments. Grandpa Joe graduated from Bloomington High School in 1931—he is dark and brooding in his yearbook photos—and took accounting courses at a trade school. He had an easygoing manner and must have had an adventurous streak; he once rode motorcycles to California with his nephew, Willie, after which he went to work as an accountant at the MaGirl Foundry & Furnace Works and met a proper young woman, secretly five years his senior, named Helen Gaull. She was Irish Catholic, and he converted so they could marry. She gave birth to Joseph Wesley, my uncle Joe, in 1941, and they took the Burlington Northern to Union Station in Los Angeles the next year, leaving a long hard history behind. My grandfather found his job at Howard Hughes's tool company, and my father was born just after the war in 1945. He excelled in school, got into the Naval Academy, realized it didn't suit his independent ways, managed to get an honorable discharge that kept him out of the Vietnam War, and went on to UCLA to become a dentist.

Along the way, the wider clan disintegrated, each nucleus of family or individual going their own way. Grandpa Joe never really knew his older brother. He went back to Bloomington once to take care of his sister Irene as she was dying of alcoholism and diabetes. When he himself was dying in 1969, three years before I was born, he waited for his older sister, Cecel, to visit him in the hospice. "I know she'll come," he said, but she didn't. Shortly after his death, she called my grandmother to get a copy of his death certificate. Cecel had apparently taken out a life insurance policy on her younger brother.

My parents came up to our house outside of Los Angeles on a Saturday to eat lunch and see their grandson, talk about the baby girl we were expecting in a few months, and, ostensibly, hear about my travels. I thought it might inspire my dad to see a page of the diary written by James Madison's very cousin mentioning his great-great-great-great-grandfather, or at least convince him this was real. "Hmmm," he said, still with only mild interest. He was more absorbed in the renovation work I was doing turning our garage into a home office. "You just put a two-by-six header there?"

We ate Thai delivery for lunch, and trying to provoke them a little, I told them I had found a Monga Maluku Mozingo in the Democratic Republic of Congo. He was the national soccer coach in the Atlanta Olympics. I had gotten his number through the foundation of the great Congolese basketball player Dikembe Mutombo and was hoping to call him that week. "Is he our cousin?" my mom asked and laughed.

I rolled with it. I didn't want to be too preachy about all this.

"I agree that he was black and all that," my dad said. "But how do you know it's an African name just because it exists there? Couldn't the Portuguese have brought it there?"

"But the name doesn't exist in Portugal."

"I'm just pretending this is all on the witness stand," he said.

"Okay," I said, though I didn't remember our Basque theory ever taking the witness stand.

"There were no records of Africa before the Europeans arrived." This was true for the area Edward came from. "So how do we know?"

"Linguists can tell what is actually an African word and what is a European word introduced there. And even the Portuguese linguists I spoke to knew immediately it sounded like an African word. It's as obvious to them as it is to us that it is not an English word."

My parents shifted around on the subject. I sensed a tension below the surface that they would never admit. For one, my dad didn't know much about his family's past, but he knew from his own youth that it wasn't illustrious. The fact that his father basically lost contact with his family suggested the family wasn't a loving, tight-knit lot. In his own childhood, my dad was constantly at odds with his parents' fussing over small things and ignoring important ones. My grandma Helen, the granddaughter of working-class British and Irish immigrants, ruled the roost with an affectation of British nobility. She had fine silverware,

Royal Doulton English china, and alabaster skin as preciously sheltered as her exact age. She hung an expensive print of Thomas Gainsborough's *The Blue Boy* over the fireplace in their living room, and watched *Upstairs Downstairs* on *Masterpiece Theatre* on her davenport at night. She focused on the tiniest bits of finery, like a blueblood, while the house cycled through bouts of squalor.

She applied wax to the windows—and then closed the curtains.

When I was young and my grandmother and uncle were living in their house, we didn't visit for years. No one did. They wouldn't let anyone in the front door because it was such a disaster inside. They did visit us, and from the moment she arrived my grandmother started complaining. She complained about the house being cold, about my dad driving too fast, about my mom's food, about all her endless aches and pains and discomforts. If she were alive today, she would most certainly claim that if I were to actually publish this story, she would have a heart attack and die. If my dad were to do such a thing, she would accuse him of trying to kill her.

So I understand why he didn't look back much. When it was time for him to leave home, he shot out like a missile. He decided who he wanted to be with no real input from the past other than as an indicator of what he didn't want. He became the ultimate do-it-yourselfer and brooked no complaints or lassitude or excuses. Working at a pharmacy in Hollywood, he paid his way through UCLA undergrad and dental school, and opened his own dental practice at twenty-six instead of working for someone else. He learned construction and enlisted my brother and me to build a big addition to our house. When I was about twelve, I was trying to whittle a piece of wood with a pocketknife when the blade jerked closed and sliced my forefinger to the bone. Instead of taking me to the emergency room, he took me to the bathroom counter and stitched it up himself. A few years later he taught me how to suture, so I could fix any deep cuts on surfing trips to remote parts of Mexico.

But my dad was a dreaming man too. He built a back office so he could paint and write fiction in solitude. And he did manage to quit dentistry for a spell to write a novel, until finances forced him back. His imagination just never focused on his past.

I suspect he didn't want me to go picking away at his family line, as if by being a generation closer to the past, he had more responsibility for whatever aberrations I unearthed there. It certainly didn't help matters when I announced that, according to census records, his aunt Cecel started out life as a boy named Cecil. And the fact that launched me on this quest—that we had an African name—only confirmed that there was something weird in his family. Who had ever heard of white people inheriting an African name?

My parents are fairly liberal and have evolved with their generation on the subject of race and social minorities, as I have with mine. They were die-hard Obama supporters, and they would not resist the simple notion that my dad had a black ancestor. But a name, especially a non-English name in a family with no dominating ethnic narrative, had a way of consolidating and defining a person's roots. This was what made it hard to fathom for me as well: our Bantu roots. Even my podmate at work, a black woman, very intellectual and versed in racial history, thought my having an African name was too far-fetched. "Are you working on your 'Black Like Me' story?" she would ask, with gentle mockery.

I gave my parents some respite over lunch and we talked about politics, family gossip, our blind dog, Dudley, and stucco removal. But I couldn't pass up the chance when my mom asked what we were thinking of naming the baby. "We were thinking of an African name," I said, as flatly as I could muster. "It seems only right. Monga Maluku maybe."

A flash of distress crossed her face before she saw I was joking.

I spent an afternoon in Bloomington while visiting Indiana and Illinois to find out more about Spencer and his descendants.

There was nothing much to see in place where a family had dissolved. I found a few prairie box homes where they had lived. At the East Lawn Memorial Park cemetery, a groundskeeper took me to Great-great-grandpa Joe's grave. He poked around in the turf with a pocketknife looking for a concrete peg with a number. The sun was bright and flat. The traffic on East Empire Street let out an endless sigh, and small planes took off from the municipal airport just across the road. "Here it is," he said. "It" was just a depression in the grass, under a cedar tree, next to the stones of his daughter Ada and her husband, Fred Lemme.

I would learn a few things about Joe from a distant cousin, Bob Inman, who met him when he was boy and wrote about him in a memoir. "We had been told not to bother Great Grandpa Mozingo . . . [who] lived phantomlike in the back room of Granma's house. He was a thin, elderly, white-haired gentleman with white goatee. He dressed in the old way, with black suit, white shirt, tie and hat. We were hardly aware of his existence. One day, while snooping around, I entered his room and there he was! . . . He seemed delighted that I had come in. . . . He smiled and his eyes twinkled. I felt immediately at ease. I said something like, 'Hi, Great Grandpa Mozingo,' and he grinned back at me. He then reached into his pocket and gave me a penny."

Inman told me Joe had joined the Church of the Nazarene at the end of his life. He was so devout that he told his family just to "chuck him in a ditch" when he died because all he needed was Jesus.

They didn't chuck him in a ditch, but they did save some money with the unmarked grave. I put a flower down on the ground and left, thinking that blank spot represented nearly every aspect of my ancestors' three-hundred-year slog through American history.

One group of Spencer's line remained fairly intact: the descendants of Henry, my great-great-great-grandfather's older brother, were still clustered around Decatur County. Since family history usually survived in tighter clans, I was eager to visit and see what they knew about Spencer and his son Joseph, our common forebears.

Unlike most of his relatives, Henry did quite well, and by the 1850s had actually become one of the most prominent farmers in the county, with fifteen children and a personal estate of at least $18,000. Henry's census record of that year is now too faded to read, but a newspaper article in 1866 said he was one of eight citizens in this township paying more than $150 a year in taxes. He paid three times in annual taxes what his younger brother had to his name. By then the development of pork packing made pigs the most profitable commodity around. Farmers no longer just let the hogs roam the forest eating acorns and nuts, but fed them corn to plump them up fast. When the animals grew fat enough, they were driven to one of the many slaughterhouses popping up on the river in Madison, after which they met their end and set off down the Mississippi as canned pork, barrels of lard, hams, slabs of salt pork, and bacon.

Henry made his money on pigs, but lost it in the 1860s, when, according to Harding's history, "through over confidence and believing all men were honest, he endorsed for men who were dishonest and by this endorsement thus lost of his hard worked earnings about eighteen thousand dollars, but enough being left to satisfy all claims."

Eighteen thousand dollars was a substantial sum. Based on average wages at the time, it would be over $3 million in today's dollars. What epic battles and tensions and rivalries played out in a family where one brother could lose that much on a bad investment and another, my great-great-great-grandfather Joe, lived just down the road with six children and $50 to his name? Maybe Henry was a callous person. Maybe he emulated how his father treated his grandfather in his dotage, leaving Spencer in the care of his neighbors. But Henry was a progressive and an ardent supporter of Lincoln, and his sons were also devoted to the progressive cause. His oldest son, Thomas, enlisted at the first call for Union troops in the Civil War and fought in one of the first skirmishes, at Philippi, Virginia, then charged into the maw of Bull Run, Antietam, and Gettysburg. Henry's third son, James, would be an active member of the Methodist Episcopal Church and the benevolent fraternal organization the Independent Order of Odd Fellows, devoted to helping those in need. They had to have some conscience to them.

Henry never recovered from his losses. He sold the land he bought in frontier days to his son James Henry for $2,200 and continued to live there. The 1870 census shows him living with his wife, four teenage daughters, and his war veteran son, Thomas. Also among them was his ninety-seven-year-old mother, Polly Clemmons Mozingo, who was born in Virginia just before the Revolutionary War. Polly haunted my thoughts, as she may have been the last person to know about Spencer (her father-in-law) and the connection to Edward, perhaps even Africa. She died in 1872.

Henry lived in the house until he died in 1888. He had a big funeral, announced by ornate cards with gold calligraphy and his name misspelled: "In Long Remembrance of Henry Mozings . . . Asleep in Jesus! blessed sleep. From which none ever wakes to weep."

The county was tamed by then, with churches and schools all about, and masonry buildings in downtown Greensburg. Mozingos helped build Mt. Pleasant Church in 1854. Citizens held county fairs and formed all sorts of societies and clubs and a growing temperance movement. A rail line came in from Lawrenceburg, and the county courthouse was even becoming famous because a tree had sprouted from a crevice on the clock-tower roof. The local paper published a photo of it in 1879. "Since that time the tree has been exhibited pictorially all over the world, and postal cards by the tens of thousands have convinced a doubting world that such a tree really exists," wrote Harding. "Some time during the latter part of the seventies, other trees sprang up on the tower, and at one time no less than seven were casting their shade over the tower."

Henry's children had nearly as many children as he did, and the family expanded rapidly. James Henry sold the farm and bought a new one. For a spell James's son was one of the biggest corn growers in Indiana. But by the Depression most of Henry's grandchildren and great-grandchildren had sunk back into the bog of poor tenant farming.

They live all over Decatur now, a close but fractious clan, divided along shifting fault lines. I had talked on the phone with Kathy Ross, the family history buff among them. "Another Mozingo came out to do family research," Kathy told me. "He was gay, which doesn't bother me none. Bud and some of the others had a big problem with it, though. So they might ask you if you're gay."

"So who's Bud?"

"You don't have earrings, do you?"

"No."

"They don't like earrings."

Kathy was trying to brace me, and also size up my motives. "Some of them are asking me if you're just going to make fun of us."

"No, no," I said, thinking, *I hope not.*

"Like we're just a bunch of hillbillies."

I again assured her I had no intention of doing so, but Kathy had a way of not actually addressing what I said.

"Amy is Roxie's daughter. Roxie was ahead of her time, very tolerant. Amy is too. You'll like Amy. She's getting up there in age. She has a lesbian sister. . . . And just so you know, Amy was, uhm, big chested."

I laughed, confused at her point.

"Then she had a double mastectomy. . . . So if you hear anything, that's what they're talking about."

"What would I hear?"

"Like Bud said he should strap a plow to her."

Kathy knew about Edward Mozingo through her research on the web, but said she didn't know exactly what her many relatives in the area knew or thought about their origins. The topic of Edward would be much too touchy. But she invited me to come to a June family reunion to meet them all and see what they knew.

I was desperate to see if I could find Polly's obituary or any account of her life. And I hoped I could get a collective pulse of Spencer's kin from them, since my own relatives were so scattered. Maybe we shared certain traits.

What I would find was the extreme of Mozingo whiteness, as if a bungee cord from Edward Mozingo to the aforementioned Bud Mozingo had stretched to its natural limit and, trembling with tension, could get no whiter or more racist. But instead of snapping, that cord was quickly recoiling.

In Greensburg, I pulled into a Walgreens parking lot next to a blue Chrysler minivan. The back door slid open. "Well, get in, goddamn it!" an elderly woman in the backseat said, and I did. She was short and pigeon-chested, with graying red hair and sharp black eyes. She wore a man's gray oxford shirt and acid-washed jeans. "You're Amy," I said.

"What did you find in Kentucky?" Kathy asked, sitting in the front passenger seat next to her husband, Ronny, at the wheel.

"I think I found where Spencer lived."

"Well, we're happy to have you here. Next time you can bring your family."

Kathy was in her late forties, with blond hair and a husky voice that didn't quite fit with her supremely kind demeanor. We turned left at a sign that said "Tree Tower" and entered the old brick downtown of Greensburg. Kathy pointed out the gnarled tree growing from the roof of the clock tower. "It's what we're famous for," she said.

"They say it's fed by a spring in the clock," Ronny quipped.

Ronny had two hearing aids, which I was told he needed because of damage from heavy artillery in Vietnam. Everyone yelled at him to turn here or stop there, and he never did.

Downtown Greensburg was tidy and vibrant, with businesses filling the leaded-glass storefronts: Minear's Department Store, Edward Jones financial advisors, Stories Restaurant, the Beach Tiki Bar and Grill. We stopped for lunch at Stories and they asked me lots of questions about my family and California, as if they were expecting some strange and exotic bird. At one point they asked me if I knew what a creek was. We ate and paid and drove on. Amy, who was seventy-eight, gave me the rundown on various family members, past and present, between cigarettes. "She's just a bitch. . . . He was the sweetest man. . . . That motherfucker. . . . He went to Indianapolis and dumped his wife and kids." She had a 40-grit smoker's voice and a big gruff laugh.

Most of the Mozingos here came down the line either from Henry's progressive son, James, or his other son, Edwin Forrest, who was said to have been in the Klan. We got out at a creek called Cobbs Fork, where the family had held an annual cookout for generations. It was an idyllic spot, afternoon sunlight spidering through the walnut and maple trees, crystalline water falling off shelves of limestone.

"The Mozingos, they fight and feud," Amy said. "You might be on one side of the fence one time, and the other side on the next. There'd be one group down there by the bridge, and one group up here by these rocks. One year, me and Maury sat right down in the middle, so we made it an integrated affair." Maury was her husband, who had passed away eight years before.

Next stop was what Kathy had primed me for, Marlin "Bud" Mozingo's home in Napoleon, along the old trace Henry walked in on. Approaching the property, I saw shoes nailed to every fence post along the road. We pulled up the gravel drive to the two-story brick house, and Bud was sitting alone on the deck in his shorts and socks, despite his wife Shirley's complaints that she had just put Armor All on the wood. He looked grumpy and stubborn, with a big lumpy head like Jerry Lewis. I would learn this was his regular demeanor, a volatile mix of facetious, cantankerous, generous, and sentimental that made it hard to gauge his true opinions. He wouldn't acknowledge that I was there for ten minutes. Finally he asked if I wanted a can of Bud Light.

"I never touch the stuff," he said. "I just keep it for visitors."

I figured he was joking and took one, then felt awkward when no one else did.

"I am the patriarch," Bud declared.

"You're not the patriarch—Dale is," rasped Amy.

Their cigarette smoke swirled above them in the fading light.

Bud repeated his claim, more forcefully.

"Oh piss," Amy said.

"Want to see my beefalo?" Bud asked me.

"Sure."

We walked over to the steel fence, where I could see one buffalo, some normal cows, and a few shaggy ones.

"You take a buffalo and breed them to a bull, you get beefalo," he said. "They got some beefalo children there."

He chased one of them into the corral and closed the gate. Bud was a horse trader who, I would learn, could sell sand in a desert. Beefalo was his newest venture. The shoes were an earlier venture. He and his brother Stan once bought a load of shoes at an auction for a dollar.

When they got home, they realized there were no pairs. First they started knocking on neighbors' doors, thrusting shoes in their hands and running away, but they had more shoes than neighbors. So they nailed them to the fence. Now the display is a local landmark, to which passersby added their own mismatched shoes.

We walked to the little lake behind his house. At seventy-four, Bud was broad-shouldered, with a girth that ended abruptly at his belt. He leaned into that top-heavy ballast impatiently, as if it would make his legs go faster.

I nursed my beer, admiring his property, wondering why I had had such a dismal view of Indiana.

"Is Los Angeles a big city?" Bud asked.

I figured he was bullshitting again. "Yeah, it's pretty big."

"I never been in an airplane."

I didn't believe him.

"You know what a Dutchman is?" Bud asked.

"Well, I guess. . . . No, not really."

"I don't like Dutchmen," he said.

He cocked his head to look at me slyly.

"I don't like queers. I don't like niggers."

"Don't use that word!" Amy barked.

"That's the word I used since I was a little boy," he replied.

"You like Tanya?" Amy asked.

"She's not one of them," he said, looking slightly hurt. "It doesn't have to do with color. You can be white and be a nigger."

"Oh, you're full of shit," she said.

Everyone else glanced at me with looks that beseeched me to please ignore him, as we sat back down on the porch. The others resumed smoking and talking about people I didn't know. I pondered my approach to revealing the family "secret." After backing down on confronting Junior in Virginia, I had committed to coming to Indiana like some avenging angel for our Congolese ancestor, armed with proof of our African ancestry, and watching the arteries on people's foreheads swell and burst. But playing gotcha didn't feel right now that I was here. These people were going out of their way to help me in my research. As a writer, I was used to staying out of people's way and just watching. My job was always to get a sense of who people were, not to change who they were. So rather than raise the issue of Bud's bigotry or confront them with Edward, I blandly asked them where they thought the name Mozingo came from.

"It's an English name, I think," Shirley said. "When Orville Holmes went to England, he looked it up. He saw cemeteries over there and Mozingo stones in the cemeteries."

"Let's call Steamer," Bud said. "He knows." Steamer was Stanley, his brother. "Just tell him you voted for Obama to get him steamed," he added, with a grin. "I voted for Obama, you know."

Shirley got him on the phone. "Oh, you say Ireland . . . England."

Bud leaned into me. "Obama is very clever."

"Yeah, he's smart."

"You notice anything you don't notice in other towns?"

"Like what?"

"There's no coloreds."

"Oh, Hungary," Shirley said in the background. "Okay."

She said goodbye and hung up, and Bud turned to her. "I was telling him how there's no coloreds here."

"They hung one of them way back and they left," Shirley said. Her tone was matter-of-fact, no sign of endorsement. She had a kind of sweet, Betty White way about her.

"They don't let them come back after sunset," Bud said.

He meant Greensburg was a "sunset town," where black workers had to be gone by nightfall. I wondered if this were true. The part about the black residents way back leaving certainly was. I had researched that. There used to be a black community around Clarksburg and black residents throughout the county. In 1880, 235 African American residents lived here. In 1960, three did. There was a race riot in 1906 that may have sparked an exodus, but such things were not reported in local newspapers, and details of the event are still sketchy. Greensburg was so white that a recent mayor was taken aback by the criticism he got when he called black people "colored" in a newspaper interview.

I gazed off as my new cousins caught up with each other and the fields turned purple and the lights of kitchen windows floated in the dark like distant beacons on a heaving sea.

We ate dinner at a diner, and they dropped me off at a Holiday Inn Express along the Interstate. I flipped on the television, exhausted, and then called my wife. "They're certainly interesting," I said. I told her all about Bud, who was the other male on Spencer's line to do the DNA test.

"Jesus," she said.

"I know. He and I have the same Y chromosome."

The next morning, I met Amy at her house, set off the gravel road in a great stand of maple and shag bark hickory. She lived alone with a poodle named Jake and so many cats I was grateful when she lit up a smoke.

Amy was a rural mail carrier for twenty-three years and an individualist truly of her own brand. She listened to a police scanner in the kitchen to hear what the neighbors were up to, fed raccoons by hand on her porch, and collected rocks. We talked family history for a spell, but she followed every tangent that popped up in her mind, uttering more names than a Russian novel.

"My dad was mean as a snake," she was saying. "He cussed every breath he ever drew. He'd look up at a hawk and say, 'Look at that son-of-a-bitch.'"

I watched a raccoon wander around on her back porch looking for cat food. "Have you seen raccoons before?" she asked.

I told her a whole pack of them lived in our storm drains, like sewer rats, except meaner.

"I need to show you something," she said. She flew upstairs and came down with a stack of photos. First was one of her smiling in a giant beige bra. "This was the day before I had my boobs cut off," she said.

"Wow," I said, unable to conjure anything else.

"They were 40 DD," she said. "I don't miss 'em too much, hanging around my waist. . . . When I got rid of them, I told Bud I wasn't going to pull his plow anymore." It struck me on this second telling that I didn't actually understand this joke.

She showed me a photo of her granddaughter, who had freckled, mocha-toned skin and straightened black hair. "That's Tanya," she said.

Amy told me the story. Tanya was born in 1974, she said. Her mother, Beth—Amy's daughter—was a sixteen-year-old dropout and alcoholic at the time, who had run away from home to live in squalor with her older sister, Lynn, in St. Petersburg, Florida. In November 1973, Beth called home to say that she was pregnant and Lynn's two kids were hungry. Amy, Maury, and Amy's sister Carol loaded up in Amy's new gray Chevy sedan and headed down Interstate 75. When they approached the house, Carol remarked that they were in the "black section" of town. Through a vacant lot, they saw Beth and Lynn in a backyard and got out. A little black boy was playing with them. The only words anyone remembers of this watershed moment were Carol's. She pointed to Beth's belly and said, "Is that ni-gro too?" Beth nodded yes.

Three weeks later, Beth had moved back home and Amy was driving her to Kentucky to get an abortion. Beth didn't want one. Amy insisted. Though Amy never shared or understood her neighbors' antipathy toward black people—she once invited a stranded black family to stay at her house while their car was being fixed, because the hotel would not take them—this pregnancy was as taboo as it got in Greensburg. The nurse took Beth into an examining room. "This is what you want, right?" the nurse asked.

"No, this is what my mother wants. I want to go back to Florida and live with the baby's dad."

"If you don't want it, we're not going to give it to you," the nurse said.

For two weeks, Amy and Beth fought. Beth cried for hours, and Amy grew sick of it. "You call that black bastard up and ask if he'll marry you." Beth screamed, "I will, then!" and she did. He said okay. She moved down to Florida and gave birth to a girl she named Tanya (the first syllable rhyming with man) because she had a tan.

Despite her fears, Amy and Maury fell in love with the baby. She choked up now talking about this, saying how grateful she was that Beth refused the abortion and calling Tanya her "greatest blessing." Amy and Maury ended up raising her in Indiana for much of her youth because Beth was a mess. Tanya was the only black child in school, and Amy protected her with a vengeance. The extended family—even Bud— embraced her, but never forgave Beth for sleeping with a black man.

I told Amy about Edward Mozingo and showed her a copy of the ruling from the Virginia colonial court describing him as a "Negro man." She was delighted and wanted a copy to needle Bud with. "Did you show this to them?"

"No. I was going to."

"Look at that," she said, studying it and suddenly tearing up. "I'm so glad because we always had to guess what it was. I'm so glad to know that for sure. I'm so happy for Tanya." She said Beth must have been "carrying along a Mozingo tradition."

Bud and his brother Stan met us for lunch at a diner in Greensburg. Stan was a thin sixty-seven-year-old fence builder with pale blue eyes, jug-handle ears, and two missing front teeth where he had had a losing match with the flying steel hook of a come-along winch. They all recommended a deep-fried piece of pounded meat they called tenderloin, and I ordered it. The salad was iceberg and blue cheese. Everyone in the restaurant seemed to know Bud, sidling up to him in eager expectation of the abuse he would heap on them.

"I'm always glad to see you," he told one woman. "I don't like you, but I like to talk to you."

"What are you doing?" he asked a woman standing over him, without looking up.

"Talking to you," she said.

"You think you'll learn something?"

He vented loudly about queers and men with earrings in front of a waiter who had a stud in his ear, and he and Stan took delight in saying "nigger" for effect. I could see other people looking askance and muttering "Jesus" and such. One visitor to our table let out a booming laugh and proclaimed, "This table is Redneck Central."

After coffee and pie, we set off to find more Mozingo graves, hoping I might find one for my great-great-great-grandfather Joseph. His father's had been plowed under, but Henry's was still around. We got in Bud's four-door pickup. The country was truly serene. Pastures lifted and dropped into steep forested tablelands and hollows. The homes were all well painted and nicely kept. White steeples rose here and there from the green. I'd say it was an idyll, except I was quickly realizing how stultifying the social dynamic was for someone not born into it. All the churchiness and long, polite, alcohol-free get-togethers. I began to appreciate Bud and Amy solely for the bombs they dropped in the conversation.

Amy at one point told me about the time her grandmother went out to the barn to find a young man having his way with her cow. She chased him off, but found him there again a couple of hours later. She screamed, and her son-in-law raised his rifle and winged him.

"Why did he shoot him?" I asked.

"He was screwing the cow!" Amy rasped. "This isn't California!"

At Sand Creek Cemetery, we found Henry Mozingo's tombstone.

"Take a picture," Kathy asked Bud.

"I only draw pictures," Bud said.

"The only thing Bud draws is flies," Stan said, and laughed heartily.

The obelisk stone offered no new details of his life: "Henry Mozingo, 1809–1888."

Stan found some pieces of wire in the dirt, twisted them into a Y, and showed me how to tell where bodies are underfoot. "You can witch water the same way." He handed it to me, and I paced forward with it. Sure enough, the wire rotated every time I walked over a grave. Stan snickered giddily. Unlike Bud, he was impeccably polite, with a faintly southern accent and the southern courtesy of saying your name in almost every sentence. But on our drive his racism proved to be even more venomous than Bud's. I asked him why he hated black people so much. There weren't even any around here to hate. He said he started hating them in the army, when a black sergeant was nice to his face then sold him out to a superior. He didn't hate all of them, though, only the ones he called "niggers."

"I have colored friends," he said. "A colored man, Jack Strode, taught me more than anyone else I know about breaking mules. . . . He could be working ten mules and he'd call one's name out and its ears would raise up. . . . 'Nigger' doesn't have to do with color. They could be blue."

"Have you ever called a white person one?" I asked.

"No, I don't think so, Joe. . . . I've been around the colored people. It's all fine when you have them outnumbered. But when they have you outnumbered, they try everything on you. I don't have a good feeling toward the black people."

What I gathered was that Bud's and Stan's bigotry had a tiny pore in its crusty skin: if they were thrust into a situation with a black person and, against the odds inherent in such an interaction, came away with a decent impression, that person would be exempted from some of their generalizations. It goes without saying, though, that they'd threaten to kill him before letting him near their daughters (or granddaughters, I would learn).

What had me thinking was the truism that you're not born racist. Certainly Bud and Stan grew up in a time when racism infected much of the society they lived in. But with no black people around at all, then or now, their bigotry retained a virulence that bordered on mental illness, and as best I could tell was far beyond the norm in Decatur County. Maybe it started with their father or grandfather. Or maybe it came all the way down through the generations of Mozingos, easing up with success, as with Henry and his son, and baring its teeth when poverty took everything but that shaky sense of "blood pride."

Perhaps this racism Bud and Stan were spouting manifested, in a twisted way, the legacy of the fear and shame of those ancestors who actually knew of their origins. Some of those ancestors no doubt overcompensated in their vitriol of blacks so that no one would suspect they had black blood, and then inculcated this hatred into their children.

Bud started talking about how big the Ku Klux Klan used to be here.

"Were Mozingos in the Klan?" I asked.

"Oh heavens, yes," he said. "Grandpa Joe was a Klan member.

Edwin was a Klan member." They must have been the only Bantu white supremacists in the United States.

I told them that there was an African man freed by the Jamestown court named Edward Mozingo, and that it was pretty evident that all Mozingos descended from him, and definitely got their name from him. I just said it matter-of-factly, no big proclamation.

"No, Joe, slaves got their names from their masters," Stan said.

"His master was a Walker," I said.

"I heard it is Italy, somewhere like that."

Bud just grinned. Neither were going to take this seriously.

"Joe, you know I have an official document about the Mozingo name I found on the computer. I'll print it up and show you."

"Okay, I can't wait to see it."

I tried to talk to Stan on this subject later several times. I told him he must have wondered about the name growing up. "It doesn't sound like Brown or Smith or Jones," I said.

"Yeah, but it doesn't sound like Obama either. Heh-heh-heh," he laughed. "I got you there, didn't I, Joe?"

I asked him if he would have a problem if it was African. "No, it wouldn't be no problem, Joe, nuh-uh. No, it wouldn't be no problem. Because the way I look at it, God made all us people. And you know, we just know it's not African, Joe. If I was colored, I wouldn't be ashamed of it, because you couldn't help it, Joe."

"But you know it's not African?" I asked

"It's not African, no. The first I heard is from Hungary, northern Italy, somewhere like that, around the Hungarian border."

I told him Edward married an Englishwoman, and about the genera-tions of mixing between him and us that made us white.

"Okay, it's not African, Joe. I ain't never seen a colored Mozingo. . . . Back when they brought the Africans over here, they had a first name but no last name. And the Mozingos used to own slaves, and they took their master's name."

The next afternoon, Kathy and Amy and I went to the courthouse. I was excited to look for Polly's obituary. I figured someone may have written one because her son Henry was so prominent in the county. She certainly was the only Mozingo in my line that came all the way from Virginia who might have had one. She was in Spencer's orbit for thirty years, and if anyone knew about his background, it was she.

I started looking through big bound books of the *Greensburg Standard*, the *Saturday Review*, and the *New Era*. My breath grew shallow flipping pages in anticipation.

"I'm tired," I remotely heard Amy say. Soon a clerk came to tell us Amy was asleep at one of the desks. Kathy walked over and checked to make sure she was all right. She snored lightly and looked content.

I really liked Amy and Kathy. In a way, I even liked Bud and Stan. I admired their self-sufficiency, a trait you didn't see much of anymore in the city or suburbs. On my block, I was one of a scattered few who mowed his own lawn, but whenever the lawn mower broke down, I checked the spark plug, kicked it furiously a few times, then took it to Sears. If Bud's tractor broke down, he pulled it apart and fixed it himself. Stan built his fences in the stifling heat of summer at age sixty-seven, and Bud kept his ranch running through ice storms and twelve-foot snowdrifts at seventy-four. There was no abstraction to their work, no ethical drift, no way to half-ass or fudge it. Like tile in my past life, you did the job right, or you scraped it up and redid it. My job now was murkier. When I came into their world, they treated me well, like family. But I was traversing a dicey ethical terrain between family and journalism. No matter how nice they were to me, no matter how discreet I was with them now about our ancestry, the story to be published wouldn't be discreet at all. There was no polite, good-kin way to write what I had to write. Bud and Stan were old racists, and I couldn't be an honest journalist and gloss over that. That was part of life in America. People argue that it's not a significant factor anymore, but they can argue from theory, not the raw details. The details here spoke for themselves. I worried particularly about Kathy. She didn't seem to have the tough skin that Bud and Amy did. I could only hope they would all forget about me and never read the stories. Before the Internet, that might have been possible.

I paged through the newspapers again and again. I dug through court records and found the grant deed where Joseph bought the eighty acres of land in 1833, and the wedding certificate of his son Joseph and Lucy Barter. But I couldn't find Polly's obituary. All I could find was Henry's, and it didn't say anything I hadn't read in Harding's book.

I sighed in defeat. She took whatever she knew with her into the ground.

We went to the reunion that afternoon, and I met dozens of people who welcomed me with a hospitality I didn't think existed in America anymore. An elderly woman with a striking resemblance to Benjamin Franklin cornered me for a good hour, telling me the family matriarch was once a madam in Indianapolis and that many Mozingo men tried to avoid the draft in World War II. "That's how they all made their money," she said. "When the other men left." When I finally slipped outside, Bud was bugging his wife by walking around with his blue underwear pulled up out of his shorts, halfway up his belly. I met his favorite granddaughter, Danielle, a social worker helping minority children. A newspaper columnist from the *Greensburg Daily News* gave me her card and said she'd like to write a column about my visit. I said sure, but groaned inside, realizing there was no way my work here was going to go down quietly.

Stan had brought a little ice chest full of Bud Light on my behalf. He had asked me earlier if I liked beer, and I said yes, but no one else was drinking, and they just finished saying grace. I told him I'd stay with my Diet Coke, and then felt bad about it. It looked like he bought it just for me. Tanya introduced herself to me as I was talking to him. He smiled warmly and didn't say anything offensive. She told me she came here just for Amy. She'd been mad at Bud ever since he called one of her sons lazy and thought the implication was racist. (Amy suspected Bud was right.)

Inside, Amy had put up big photos of Tanya and her three black children on a mantel to preside over a reunion otherwise white as yogurt. No one said a word. Why was it so hard for us to accept that white people could descend from a black man, after many generations of mixing, when we accepted the opposite without a thought? Here was one white line of people turning black, by their definition, in a single generation with Tanya, and even blacker in two.

I read a framed printout next to the photos, titled "The Surname History of the Family": "The Italian surname MOZINGO was from the English given name, James, which spread widely throughout Europe in many forms including JAQUEME, GIAMELLI, IACOMELLI."

Stan handed me a copy of his promised document, titled "Historiography of Mozingo." "The surname Mozingo . . . is believed to be associated with the Spaniard's, meaning, 'one who was young in appearance.'" In the free-for-all of the Internet, these absurdities carried as much credibility as any document at the Library of Virginia.

I watched everyone talking and laughing and griping, the children playing outside, throwing water balloons at Bud, who feigned outrage and muttered "you little sons of bitches" but smiled a pure happiness when they weren't looking. I thought of the scene as Spencer's epitaph, for better or worse.

Early one afternoon, a few of us walked down a wet-leaf path through the forest behind Rodney Baptist Church to the creek where people had been baptized for 150 years. Amy sang a hymn: "Shall we gather at the river, where bright angel feet have trod?"

The creek ran through a deep hollow, flowing over shelves of bedrock, falling off steps into ponds where waterbugs scrambled between the bubbles on the surface. The current had carved and polished the stone. Pebbles spun in the eddies.

After my relatives left, I floated under a three-foot cascade in the cool, tannic water, watching the world. The creek came warm and shallow off the shelf, heated by the sun over the rock. I lay on my back, inhaling to stay afloat, exhaling quickly and drawing the air back in before my face went under. The water below gurgled like the plumbing in an old hotel. The maple leaves above glimmered with the ripples of sunlight reflected off the pond. These creeks were immortal.

I closed my eyes and saw the orange light glowing through the blood in my eyelids, content that it was my turn, and my children were just beginning.

Chapter 12

Back to the Northern Neck

> As he accepted the alabaster Christ and the bloody cross—
> in the bearing of which he would find his redemption, as,
> indeed, to our outraged astonishment, he sometimes did—
> he must, henceforth, accept that image we then gave him of
> himself: having no other and standing, moreover, in danger of
> death should he fail to accept the dazzling light thus brought
> into such darkness.
>
> James Baldwin, *Notes of a Native Son*

A s I contemplated my travels, it still perplexed me that the
Mozingos born and raised in the same corner of the Northern
Neck where Edward and Margaret settled could so thoroughly
have lost or buried any trace or connection to him. I decided to go back
to Virginia to see if I couldn't find some glimmer of recognition, some
faint vestige of awareness, or at least understand when it was lost. On a
deeper level, I had a different goal. I knew so much more about our entire
story than when I first visited the Northern Neck. I hoped now that I
would feel that sense of connection that eluded me on Pantico Run.

When I arrived in the Northern Neck, the June air was humid and
electric, almost delirious. Cobalt dragonflies bobbed over the tall grass,
and cicadas sputtered off in the forest like wind-up toys. A thundercloud
was waking up in the distance, and a restless breeze set the entire landscape in motion.

I pulled up to Rhodie Mozingo's small ranch-style home on Fallin Town Road, set under two great maples, about ten miles from Pantico Run. I had briefly met Rhodie on my earlier trip, after visiting Junior, his very different older brother. For twenty years Rhodie sold insurance door-to-door and now did commercial sales at a Lowe's in Fredericksburg, where he lived most of the time. He was raising a grandson, struggling with chronic lung disease, and dreaming of retiring to Myrtle Beach. He struck me as being open-minded and thoughtful. He thanked the army for showing him the wider world, remarking that if he hadn't enlisted he'd still be "chewing tobacco and being the biggest redneck in the world." I had told him about Edward earlier, but had hedged on whether the ancestry was certain. I wanted to hear more of what he knew before he shut down on me. He kept his father's house in the Neck and visited now and then, and he had agreed to meet me here to show me around Mozingo country.

Edward was Rhodie's seventh great-grandfather. By the late 1700s, tax lists identified Rhodie's fourth great-grandfather John, Edward's great-grandson, as white, as they did his three brothers. But the brothers also appear on a registry of "Free Mulattoes" in Westmoreland County in 1801. John had moved back to neighboring Richmond the previous year and avoided the list. He also had more money and even owned a slave, so he might have had more clout to claim his whiteness.

There was no science to who was white, just as there is none today. When Sally Hemings was freed from slavery upon Thomas Jefferson's death, she moved to Charlottesville to live with her freed sons. All were born as slaves, and all were listed as white in the 1830 census. By any biological measure, they would be. Sally Hemings's father was white, and her mother was half-white. Her sons therefore had a mother who was three-quarters white and a father who was most likely Thomas Jefferson. Still, when they were slaves, they were colored. They had to be. There were no white slaves in America.

The area where Rhodie's ancestors lived around Farmers Fork had free black, white, and biracial families. In 1850, among the nine heads of households around them were a white tailor named Thomas Mason, who had no land; a free black farmer named Thaddeus Kelly, who had a little bit, worth $100; a mulatto farmer named London Maiden with half that; and a wealthy white planter named Thomas Omahundro. Rhodie's great-great-grandfather John owned a patch of soil worth $205. In 1860, he acquired more, worth $600, doing much better than my ancestor Joseph in Indiana at the time, and kept it through the Civil War.

By then, family reputations had long calcified, as had the lines between races. The late nineteenth century saw the birth of the eugenics movement, which, during its ugly half-century trajectory to the Holocaust in Europe and forced sterilizations in America, spawned the "one-drop rule." One drop of black blood and you were polluted; you could no longer be a member of society. In 1912, a virulent eugenicist named Walter Ashby Plecker took over at Virginia's Bureau of Vital Statistics and ran it for the next thirty-four years. He fumed and foamed over "mongrelization" and fought doggedly to prove Melungeons and other people claiming Native American ancestry were mostly black. With his advocacy, Virginia passed the Racial Integrity Act, which put into law the one-drop rule. The legislature made one exception under political pressure: it allowed a person to have one-sixteenth Indian blood and still be considered white, so as not to alienate the storied descendants of John Rolfe and Pocahontas.

Now everyone in Virginia fell into two categories, white or colored. Plecker pulled children from white schools if his office deemed they were mixed, rejected marriage licenses because one of the parties could not prove he or she was white, even disinterred suspected black corpses from white cemeteries. Nearly three hundred years after the colonists had routed and marginalized the Indians in Virginia, he all but officially erased them as a people.

Rhodie's family never came under scrutiny, as best as anyone knows, and it's hard to imagine that the Vital Statistics Office, even if it tried, could have ferreted out his connection to those ancestors on the "Free Mulattoes" list. But Plecker had people trained to do exactly that, and the records were there. The truth is, no one has really assessed how much Plecker and the Racial Integrity Act affected most Virginians. If nothing else, they ingrained the notion that God set down firm divisions among the races based on biology—and a wave of paranoia that man was erasing them.

Rhodie and Junior's father was born out of wedlock in 1922, two years before the act was passed, and got his surname from his mother, Josephine. Their dad managed only about three years in school before he had to help his mother in the gristmills, and never said a word about their roots. Rhodie didn't have a clue that he'd spent his childhood within a mile of where his ancestors settled in the late 1600s; he even fished on Pantico Run with a cork bobber and cedar pole. But he started wondering about the family when his father died in 1991. Rhodie had a photo of Josephine that always intrigued him. She looked Native American, with high cheekbones, dark hair, and dark eyes.

His sister Betty had those same features, and she joined us at his house that morning. Rhodie asked what I'd learned since we last spoke.

I showed him a printout of his lineage straight to Edward Mozingo and the Virginia court ruling from 1672. He looked briefly at the papers, smiled, and sighed. "I've been told my mom was Indian," he said. "I thought the *name* was Italian. I met some people from Italy who came over here when I was in the insurance business. They owned a restaurant and they treated me like gold. If I'd go in and order something, I'd notice I'd get more than everyone else on the plate. They'd come to the table more often. I finally found out why. They said the name was from Naples." He looked at my papers again. "We're probably a mixture of every race there is."

Betty smiled and didn't say too much, but showed keen interest.

"I'm starting to wonder what Uncle Milton knows," Rhodie said. "The other day he said, 'Some people keep searching. Well, you might find something you don't want to know.'"

He offered to take Luis and me on a little tour of Mozingo-dom in the Northern Neck. Betty came along for the ride as we first headed to the Buck Mozingos, who lived around Haynesville. Rhodie did not know their relation to him. A vague story fluttered about that they had landed in a boat at Farnham Creek back when people still just landed places and, just as Junior had mentioned, they all had one blue eye, one green eye, and a streak of white hair. We followed two-lane roads through rolling fields of corn and soybeans and stands of forest tangled with creeper.

"Back in the fifties or sixties this would have bugged the hell out of me," Rhodie said. "Today, things have changed so much. There's not just one race anymore. I have a son that this would probably bother because he's what we'd call a redneck. Pure country, living in the 1940s. There's a percentage of this county that can't accept a mixed president. If he does a good job for me, I don't care if he's purple."

He said blacks and whites were mostly separated when he grew up. There was Coles Point Tavern for whites and Burton's Corner for blacks. The drive-in theater was divided down the middle. But everyone was poor, and they all worked together in the mills or fields and shared some common experiences. A cluster of black families lived in the pines not far from Rhodie's house, and he and his friends would walk there to play baseball with them on their diamond. "The blacks felt like they were better than the whites, and the whites felt better than the blacks," he said.

We pulled up to a double-wide on Drinking Swamp Road. Earl Buck Mozingo, age seventy, looked up from under the hood of his Ford pickup as we got out of the car and walked up. His dog, chained to another truck, lunged and barked with raw fury. I couldn't see the streak of white in Earl's hair because he wore a cap with a Confederate flag above the brim. Within seconds, using just the sound "nuh," he conveyed that he didn't know anything about the Mozingo name, never cared. By now I knew better than to try to induce a tree stump to speak, so we stepped inside the vinyl-sided home to chat with his sister, Madeline, sixty-eight, who wore shorts and flip-flops, showed none of the rumored traits, and was as cheerful as her brother was curt. She said her sister in Florida had been researching the family tree. "I said, 'Quit digging!' I'm going to find out I'm my own grandma."

Her boyfriend chuckled slyly from his recliner. Rhodie got right to telling them, in a quaintly tortured way, about Edward. "He was a dark-complected man. We don't know if he was Portuguese, Italian, Indian, or Negro."

"That's why I told my sister to quit digging!" Madeline said.

"If he was Negro, he probably worked for a Mozingo," her boyfriend said.

Rhodie looked at me expectantly for a moment, as if this might settle the issue and get them off the hook.

"No, he worked for a Walker," I said.

"Oh," the boyfriend said. I asked about his British accent. He said he fought in the Falklands War and got a raw deal in his pension that so incensed him he ditched England and moved to America.

Madeline brought out printed emails from her sister that told three stories about our origins. One said our name used to be spelled d'Monzangeau, "which means Mount Zangeau." Another said there were several "historical Italian figures with this name," but didn't identify them. The last read like a children's fable: "In the land of Italy there was a family by the name of Mozingo. They left Italy and went to England. The son, Moses, made friends with some other boys and decided to run away from school. They stowed away on a ship by the name of the *Queen Mary*, a sailing vessel. After the ship was out to sea, the boys were discovered and carried before the Captain of the ship. He threatened to throw them overboard, but they begged him not to, promising in exchange for sparing their lives they would work to pay for their passage. He agreed to this, and they worked for seven years before he released them. When they were finally put on land it was America and Moses was grown by then. He settled in Richmond County, Virginia and became a farmer." This was the most detailed myth I'd heard yet, and so folkloric—stowing away, held hostage on a ship, seven years of servitude.

We shifted our talk back to the Jamestown court record. Madeline grimaced and shook her head while keeping her humor. She turned to Rhodie and said exactly what his Uncle Milton had told him: "Dig too much and you'll find something you don't want."

"I don't care," Rhodie said. "My grandkids keep asking me, 'What are we? Where do we originate?' I want to tell them."

Madeline cast her eyebrows skyward and gave a vigorous, discounting wave of the hand.

"Well, at least you'd have a healthy genetic mix," I quipped. "You could have been inbred."

Her boyfriend turned to me with wide, serious eyes. "There's definitely some of that around here," he said. "*Moonfaced.*"

We were pulling out of the driveway when Madeline yelled something. Rhodie rolled down the window to hear. She poked her boyfriend in the belly and screamed, "He just called me a nigger!"

I had a sense we left something heavier behind than a crude joke. In redneck territory, we were like a Publishers Clearing House crew with news no one wanted to hear. I imagined hurtling around in a primer-black van, racing up to Mozingos at their mailboxes, and handing them a folder of documentation labeled "By the way, you're black!"

I would later learn that Edward was the sixth great-grandfather of Earl and Madeline. Their most recent common ancestor with Rhodie was the "white" John Mozingo whose brothers were "Mulattoes."

We stopped by Uncle Milton's aluminum-sided house on Route 360. Rhodie said he had a certain resentment of his uncle, feeling that he always acted like he was better than the rest of them. He couldn't really explain how. Milton was eighty-eight now, and we interrupted a midmorning nap in his lounge chair. The heater was on, even though the temperature outside was over eighty. Milton had a sunken mouth and pale blue eyes. He was dressed nattily for his nap, in pleated khakis and a plaid shirt, neatly tucked. He gamely told us about growing up in the area so long ago. "Granddad ran a gristmill for years. I never started working until I was sixteen years old, and then worked in a sawmill for thirty-eight years. It'll make a man out of you or kill you."

Rhodie started in on our roots—I suspect, to bug his uncle more than to get any information from him. He had the Edward pitch down pat by now. "There was a man named Edward back in 1672. He lived right up by Farmers Fork. This one was supposed to be of dark complexion. It doesn't say if he was Portuguese, Negro, Italian."

Milton's pupils sharpened, just as Junior's had when I raised the subject. It was obvious which one of those three possibilities pricked his emotion.

"Sixteen hundreds," he said abruptly. "That's before I was born." He looked down at his lap and moved his lips as if he were trying to dislodge something from his front teeth. He looked back up. "Negro," he said, and furrowed his brow and curled the corners of his lips in vague amusement, as if we were children. I saw the condescension Rhodie was getting at. "No, I always heard it was Italian."

I asked him if he was curious about the origin of the name.

"No indeed," he said. "No indeed. . . . What I'm curious about is where I'm going. I'll be eighty-nine next month."

We decided to stop bothering the old man and headed to Pantico Run.

"You see that look in Milton's eyes when I said Edward was from a dark-skinned race?" Rhodie asked Betty.

"He remembers what he wants to," she said.

"I really wanted to say that to him."

The forest around Pantico Run was too tangled with vines and nettles to get to the creek, so we drove over to Mozingo Road and walked through the old pasture that sloped down to the creek from the south side. The empty field was part of the tract that Colonel Walker once owned and Edward surely treaded.

We passed the pile of bricks I had mistaken for some ancient Mozingo homestead. Thunder was approaching. The June sun suffused the leaden sky in a way that turned the foliage an iridescent green, like polished jade. The old cemetery was overgrown with vines now, invisible. Wildflowers streaked the pasture in purple, yellow, and white. The cicadas in the trees sounded like a miniature sawmill. Bloated neon dragonflies helicoptered over the field. The rain started, falling sparsely in swollen silver drops that landed strikingly cold.

"Better get back to the car," Rhodie said.

I held back as they paced down the dirt road. A sound was running through my mind, the repeated metallic clink of a hoe working rocky soil. Thunder grumbled lowly, a dog having a bad dream. Down at the far low end of the field, near the edge of the forest, I saw a dark figure lean on his hoe and look at the sky, a phantom. He called to someone in the trees that he'd be inside soon.

I could see him, just this conjured glimpse.

I jogged to the car as the rain came in.

On the drive back to his house, Rhodie was still trying to get his mind around Edward Mozingo. "It doesn't bother me none," he said. "Why would I care? It doesn't change who I am if he was of the dark race."

It was clear, though, as we talked further, that his ancestor's race was not a fact for him to embrace so much as a painful truth to accept. He grew up having, in his mind, only black people between himself and the bottom.

He knew society had changed, and he was doing his earnest best to keep up. This struck me when we pulled up at his house and I met his son, who lived in a trailer on the property with his young family and clearly did not have his father's desire to keep up with mainstream thinking. He was about my age and wore a camouflage cap that said "I probably don't like you either." His arms were heavily tattooed with snakes and spiders and skulls and at least one "Fuck Off."

He was picking raspberries and, learning that I was curious about the moonshine in these parts, went into the trailer to get me a taste.

I wasn't about to touch the race issue with him. Rhodie was right.

I didn't even feel like touching the subject with Rhodie anymore either. He had a vague sadness about him, a heaviness that spoke of many disappointments. This wasn't the story of his roots that he wanted to tell his grandchildren. On the phone with me sometime later, he mentioned the *Queen Mary* story. "Your research says black. Hers says Italian. I don't think we'll ever know."

"Yeah, probably not," I said.

The Riverview Mobile Estates sat just off U.S. Route 17 west of Tappahannock. A couple dozen single-wide trailers rested on the dirt. There were no bushes or fences. Black families were milling about in the warm afternoon, eyeing me warily as I approached. I opened my rental car's window. "Do you know where an Elvis Mozingo lives?" I asked.

Their hard looks gave way and they pointed to the gray, wood-paneled trailer at the end of the road, under big gum trees along a creek.

Elvis, Junior's son, didn't have a working phone or email, so I was arriving unannounced. I had heard Elvis's grandchildren were all mixed race and was interested to hear how he felt about that.

A little boy was playing in a puddle in the dirt next to the house, filling up his diaper. "Get out of there," barked his dad, one of Elvis's sons, or stepsons, working on his truck. The boy was black by America's current standards. His dad was white.

I knocked on the door. "Yes?" a woman's voice came through the screen.

"I'm looking for Elvis Mozingo."

"Oh yes," she said, and called out, "Elvis!"

Mild groaning and shuffling emanated from the back. He pulled a shirt on and opened the screen door. He looked nothing like his father, or what I expected. He had a slight build and a kindly pale face.

"I met your father awhile ago, when I was doing research on the family," I said.

"Oh yeah, come on in."

He cleared some baby toys off the couch for me to sit. His wife, Pat, much larger than he, sat in a plastic chair. I gave my pitch about looking into our origins.

"I always thought it was Indian," Elvis said. "When I was a young boy we were told we were Cherokee Indians."

There was a quiet politeness in the way he spoke. When I had first heard about Elvis, and all the deer he shot, I pictured a caricature of an angry redneck. Now I winced at that easy stereotyping.

I told him about Edward, trying to make a connection to his having mixed-race grandchildren. That's what I wanted to hear about.

"I have five children, and all of them have black children," said Pat. This was delivered as objective fact.

"So what do you think of your kids having black children?" I asked both of them.

Pat chimed in first. "It didn't bother me because when I was growing up my grandfather raised me. He had black people working for him and with him. So I was around them and realized they weren't bad." She said her best friend, Sarah Dixon, was black.

"What about you, Elvis? How old are you?"

"Forty-nine."

"When you grew up, this would have been kind of a scandal, right?"

"I didn't agree with it at first," he said. "But what can I do? I can't change it."

"Does it bother you at all?"

"No. Not no more it doesn't."

"Did you struggle with it for a while?"

"No."

Their seventeen-year-old daughter, Cindy, came in wearing a tight tank top and shorts that were both wrestling ample snow-white flesh with lots of piercings. She had a nine-month-old girl named Neh-Keila, whom Pat was holding and who must have weighed thirty pounds. Elvis's other mocha-toned grandchildren were in the trailer and yard: Quentin, Tra'Shon, Kearra, and Tylor.

I'd seen mixed-race couples all over Tappahannock, and I was curious about how such a rigidly divided society had so quickly turned into a mixed-race free-for-all. Elvis's brother had told me it started in the trailer parks, where everyone lived close by and shared much in common. But I had no idea how to ask about it.

They were staring at me, wondering what I was doing there. I stalled just like I had with his father, telling Elvis his trailer was surprisingly roomy.

"Why don't you ask her?" Pat said. "She only likes black guys."

"So that's who you mostly date?" I asked Cindy, struggling for words. Inside I was dying.

She shrugged and looked like she was laughing at me inside.

"So"—I knew as I was uttering it that this was undoubtedly the lamest question I had ever asked as a journalist—"what is it that you like about black guys?"

She shrugged again, lingered for about twenty seconds without saying a word, and then bolted out the screen door.

I thought for a fleeting moment how this interview might have gone in 1705 with Edward's wife. "So, Margaret, what is it that attracted you to this Negro man?"

Elvis Jr., who was twenty-four and looked like someone in a 1990s boy band, had stepped in and was sitting there smirking. "He only likes black girls too," Pat said.

I glanced at him, hoping he might pipe up. He looked at me like I was a freak and was gone within the minute.

I was on such nakedly false ground, trying to dissect basic human attraction as if it were some strange phenomenon and not just the natural order when the color line fell away. Race simply lost its status. It was a deflated concept, and I was trying to analyze the absence it once filled.

More than three centuries after whites and blacks were forced to stop mixing in this part of Virginia, they were blithely doing it again. It struck me that America, finally easing away from its cursed preoccupation with race, was looking forward to some grand moment to proclaim the battle was over, when really it might finally just sputter out like this, quietly, family-by-family, with a shrug.

Not no more it doesn't.

During the course of my research, when I told people the story of my name I often got, in one form or another, the same question: Did I feel the blackness inside? I always laughed them off. *How is that supposed to feel?* I thought.

Not that I felt people do not viscerally feel their race or ethnicity, based on the experience they lived. My wife keenly connects with the Japanese inside her. She was raised to appreciate it and found pride and solace and solidarity in it when it became the subject of abuse. When she was a child and her Japanese features were stronger, she had to cope with endless questions about why her father didn't look like her. She had to endure taunts and shoves and derogatory "Chinese-Japanese" rhymes. She never really felt white because society didn't see her that way, even though her father was white, with blue eyes and sandy hair. She felt American, but never any one race. When she went to Japan, she felt like "the other" there, even at Japanese school on Saturdays, where a group of the "pure" boys were her worst tormentors. All this was imprinted on her psyche. It was not in her blood.

My friend-since-childhood Erik, whose mother was Mexican American but whose own features didn't announce that he was "different," never felt any of that. I'd never heard him once call himself Latino. When he met his future wife, who was Chinese American and took a number of race studies courses in college at Santa Cruz, she was annoyed that he was in denial, as if white Republican Orange County had brainwashed him and made him ashamed of who he *really* was.

Latino or Hispanic is even more difficult to pin down in terms of "blood" than Japanese or black. The terms include anyone with roots from the Straits of Magellan to Tijuana, including pure Kanjobal Indians in Guatemala who speak no Spanish and blue-eyed *chilangos* who vaunt their pure Spanish blood. Anyone north of the border with ancestors south of the border is Latino. This is not a race or ethnicity or culture, all evanescent terms themselves. But it is something.

I truly grasped now, from all this digging into my family's story, that the biological aspect of race is minimal to the point of meaninglessness, that race means what our society has taught it to mean, that we see it through the distorting lens of expectations or expediency or self-preservation. But the meaning imparted to it becomes its own reality, a tangled, layered, long and violently conflicting reality, particularly in a people whose past has been stolen.

He must, henceforth, accept that image we then gave him of himself: having no other.

In 1963, James Baldwin wrote a compelling letter to his fourteen-year-old nephew on the hundredth anniversary of emancipation, hammering home how this fraud of white supremacy twisted the psyches of black *and* white America:

> You were born into a society which spelled out with brutal clarity, and in as many ways as possible, that you were a worthless human being. You were not expected to aspire to excellence: you were expected to make peace with mediocrity. Wherever you have turned, James, in your short time on this earth, you have been told where you could go and what you could do (and *how* you could do it) and where you could live and whom you could marry. . . .

Take no one's word for anything, including mine—but trust your experience. Know whence you came. If you know whence you came, there is really no limit to where you can go. The details and symbols of your life have been deliberately constructed to make you believe what white people say about you. Please try to remember that what they believe, as well as what they do and cause you to endure, does not testify to your inferiority but to their inhumanity and fear. Please try to be clear, dear James, through the storm which rages about your youthful head today, about the reality which lies behind the words *acceptance* and *integration*. There is no reason for you to try to become like white people and there is no basis whatever for their impertinent assumption that *they* must accept *you*. The really terrible thing, old buddy, is that *you* must accept *them*. And I mean that very seriously. You must accept them and accept them with love. For these innocent people have no other hope. They are, in effect, still trapped in a history which they do not understand; and until they understand it, they cannot be released from it. They have had to believe for many years, and for innumerable reasons, that black men are inferior to white men. Many of them, indeed, know better, but, as you will discover, people find it very difficult to act on what they know. To act is to be committed, and to be committed is to be in danger. In this case, the danger, in the minds of most white Americans, is the loss of their identity. Try to imagine how you would feel if you woke up one morning to find the sun shining and all the stars aflame. You would be frightened because it is out of the order of nature. Any upheaval in the universe is terrifying because it so profoundly attacks one's sense of one's own reality. Well, the black man has functioned in the white man's world as a fixed star, as an immovable pillar: and as he moves out of his place, heaven and earth are shaken to their foundations.

This was why Edward's origins were so hard for some Mozingos to accept. They woke up to find the sun shining and all the stars aflame, a people who were mostly white emerging from a black man, carrying his name from Africa and across the continent.

The Mozingo story was buried because of race, and I was unearthing it because of race. The hook of it, the surprise of it, the paradox of it, revolved around race.

But in the clear-eyed view of a new millennium, the story no longer felt strange or startling to me. I understood the history now, the fleeting years of intermixing, the fluidity that ran throughout America's past and continues in its present. I'd seen black families turn white and white ones turn black, and knew many landed somewhere between those two labels that didn't mean much anyway.

I did feel a connection to Edward now. His race now did not separate us as it first did. But my view of him, and our origins, was limited to the moment when the notion of white superiority rained down on him. I was trying to understand my family and myself from our past, but I didn't understand Edward's past. His separation from his people and his past, from Africa, had to be at the heart of his story and ours.

Virginia was the soil to which he was transplanted and forced to adapt in the most hostile of settings. It was not the homeland. The line just passed through there.

I needed to go to Africa.

Chapter 13

I Too Was Told Mozingo Was Italian

I started researching the slave trade while I worked on my story for the newspaper and attended to the new Mozingo who came into the world in July. Lucia Louise. (Latin names sound good with Bantu.) Her brother Blake was three and I was thirty-seven. It was a strange time in my life to be hunting gravestones and digging for the dead. This was supposed to happen in the fading of life, this recognition that ancestry, posterity, and one's life were not just connected, but different vantages of the same immortal system.

Children made you see your part in this system, this chain, as much as death. Already I longed for the days when Blake was two in a way I could never care about my own years passing. Yet there was nothing like a child to ease the grief when a parent or beloved relative died. They provided an existential comfort, seeing new life grow.

With Noaki home on maternity leave with Lucia, and Blake home from preschool at lunch, I holed up in my garage office, with the chattering, chirping swirl of family around me. The writing emerged as gracefully as a fit of dry heaving, then I threw it out there for the world to see, with my email address attached to the bottom. Knowing that readers who email newspaper reporters often start with greetings like "Hey

Moron," I was tensely coiled, realizing how much more vulnerable I felt writing about myself. I didn't think I could take dozens of emails with the likes of "Who gives a shit about your family?" in the subject line. Hovering above that paranoia was the dread of a cascade of repercussions: Kathy and Amy feeling betrayed. ("After all we did for you, you write that my house smells like cat piss?") Some historian sending me a link to the oil portrait of the great Sienese glassblower Spencer Mozingo hanging in the Uffizi. Getting death threats from redneck Mozingos who got flushed out of their KKK meetings in the pines.

The editors decided the story would run as a three-part series. The first ran above the fold on the front page on a Sunday in May, headlined "In Search of the Meaning of Mozingo." Part 2 ran on Tuesday, part 3 on Thursday.

Emails flooded in, long ones. I'd never received so many, over a thousand in the end, many of the writers telling me of their own journeys into their past. They riffed on race, on identity, on history, on the quirks of their own family trees. But what caught me most off guard was the reaction of Mozingos from around the country. By writing the story in the newspaper, and putting it out on the web with the imprimatur of the newspaper, I was essentially driving that Publishers Clearing House van up to every Mozingo house in America. To my surprise, by and large, they took the envelope and said, "This is wonderful."

"I have to say, what you wrote about has been something that I've been trying to figure out myself," wrote Mark Mozingo, an actor in New York originally from Kentucky. "I too was told that Mozingo was of Italian origin, possibly Sicilian. But a friend of mine's mother who is first generation Italian said she had never known of the name Mozingo in Italy. I joined a Facebook group trying to figure out more information. There I was told we are Spanish Basque . . . which seemed to me way more fun than Sicilian. Around the same time, I came across the same information you did about the coach from Zaire with the last name of Mozingo and it really puzzled me. I had a co-worker from Ghana tell me that he knew someone from Kinshasa with the last name Mozingo. I'm really pleased with your article about our last name, and think it makes complete sense that somewhere down the line the 'white' Mozingos from the South chose to cover our true roots."

"I was in complete awe, so excited, with chill bumps as I read it," wrote Amanda Mozingo, born and raised in Mississippi. "I kept my maiden name Mozingo, mainly because I have always been proud of it. I too originally was told the story of us being Italian, but then later we learned the name had been shortened from 'Montzingeaux' . . . so must have been French. I even had a professor in college tell me he thought it sounded African. And of course, there was always some 'rumor' that we may have black ancestors. . . . This makes me even more proud! Thank you so much for putting in so much work to help all of us better understand our history. There is no better feeling."

"Loved the article—it confirms much of what I've come to believe about our origins," wrote Charles Mozingo in West Virginia.

It turns out Mozingos around the country have been quietly, individually exploring this topic and eschewing the myths for the truth. Many were from the South; one even played a Confederate soldier in reenactments of what he called the War of Northern Aggression. Another man admitted that it bothered him the name was African, but said he'd rather know the real history than not.

As for deniers, I got two emails with this exact sentence: "We are from South Carolina and have traced way back and have not found any evidence of blacks in our family." That was it, no sign-off even.

One Mozingo, perhaps rightfully, complained that I didn't include any educated professionals in the story. So here it is: there are many doctors, lawyers, professors, engineers, politicians, dentists, geologists, nuclear power plant operators, and journalists among Edward's descendants. There are Mozingos who have written and cowritten papers such as "A Multicenter Review of Toxic Epidermal Necrolysis Treated in U.S. Burn Centers at the End of the Twentieth Century" and books such as *Shrubs of the Great Basin: A Natural History*. There is an iconic music shop outside St. Louis called Mozingo Music. Perhaps the most noted Mozingo was a trial attorney in South Carolina famous for his courtroom oratory, James "Spot" Mozingo, who headed the national plaintiffs' attorneys association in the 1950s and became a state senator.

There were some humorous responses too. One subscriber to the paper named Mozingo told me he sat down for his normal Sunday read and thought, "My life just took a strange turn." He had never had an inkling of the family history. A woman wrote saying her husband's family had features like the "Buck Mozingos" and she wondered if they also suffered hearing loss. And a bank manager from Kenya reached out to me to help unfreeze millions of dollars in the account of Dr. Kevin Mozingo, who allegedly died in the Seychelles: "My colleagues and I have decided to look for a reputable person to act as the next of kin."

I came across a debate about my series on a white supremacist web forum called Stormfront. A member screen-named "Tuffield" posed the first question: "There are now thousands of Mozingos in the US, mostly in the South, and judging by a quick look on Facebook, almost all appear to be a phenotype that most would eyeball as 'white.' Should such people be accepted as White Nationals, should they be so inclined?" In the photo posted, Tuffield's phenotype was blond, tiny-faced, with fine features.

"DeutscheTreue" piped in with some wisdom: "No, they are all mongrels when they tell the truth. When we would accept them, we can accept for example Heidi Klum's black son, in a few generations his offspring is 'white' enough. One drop of non-white blood is not acceptable." Apparently they had stricter standards than the Klan.

"Loland" had some insight: "How would you go about inheriting a surname from a slave. It's not really the type of thing you want to boast about, 'My daughter ****ed my pet monkey! . . . This guy is full of ****,' Mozingo is of obvious Italian origin and he just wants to drag everyone to hell with him."

"Tuffield" came to my defense. "I dunno. Searching Google, I can't find any Italian Mozingos, but many African ones." I wondered if this "Tuffield" was a provocateur; there was no way she found many African Mozingos on Google.

"Sparrow" said the debate over whether someone like me could be accepted into their group came down to two theories: creationism and evolution. "The Creationists believe that some divine power created the 'white man' perfect and complete, and that any mixing is a degeneration of the proper product. . . . The Evolutionists believe that the 'white man' is an evolutionary adaptation, in other words, there is no original white man, but a spectrum of ancestors who separated from the great mass of proto-humanity and that spectrum carved out a unique racial niche. . . . Under the Evolutionists view, the person with a small strain of black blood might be considered sufficiently within the 'family.' . . . I tend to agree with the evolutionists." Lest you think Sparrow was sounding reasonable, she finished: "having 'one-drop' of black blood won't save the Mozingos or any other family from the terror that will occur if whites lose their majority and power shift completely to the Jewish Supremacists and other anti-white groups."

"Castanea" questioned, "So our cause is almost white, kinda white, mostly white?"

"Master Baphomet" piped in with some research for the members who doubted the premise of my story. He found Samie Melton's website and posted Edward Mozingo's court records. He then pointed out that unwed mothers often passed their name to their children, by means of explaining how I didn't have an African Y chromosome.

There was a long, technical discussion of how much black blood I would actually have, after which "Raised by Wolves" raised the level of debate even higher. "DNA supports him being white and the percentage does. The guy is a retard. Theres no way if I was him and under these circumstances would I have said a damn thing. He sounds to me like he wants to be black."

Referring to DeutscheTreue's one-drop comment and others, "Odhin" wrote, "Comments like this are what makes the whole Stormfront look bad, honestly. Accepting a guy with a drop of black blood from 1600 is the same as accepting a 50 percent black person? Give me a ****ing break. If you expect the white race to survive with that mindset you better shoot yourself in the head right now."

That pissed off DeutscheTreue. "Grow up, of course it is the same. In a few generations the half black offspring is white enough. White power.

What you are talking about is not White Nationalism, it is 'White Skin Nationalism.' I don't need to shoot myself, we Germans are really rarely mixed with nonwhites. ;) I would bet, most of those who defend non-whites here, know they have nonwhite blood in them. I saw here even a 'White Person' with a native as a mother."

Master Baphomet jumped in, after more digging, having discovered my hidden agenda. "According to an interview he did . . . wait for it . . . the reporter's wife is . . . bi-racial."

This was the domain of what were once mainstream ideas, now a bunch of weirdos too scared to use their real names, practically masturbating to their own "whiteness," and plotting the takeover of America like children planning a trip to Mars. And even they, the white nationalists, can't seem to agree on what a white person is.

Now the extended family started chiming in about the stories. I heard from Amy's daughter Beth that Amy had not read the story but was told what it said, and was furious, and that Kathy would never talk to me again. Beth loved the story and seemed more than delighted that it had agitated an extended family that had alienated her. Amy, she told me, thought I had insulted her when I said she lived down a dirt road, when in fact it was a gravel road. The supremely kindhearted Kathy didn't understand why I had to say Bud had a "big, lumpy head," but she said she forgave me.

The following Saturday my family and I were eating burritos at a little taco shop near our house when I got a Facebook message on my phone. "Hello, Joe, my name is Danielle. I met you last year at the Mozingo family reunion here in Indiana." I knew who she was: Bud's favorite granddaughter, the social worker. *Here it comes*, I thought. I put the phone in my pocket, not wanting her inevitable rant to sour my lunch.

Back at home, I put the kids down for a nap and logged on to Facebook to read further. "I'm writing you because my grandfather, Bud Mozingo, is the most racist man I know. I was previously his favorite, but that is not the case anymore. I told my family that I have a black boyfriend. (He's an officer in the navy and stationed in San Diego. . . . I've been dating Jason for a year now and my grandfather has quit talking to me. They've said some pretty hurtful things to me, unable to accept my decisions. I'm anxious to see if your article has any effect on him or if he will continue to carry out his intolerant ways. The most I can say right now is thank you. If for nothing else, this has brought a smile to my face. Life is funny how it comes around."

The Facebook picture of Jason looked like Bud's nightmare: dark black skin, close to three hundred pounds of what appeared to be solid muscle, diamondlike stud in his left ear.

I messaged her back and congratulated her on the courage of her convictions. I could only imagine how hard it would have been just to write the story if my grandmother were alive, and here Danielle was defying her entire family—a tightly woven one at that—in a most visceral way.

I asked her how people out there were coping with the articles.

"People at my work requested that you return to interview some 'normal' people from Greensburg. I think it's more of a generational thing. Younger people are more accepting of differences than our parents or grandparents. . . . I don't think that Grandpa read your article. He said he didn't anyway. Grandpa and my grandmother are in complete denial and avoid all proof that may go up against their belief system. They threatened to beat Jason up. The visual of that makes me smile. Jason is cut! Grandpa, Stan and Earl are unapologetic about their racist beliefs. My grandmother told me I was living in sin because God wants us to stay with our own kind. I told her Jason wasn't an elephant."

I called Amy, who still hadn't read the story—and I suspect never would. She quickly forgave me for the dirt road mistake. The impact of my grenade was quickly forgotten under the mushroom cloud of Danielle's atom bomb. Danielle's father said he would shoot Jason if he ever came on his property. Bud cursed and spat on the phone with Amy for a straight hour. Amy tried to talk sense into him, but he just kept repeating the epithet he said to me when I first met him.

Danielle and I exchanged notes over the next few months as I was preparing for my trip to Africa, holed up in the libraries and my garage office researching the slave trade. Jason ran nuclear power plants on navy submarines. They met on a cruise that her mother took her on a year ago. They were serious and talking about getting married. She was angry that her parents were not accepting this. "I was a really good kid, never a rebellious teen or anything. I was third in my high school class, involved in sports and clubs, and I got a full ride to college. I've always been responsible. I think I've earned my family's trust. When I told my dad about Jason, he said that I could run off and get married but don't expect him to be there. He understood that I could make my own decisions, but he did not want to be part of it and was sorry that I was choosing to ruin my life. He said he does not want to meet Jason ever. Now we get along fine, my dad and I just don't talk about it."

Danielle said her mother (Bud's daughter) fell into a state of crisis. "She invited me over to have dinner on my birthday. She told me that she used to be proud of me, but now thinking of me made her nauseous. It was my fault that she hasn't been able to eat or sleep. She's ashamed that I'm her daughter. . . . I've never heard my mom make one racist comment. I've even seen her go out of her way to help. When I was in the sixth grade, I got off the bus to find three black boys playing in our backyard. Their family was living in their car, on their way to a homeless shelter in Indy. Their car broke down on the Greensburg exit, of all places! She brought the kids home, made the family dinner, and paid to fix the car. She really is a wonderful person. She tells me that I just don't understand, which is completely true."

Danielle and I met for breakfast on the pier in San Clemente when she was in California visiting Jason. I spotted her instantly, as she was white as porcelain from the Indiana winter, with freckles and striking red hair.

She and Jason were now officially engaged. He was thirty-four and she was twenty-six. They were going to have the wedding in Virginia Beach, where they planned to live, and a reception in Greensburg. "My dad and my grandpa already said they're not going to either one," she said. "This is all their choice, not mine."

Each time we came back to this point, she shrugged coolly, but her brow flickered and her face fleetingly tightened as if she were about to cry. She knew her father's and grandfather's beliefs were hardened. She just hoped that they would come around for her, particularly when they realized no gamesmanship on their part would change her mind. But it didn't look like they were going to. Their hatred had ossified into their very skeletal system.

"So Bud was a really good grandfather?" I asked.

She gazed off at the sea, pale and smooth under a bright and lifeless sun. She looked back at me obliquely. "I keep remembering when I was little, sitting by the fireplace, and he'd be playing with us and holding us and reading us stories. He'd always have a story. When I was older I always took my friends over there because he's a riot. He'd take us on tractor rides, or we could fish on his dock. He'd let you help bottle-feed the calves. He'd bend over backwards for you. I locked my keys in my car once and called him, and he came. He sat there and picked on me—'Why don't you have a hide-a-key?'—until the police came. If you're going on vacation, he'd give you some money and say, 'Why don't you do something nice?' I think he'd really like Jason if he'd let himself meet him."

She said her aunts and uncles on both sides had been very support-ive. In particular, her aunt Suzanne, her dad's sister, and her husband had steadfastly stood by her and given her encouragement. Her mom was slowly coming around. She was going to the wedding and reception.

Her dad wouldn't budge. "I'm a little worried he might show up to the reception with a shotgun."

"He wouldn't really do that, would he?" I asked.

"Just the fact that I keep asking myself that same question makes me anxious."

After breakfast, I headed up to the library at University of California at Irvine to find a couple of obscure books on the slave trade. I knew in that long and sordid history lay the stitches of information I needed to follow the thread of my family line across the sea. But could they be found? Since I started researching it months before, the trade's duration and complexity had overwhelmed me. It was no wonder few African Americans crossed the breach of the Atlantic in building their history. With their pasts erased by slavery, they were left no clues to guide them to a specific people or place of their ancestry. Alex Haley's claim to have connected his ancestor Kunta Kinte to his parents in the village of Juf-fure, Gambia, was torn to pieces by academics who retraced his research. His spectacular novel remained well-researched fiction.

But Edward Mozingo bestowed on us a remarkable clue by keeping his name and by suing for his freedom in Jamestown, where a clerk recorded the likely year he crossed the Middle Passage.

Chapter 14

South of the River of Prawns

Long before Columbus set sail across the Atlantic, the Mediterranean ports of North Africa teemed with spices, gold, and silk, and fanciful tales of mysterious kingdoms to the south and east, all delivered by great camel caravans a thousand miles and more across the deserts. The galleys of Genoese, Venetian, and Catalan merchants tied up next to Arab feluccas, while Jewish traders from Europe established routes with Jewish colonies throughout Moorish North Africa. The trade linkages were expansive enough that European cloth, horses, saddles, and spurs were found in remote bazaars beyond the Sahara long before any white man was known to set foot in them.

The Europeans wanted to get to the source of the baubles that came to these bustling harbors. Marco Polo had opened briefly routes east through the Levant and Central Asia to the fabulous luxuries from China and India. Rumors of lands south of the burning wastes of the Sahara promised equal riches. But the spread of Islam had cut Europeans off from both parts of the world as Muslims controlled key segments of the routes. An enduring legend in Europe had that a Christian nation ruled by a king named Prester John still existed somewhere out there, severed from the rest of Christendom.

The journey south by sea was treacherous, the waters little known past Morocco, current and wind making it hard to get back. Medieval

Arab mariners called the ocean beyond Cape Bojador on the Saharan coast the "Green Sea of Darkness," thought to be a place of sea serpents and ogres, whirlpools, deadly reefs, and boiling water that turned the skin black. By the beginning of the fifteenth century, the great kingdoms of Europe were beset with internal strife that held them back from exploration.

Only little seafaring Portugal, perched at the natural launching point to the new worlds, found itself relatively unbothered. Generations of war to wrest its territory from the Moors and try to control Spanish Castile had ended. The royal coffers were depleted, and King João I needed riches to shore up his power and create estates for his five sons. Out there, at the western end of the continent, he and his princes had nowhere to look but south.

João launched a crusade in 1415 to capture the port of Ceuta, on the northern tip of Africa, just across from Gibraltar. The king's son, Prince Henrique, orchestrated the conquest and, according to his hagiography, played a hero's role in the battle that inspired his pursuit of exploration and the crusade against infidels for the rest of his life. Ceuta was the terminus of several African caravan routes and a nexus of the gold trade. A hillside city of striking arches, minarets, and gold-leafed domes, its bazaars were filled with sacks of gold dust, head-high pyramids of elephant tusks and rhino horns, mounds of jade and amber, oryx skins and ostrich feathers, silks, incense, and pearls, as well as anguished, dark-skinned slaves. Henrique walked the narrow alleys marveling at it all. He pressed war prisoners for information about the trade routes and the royal cities on rivers beyond the scorching sands: Gao, Canton, Timbuktu. European traders had heard of such places, and cartographers made spectacular maps. There was a rumor of salt mines in the middle of the Sahara and people who carried salt blocks south to Timbuktu to exchange for gold, which itself came from a people farther south, who had the heads and tails of dogs.

Henrique attempted to bully his way through North Africa, leading his troops on an assault on Tangiers that ended in disastrous defeat by the Moors. Eventually, he set his sights on flanking them and the desert by sailing down Africa's west coast to reach the great cities. Already the

Portuguese had conquered the Canary Islands, which made a convenient stepping stone. Henrique built a base on the juniper-dotted outcropping of the port of Sagres, the arthritic toe of southwest Portugal, sticking out into a windswept ocean whose boundaries were unknown. From there the clumsy, square-sailed vessels of the day launched, first to the uninhabited archipelagos of Madeira and the Azores, and then made deeper probes south along the African coast. Henrique cloaked his ambitions in a scrim of idealism, converting pagans and Muslims and seeking Prester John's kingdom, which would justify the very un-Christian deeds his people would soon commit.

One of his captains rounded what he suspected was Cape Bojador in 1434 and sailed into the Green Sea of Darkness, discovering that the sea didn't boil and his sailors did not turn black. Subsequent expeditions passed a headland a couple hundred miles south and found a market run by dark-skinned Muslims in Berber garb, with camel caravans resting and drinking after long journeys from the interior. The sailors traded for some ostrich eggs, gold dust, and twelve black Africans to show Henrique.

Portuguese explorers reached the banks of the Senegal River in the 1440s and crossed into what they viewed as the true land of the blacks, os negros. "It appears to me," wrote the Venetian adventurer Alvise Cadamosto, traveling with a license from the Portuguese king, "a very marvelous thing that, beyond the river, all men are very black, tall and big, their bodies well formed; and the whole country green, full of trees, and fertile, while on this side, the men are brownish, small, lean, ill-nourished and small in stature." The explorers were offered elephant meat and ivory.

This was the beginning of their conquest of the coast they called Guinea.

Henry the Navigator, as the prince Henrique came to be called centuries later, didn't actually do any navigating. He never embarked on any of the voyages down the African coast, but his funding and expansionist zeal would set off the Age of Exploration and establish the transatlantic slave trade. He brought a handful of Europe's best astronomers, cartographers, compass makers, mathematicians, and shipwrights to Sagres. Princes and merchants came to invest in expeditions. He built a fortress, church and library, and dockyards fifteen miles east, in Lagos, where the expeditions launched. Seeking a faster ship, his builders borrowed from local fishing vessels and the Arab feluccas and came up with the agile caravel, which could sail close to the wind and navigate shallow coastal waters and rivers. The caravels' speed and ability to tack upwind with lateen sails allowed them to make much longer journeys and kept Portugal in the vanguard of discovery for years.

While the explorers primarily sought gold markets, they reaped a more reliable commodity by stealing the Africans. They snuck up on their fishing villages or lured them aboard their ships to trade. They carried off women and children and tried to ransom men of importance. The trade developed quickly.

Under license from Henry, a private trading company organized one well-documented slaving expedition in 1444. The company hired the captain who had first passed Cape Bojador, this time to lead six caravels to the island of Arguin just off the Saharan coast. Villagers fled from their houses in hysteria when they saw armed white men approaching in rowboats at dawn. The sailors, "shouting out 'St. James,' 'St. George,' 'Portugal,' at once attacked them, killing and taking all they could," wrote the chronicler Gomes Eanes de Zurara. "Then might you see mothers forsaking their children, and husbands their wives, each striving to escape as best he could. Some drowned themselves in the water; others thought to escape by hiding under their huts; others stowed their children among the seaweed."

The kidnappers returned to Portugal with 235 captives, who were taken out into a field at Lagos on the morning of August 8 for the great Henry to see and take his fifth share. Some kept their faces down in tears, some groaned in pain, others stood with their eyes fixed to heaven, "crying out loudly, as if asking help of the Father of Nature," according to Zurara.

And though we could not understand the words of their language, the sound of it right well accorded with the measure of their sadness. But to increase their sufferings still more, there now arrived those who had charge of the division of the captives, and who began to separate one from another, in order to make an equal partition of the fifths, and then was it needful to part fathers from sons, husbands from wives, brothers from brothers. No respect was shewn either to friends or relations, but each fell where his lot took him. . . . So soon as they been led to their place the sons, seeing themselves removed from their parents, ran hastily back towards them; the mothers clasped their children in their arms, and holding them, cast themselves upon the ground, covering them with their bodies, without heeding the blows which they were given.

Watching from on high on his "powerful steed," Henry was so impressed by their capture that he made the man who organized the venture a knight and rewarded him and his captains with great "benefits." Henry took forty-six of the slaves and uttered no quibble about the children and parents being torn apart, but reflected with great pride upon the "salvation of those souls that before were lost"—a sentiment with which Christians would legitimize the slave trade for centuries.

Slavery was new neither to the Europeans nor the Africans. In ancient Athens thousands of Scythians from the steppe north and east of the Black Sea had been enslaved; Egypt enslaved Jews from the Levant and Nubians from Sudan; and the Romans plundered Gaul, Britain, Iberia, and Germania for their slaves. The Vikings took slaves from all over Europe and established a major slave market in Dublin. Slavery was so rampant among Anglo-Saxon warlords that it is estimated a tenth of Britain's population was enslaved in the eleventh century. Muslims brought black slaves up the Saharan caravan routes from the forests and savannahs of the south, and they raided coastal villages in Spain for white slaves. In the sixteenth century, there were an estimated thirty thousand Christian slaves in Tunis. At the same time, the Portuguese raided North Africa for Muslim slaves.

Each of these societies arrived at its own version of servitude, with varying degrees of dehumanization, from serfdom to chattel slavery. Some allowed slaves to have families, property, freedom of movement and commerce, and even respected positions, such as being members of the palace guard. Others drove and managed the enslaved people brutally, as if they were oxen. The slaves taken to Portugal were usually made household servants for wealthy families or worked alongside serfs.

In two papal bulls of the 1450s, Pope Nicholas V gave Portugal all rights to the territory it discovered in Africa and authorized the permanent enslavement of any Muslims, pagans, and "enemies of Christ." But as word about the raids spread along the African coast the Portuguese captains found it increasingly difficult to kidnap people. Warriors came out in canoes that could outmaneuver the caravels, with poison arrows that could pierce their chain mail armor and kill them with even a glancing blow. Zurara described one dicey expedition in Sierra Leone:

> The next day they landed a little further along and saw some Guinean women who seemed to be collecting shellfish on the shore of a little inlet. They seized one of the women who must have been about thirty years old, with her son who was two, and also a young girl of fourteen, who did not lack a certain elegance of form and, for a Guinean, a certain beauty of face. The strength of the woman was astonishing because the three men who seized her had great trouble getting her onto the boat. So one of our men, seeing the slow progress they were making, which might allow time for some of the inhabitants of the land to surprise them, had the idea of taking her child and carrying him to the boat, so that her maternal love made her follow him.

They continued on and caught another woman. Then four or five canoes of men came after them, and the Portuguese immediately retreated, in fear of poison arrows. One canoe drew close, and a warrior shot an arrow that hit the captain in the leg. He pulled it out quickly and washed the wound with urine and olive oil, but still fell ill and almost died.

The Portuguese ultimately concluded it would be more prudent and expedient to trade for captives than to kidnap them. The inland mullahs and local chiefs and merchants had sold prisoners of war and criminals as slaves to the Barbary ports and Arabia for many years, and were just as willing to sell them to the sailors, trading them for goods from all over

Europe: spiced wine, brass basins, horses, swords, copper bars, candles, cloth, wool, wheat, beads. The chronicler Cadamosto offered a vivid record of the status of human lives in the hierarchy of trade: "A harnessed horse with its accoutrements fetches between nine and fourteen slaves according to its quality and appearance." Owning a horse was such a status symbol in West Africa that buyers even valued the dead ones. A German traveling on one of the slaving missions wrote, "Even if the horse is ill and he knows that it will die the next day, he buys it all the same because everyone keeps the tails and these are hung up in their houses. And when they go to a festival, the women carry the tails in their hands to let it be known that their husband has possessed so many horses."

The caravel captains continued down the Guinea coast as it turned east. Henry was ecstatic to hear the mistaken news that the southern end of the continent had been reached. Many had thought Africa extended to the ends of the earth. Now it looked like the Portuguese had found the long-sought seaward passage to the Orient.

All along the way, the Europeans were coming upon cultures far more connected to the broader world than most of those they would find in the Americas in years to come. This was the frontier of Muslim civilization, which at its core was more advanced at the time in science and scholarship than Europe. Out on its rugged edges, many of the West Africans had moved well beyond subsistence farming, and trade routes extended from the equatorial rain forest to the Mediterranean and Middle East. They smelted iron and copper and produced high-quality steel and gold jewelry. Many families owned metal knives, hoes, and axes, intricate basketry, ceramics, and ivory carvings. The larger kingdoms boasted complex power hierarchies and alliances.

When Prince Henry died in 1460, exploration briefly lagged, as his nephew King Afonso V had little interest in it. Nine years later he decided to franchise the Crown's monopoly on Africa to a Portuguese merchant named Fernão Gomes, who resumed the push east for a route to the Orient. Shortly after, in 1472, the captain Fernão do Pó sailed around the bulge of the Niger Delta, through a channel between a towering island volcano and an even taller mainland mountain—

Mt. Cameroon today—to a wide river he named Rio de Camarões after the swirls of prawns he saw there. Continuing along the coast he discovered that it eventually turned south again, dampening hopes for an easy route to India and China. Africa had another three thousand miles in her. But there was plenty of money to be made from the continent itself now. Slaves had become highly profitable. Sugar plantations on the offshore islands of Cape Verde and Madeira had opened up a booming market for labor. The Portuguese tapped into an internal slave trade as well, discovering they could buy slaves cheaply along the creeks of the Niger Delta and sell them for gold to the west.

In 1482, on a rocky hook of land in present-day Ghana, the Portuguese built their west coast headquarters, São Jorge da Mina Castle, a huge stone fortress, to warehouse goods and slaves and guard nearby gold mines. One visitor to the fort shortly after its construction was a young Genoese sugar buyer who had lived on Madeira and whose Portuguese name was Cristóvão Colombo. Ten years later, he would be the first to sail straight across the Green Sea of Darkness.

The year Colombo visited the fort, the mariner Diogo Cão passed through, under orders to look for a way to the Indian Ocean. As the coast turned south at the River of Prawns, he fought the prevailing northerly current and winds, slowly luffing in the tropical heat. Past the equator, he came upon reddish sea and drifting islands of vegetation and water so fresh it was drinkable fifteen miles from shore. He took out his spyglass and saw two spits of sand, like pincers, protecting what looked like a vast harbor. Sailing toward the harbor, he found he was running against a current as fast as a man jogged, pouring out of an inlet six miles wide.

This was not a harbor, but the mouth of a mighty river, the most powerful the Europeans had ever seen. The banks were low and lined with mangrove and palm. The ocean waves bending away from the current broke a translucent orange on a red mud beach. Faint blue mountains rose from the forest far in the east.

A leadsman on the bow dropped a weighted line and shouted back a substantial depth. Cão fought the current to a point a couple miles up the river, where he put ashore on the southern bank. Natives emerged out of the mangroves to greet them. Cão had brought along several baptized Africans from Guinea to interpret, but they struggled to understand the language. Cão dimly gathered that the people were *kongo* and had a ruler nearby and a greater king many miles inland. The locals called the river Nzere, which they conveyed through gestures as "the river that swallowed all rivers." Cão dressed the four Guinea translators in Portuguese finery and sent them off as messengers to meet the king. He then sailed farther south, and returning weeks later found the messengers hadn't returned. So he apprehended four natives and took them back to Portugal.

This was the inauspicious beginning of a relationship between the Kingdom of Portugal and the Kingdom of Kongo that would unleash the first great torrent of slaves to the Americas. In Lisbon, word of a great new kingdom sparked the Crown's imagination, and Cão sailed back to the Congo River in 1485, with his captives, who now spoke Portuguese. He sent them, bearing gifts from King João II, on the hundred-mile journey inland to the native king's mountain palace, called M'banza Kongo. Cão meanwhile sailed farther up the river to find a great impassable rapid a hundred miles in. It is unclear what happened after this, as he disappears from accounts. All that is known is that at some point his ship returned to Portugal carrying gifts and an official envoy of noblemen from the Kongo king, whose main ambassador converted to Christianity in Lisbon. In 1491, João sent the envoy of men back to Africa with a contingent of soldiers and more lavish gifts, including horses along with priests, stonemasons, carpenters, and female housekeepers to teach the natives the ways and skills of the Portuguese. The plague killed many on the journey, including both the Portuguese and Kongo ambassadors, but when the survivors arrived at the river mouth, they were met by a great celebration, held by the local ruler of the Soyo people, who were vassals to the Kongo king.

According to the chronicler Rui de Pina, the party feasted for three days, performed baptisms, and then set off for the capital, following footpaths and crossing vine bridges over rivers and ravines, through the savannah and low mountain forest, and arrived twenty-three days later. The city sat at the top of a rounded mountain, 1,700 feet above sea level, overlooking wide valleys on all sides. It boasted no large buildings or markets filled with exotic riches or slaves. The kingdom was certainly not as grand as had been conjured, or as would be later depicted. European renderings would show a grand castle on a bluff over a navigable river that didn't exist.

The Kongo people were an agrarian society, practicing slash-and-burn cultivation, growing bananas and yams, raising goats, pigs, and cattle, and hunting and fishing, mostly for themselves. They had slaves from neighboring tribes, though it is not as they were far to the south of the Arab influence and the caravan routes that made slaves such a valuable commodity.

But the king was indeed a powerful man. He ruled six principalities covering land as far as two hundred miles away through an elaborate feudal system of tribute and nobility, with "tribute roads" connecting to all parts. He was said to have twenty thousand professional soldiers at his command and could summon an army of a hundred thousand if he sounded war drums. More important, perhaps, he controlled the currency of *nzimbu* shells, mostly collected on a barrier island on the southern end of the kingdom and treated like gold coins throughout the land.

The king housed the Portuguese in some new huts and sent them "many courtiers who danced in a demented manner," wrote Rui de Pina, "and after them an infinite number of archers and lance bearers and others with warlike arms, and also countless women all arranged in companies with ivory trumpets and drums and other instruments, all singing the praises of the King of Portugal and, with great joy, extolling his greatness." They led the Portuguese to a large square shaded by a giant fig tree. In front of the outer wall of the palace, a palisade of stakes entwined in vines, the king was sitting on a raised throne of wood inlaid with ivory. He was about sixty years old, bare-chested, shoulders draped in leopard and civet furs, arms laden with copper bracelets. A bow and arrow sat in his lap and a zebra tail hung from one shoulder. Over his palm cloth skirt rested a damask cloth Cão had brought him from the king of Portugal eight years earlier.

The earliest known mention of the king's native name came in a reference written by Damião de Góis in 1545 to the king's son, Mobemba amosinga, which in the manner of Kongo names meant *Mobemba, son of Amosinga.*

Spelling across the Western world was terribly inconsistent until the nineteenth century, even within the writings of one person. Gomes Eanes de Zurara was also Gomes Eannes Azurara, and Alvise Cadamosto was also Alvide da Ca' da Mosto. The lack of consistency was worse when Europeans were trying to take down a language they didn't remotely understand, not to mention a tonal dialect in which the pitch of a syllable changed the meaning of a word.

In a paper for the *William and Mary Quarterly*, one of the foremost experts on Kongo history, John Thornton, called that first A of *Amosinga* a link between the two elements, so that the name would more accurately today be written *Mobemba a Mosinga.* The Portuguese often pronounce an *s* between two vowels somewhere between an *s* and a *z*, as in *José*, and the spelling of the name in the Kongo would later take on the *z*. Thornton, a professor at Boston University, discussed this with me at length. He said the name probably landed on European ears sounding like *Muh ZING uh*—*uh* sounding like the *u* in *put*, except shorter.

The language changed in the seventeenth and eighteenth centuries, as languages always do, with the first *b* of *Mobemba* taking on a *v* sound, the initial vowels being dropped in both words, and the *m* in *Mosinga* becoming more nasal. The modern orthography of the name—the one in the history books—is *Mvemba Nzinga.*

Thornton was convinced the American Mozingo was the earlier variation of this Kongo name, preserved by coming to Virginia and getting rooted in English record keeping.

The Portuguese captain leading the expedition, Rui de Sousa, kissed the king's hand and flattered him with "Spanish ceremonies . . . which [the king] showed that he received with great pleasure. And as a sign of his satisfaction, he took earth in his hand and ran it down the captain's breast and his own, which is the greatest sign of respect that the king could give." After the festivities, he dismissed his guests to rest. They met again later to present the gifts from Portugal: gold and silver jewelry, "cloths of silk and velvet and others of many colors, and satins and damasks and scarlet and pieces of Holland, and horses' tails decorated with silver, which he valued above all, especially some which were light brown, and large bells and other things of this kind."

From his emissaries, King Mosinga already knew of Portugal's great cities and ships and weaponry. He undoubtedly hoped to gain immense wealth and power from the alliance and from their religion. He immediately agreed to be baptized, and, with elaborate fanfare on both sides, work began on a stone church near the king's palace. One thousand Kongo men joined the labor, carrying stone and lime and timber from miles away.

But before the church was finished, the king learned of an insurrection in the north. To seal the alliance, a priest hastily baptized King Mosinga under a wooden altar, and he took the name of the Portuguese king, João. Forced to pick which of his many wives he wanted to be his Christian one, he elected one who became Eleanor, the name of the Portuguese queen, while their oldest son took the name Afonso, that of the heir to the Portuguese throne.

Rui de Sousa ordered his soldiers to fight with King João's army to put down the insurrection as if they were embarking on a crusade against Muslims. And they did, showing the power of their firearms and returning to M'banza Kongo with prisoners and plunder. De Sousa departed for Portugal content with his work, leaving behind a contingent of priests, soldiers, and artisans.

But the relationship between the two kingdoms would falter. The priests became overzealous in extinguishing the native beliefs and practices, notably polygamy—even as they themselves impregnated Kongo women. Just four years after his baptism, the king renounced Christianity and banished the Portuguese and his own Christian son, Afonso. But upon his father's death in 1506, Afonso seized the throne, and the white men returned, setting up an embassy in M'banza Kongo and a trading post at Mpinda, at the mouth of the Congo.

The new king exhibited a born-again's fervor for Christianity and European culture. Dom Afonso read volumes of theology and Portuguese law. Catholicism became the state religion, and the church opened schools to teach Portuguese and Christianity. Dom Afonso sent youths to be educated in Lisbon and Rome, including his own children. His son Henrique went to Rome and became the world's first black Catholic bishop, serving in Madeira.

At first, the Portuguese were mostly interested in trading for ivory and high-quality copper that came from the northern frontier of the kingdom. But the world was rapidly expanding. Six hundred miles from the mouth of the Congo, the Portuguese were growing sugar on the island of São Tomé, a former penal colony full of ex-convicts now run by a trading company. The Spanish were also just starting to plant the transformative cane in the newly discovered islands of the Caribbean. By the 1530s, mills and gold and silver mines were to be found all over Hispaniola, Cuba, Puerto Rico, Mexico, Brazil, and Peru, and all these colonies would be clamoring for slaves.

The Kingdom of Kongo had strict laws restricting the taking of its freeborn subjects as slaves; only criminals and foreigners could be sold. But Afonso swooned for the shiny European goods, and he decided to raid his neighbors to the east to round up slaves for exchange, buying them at inland markets with *nzimbu* shells. His hold on the kingdom was fragile, though, and he didn't have the army to acquire the numbers of slaves the sugar growers needed. So the proprietor general of the São Tomé sugar colony, a roguish sort who routinely ignored the Crown and was by most accounts a vile man, set up his own slave-trading posts and sent his armed men inland to trade directly with whomever they found.

Afonso sent numerous letters to King João III of Portugal complaining that his subjects were being kidnapped by illicit traders he called "thieves of men without conscience." He said he wanted more teachers and priests from Portugal, not more traders, and even mentioned abolishing the slave trade altogether. But sadly, he knew it was too late for that. Slaves had become the very currency for dealing with the Europeans, and the lords of the provinces and the lesser chiefs found the European goods too enticing, the trade too lucrative. He knew they would continue selling slaves to the Portuguese, striking their own alliances, and the kingdom would fall apart if he tried to thwart them.

In the end Afonso regained a measure of control as a major slave market opened in the area known as the Malebo Pool, beyond the rapids of the Congo River, where his father had put down the insurrection. By 1540 he was touting his slave trade to the Portuguese king. "Put all the Guinea countries on one side and only Kongo on the other and you will find that Kongo renders more than all the others put together," he wrote. But when he died in 1543, lords, chiefs, and even village headmen resumed striking their own deals with white men. The mixed-race offspring of Portuguese men and Kongo women often brokered the trading; called *pombeiros*, they were becoming a sizable merchant class throughout the kingdom.

As the land hemorrhaged slaves, the Portuguese spread their reach. On the southern border of Kongo they had made friends with a former Kongo vassal, the Kingdom of Ndongo, and began trading for slaves at a great natural harbor there. The Kongo king claimed the bay and barrier island—the major source of *nzimbu* shells—and maintained a long toll road from the bay to M'banza Kongo, traversing two hundred miles as the bird flies. The Ndongo Kingdom lay inland of the bay and procured its slaves by attacking smaller tribes to the south and east, as the Kongos had done to them. The two states traded extensively with the white men, and soon the Portuguese established their first true colony on the bay, calling it Luanda. But relations deteriorated with the Ndongo king, the *ngola*. (His title would be adapted by the Portuguese as a name for the kingdom, which would become, in the broader Atlantic world, a term used for much of the west central African coast.) Large-scale war erupted. It was a long campaign, with attacks and counterattacks lasting nearly twenty years. With help from the Kongo army and alliances with shifting Ndongo vassals, the Portuguese eventually won and greatly expanded their territory, harvesting slaves along the way.

In Kongo and the thorny hinterlands of Luanda, lumped together in Europe's distant view as Angola, insurrection, internal strife, outright pillaging, and civil war would continue into and throughout the seventeenth century. Captives poured into Luanda and Mpinda, feeding a voracious demand in America.

From 1575 to 1600, roughly 105,000 slaves were taken from the region. In the following fifty years, during which time Edward left Africa, the number was more than 563,000. That latter number represented 84 percent of all the slaves taken from Africa up to that time.

Chapter 15

A Thousand Miles of Bantu Coast

All the evidence seemed to point to Edward's having come from the Angola region. The kings were named Mosinga, and the slave route from Malebo Pool actually passed right through an area called Mazinga. The queen of Ndongo when Edward arrived in Virginia in 1644 was called Queen Nzinga, and so many slaves were coming from her country that the Brazilians briefly called them Zingas. And the only known origin of the slaves arriving in Virginia in the years prior to Edward's arrival was Angola.

But the more I researched, the more the realm of possibilities for Edward's homeland grew. Bantu experts said that Mozingo was, without a doubt, a name from the Bantu group, but that included more than two hundred languages that were spoken across much of southern Africa. And could these experts be sure that the name didn't also exist in other African languages to the west, in Guinea and Senegambia? Could it not also sound like a word in Igbo (Nigeria) or Akan (Ghana) or Yoruba (Benin) or Wolof (Senegal)? It sounded Italian, for God's sake. Ultimately, I was to find that there were more than a thousand languages in West and Central Africa from which the name Mozingo could have emerged.

I assume Edward departed Africa in late 1643 or 1644, but he may have left earlier and spent time in Barbados or elsewhere in the Caribbean. And the clerk who noted in 1672 that Edward's term of twenty-eight years of servitude had expired didn't say exactly how long ago it had expired. So he might have been in Virginia earlier than 1644. But most likely that was the year he arrived, a few months after leaving Africa.

There were several different routes he might have traveled to Virginia. In 1641, the Dutch took control of the Portuguese ports in Angola, and for a variety of reasons, the slave trade there briefly slowed. In 1642, only 783 slaves were documented leaving Angola, a quarter of the number taken five years before, while 895 left Ouidah, Nigeria, and 365 left Calabar. But the trade ramped up again, with 4,336 embarking in 1643 and 4,325 in 1644. In these years the Angolan slaves were shipped mostly to Brazil, so if Edward had landed in Brazil, I felt I could say with near certainty that he came from Angola, but he had landed in a backwater British colony. By the mid-1640s, the British had made their first push into the slave trade and were picking their "pieces" all along the hundred-mile stretch of coast around Calabar and Cameroon. They also took slaves from thousands of miles northeast in Senegal and at many points in between. He could have come from any of these sources of trade.

The existing DNA data also didn't help pinpoint his origins. The testing of modern-day Africans was too scant to know which peoples had which genetic markers, not to mention that Africans had migrated substantially within Africa since 1644, so a concentration of a genetic marker found in one area today wouldn't mean that tribe had lived near there more than three hundred years ago.

But as I reached out to university experts on the main language groups in the slave-trading regions, more and more of them assured me the name was Bantu. "Mozingo does not sound like a name in any Gbe language," wrote James Essegbey, an assistant professor at the University of Florida. "The Bantu connection seems more compelling for historical and linguistic reasons." Response after response echoed this, basically saying, nope, sounds like Bantu to me.

This gave me the confidence to focus on the thousand miles of Bantu coast between Calabar and Luanda. But that was still a vast territory, the distance from New York City to Miami, with seven countries in it. I taped a giant Michelin map of West and Central Africa to my wall, circling the slave ports of Calabar, Rio del Rey, Bimbia, Loango, Mpinda, Luanda, and Benguela. I also circled the word *Mazingo*, sitting on a blank green swath of the map in eastern Gabon. Maybe this tiny village was Edward's home.

The more I researched, the more I wanted to go to Mazingo. Gabon looked gorgeous, with pristine rain forests and game preserves, the only country where big mammals from the heart of the Central African rain forest and savannah still reached the Atlantic coast. Hippos wallowed in the surf. Elephants wandered the black sand beaches. This village bewitched my imagination: I would find a chief there who led a secret Mazingo cult. After trekking through the jungle to find him, and after his warriors put down their poison arrows and he saw the name Mozingo in my passport, he would immediately embrace me as one of his own. But how would I get there? It turns out the village was at the heart of an Ebola virus outbreak, and a few Canadian and American scientists had traveled there extensively to study the cause and other ecological issues. One had actually taught at my university in San Diego when I was a student. She was supremely helpful and offered to let me go along when she went there again. She said it would be a two-week journey to the village once I arrived in Gabon.

But logic began to regain its hold on me. The stretch of coast where a slave from deep in the jungle around Madjingo, as she said it should be spelled, would have been taken was really not frequented much by the Europeans in the 1600s. Edward didn't come from there. I knew it. But I still wasn't sure about Angola.

One night soon after this conversation, I was in Haiti sitting at the bar of my hotel during elections, drinking Barbancourt rum, when a man in the tailored suit of a high-level diplomat sat next to me. He was with a woman, and they were speaking in English. Eavesdropping, I learned that he was from Cameroon. When they finished their conversation, I pulled my passport from my pocket.

"Excuse me, I heard you mention you're from Cameroon."

"Yes."

"I have a strange question to ask." I showed him my name. "Do you have that name in your country?"

He looked at me askance, then back at my passport. "Yes . . . yes, I have seen this name," he said. "This name is very common in my country."

"Do you know what part it comes from?" I asked.

"The capital area, I think."

When I got back to California, I dug into the Trans-Atlantic Slave Trade Database, which brought together all known records of European slave ships. The slavers never recorded the names of slaves. But when the British abolished slavery in the nineteenth century and the Royal Navy began to intercept illegal slave ships, clerks recorded the slaves' African names, as they heard them. I found the record of an eight-year-old boy named Masingah from "Cameroons River"; a nine-year-old boy named Mahsinga from Bimbia, Cameroon; an eleven-year-old girl named Mosingah from Cap Lopez, Gabon; a twenty-six-year-old man named Masinga from Congo; and an eighteen-year-old boy named Mujingo from Congo. There were also seven Singas from Congo. (The *mu* syllable at the beginning of Kongo names is a prefix that fell away in some cases, so Masinga and Singa were not necessarily different names.)

The planters in the British colonies also reacted to abolition by registering the "lawful" slaves they already had. I found the record of a Mazingue Coigna in Trinidad, thirty years old and owned by John Garcin in 1813. Two decades later, he showed up with a new owner, Duncan Hovart. He was listed as "African Congo" and had "country marks on his body and face."

All of this only convinced me that I should focus on the thousand-mile stretch of coast from Calabar to Angola, with the two ends of that span the most likely candidates for Edward's homeland.

As I mentioned, in 1643, over four thousand slaves left Angola, while 624 slaves left Calabar and the adjacent estuaries of Rio del Rey and Cameroons River. In 1644, roughly the same number came out of Angola, while the documented number out of the Calabar-Cameroon region was 392. Yet 1,988 slaves came from "unknown" regions and landed mostly in Barbados, a known transshipment point to Virginia.

And documentation of a strong Calabar-to-Barbados trade would start the next year. Dutch or Portuguese merchants in Angola, with a colonial government on site, likely documented their commerce better than those dealing on the lawless, contested coast.

I decided I'd visit both areas and see what I found.

It turns out you need an invitation to visit much of Africa. I got the feeling right from the beginning that Angola didn't want me—at least its government didn't. I was told only the minister of culture could invite me, and she ignored my entreaties for months. She also ignored letters from her own museum directors and American anthropologists with whom she had worked closely. She ignored entreaties from the U.S. Embassy even though the United States fully supports her repressive, nondemocratic government. It was not that she was too busy. She just had no reason in the world to desire my presence there. Every journalist I talked to who had covered Africa complained that Angola was one of the most difficult countries to get into, get around in, get any answers from. The government doesn't want eyes on what it's doing. "We got word from an aid-worker friend that we better leave," a photographer told me about her visit there. "For our safety."

Cameroon was a little easier, largely because a history professor at the University of Buea, Walter Gam Nkwi, took an interest in my work and sent me an invitation letter in short order. Another benefit of Cameroon was that the region I needed to visit was English-speaking.

I sent off my visa application with my passport and a $150 fee, and bought my $1,000 ticket to Paris and another $1,000 ticket to the Cameroonian city of Douala, and off I went, groping into my own Green Sea of Darkness.

Chapter 16

You Are Coming to the Source

I had driven across the deserts of the American Southwest many times, in awe at how vast and empty they still were. Even flying over them, I would find myself staring out of my window, thinking what a feat it was that explorers and pioneers ever got across them. Flying from France to Cameroon takes you over some 1,500 miles of land that makes the Southwest look suburban. For an entire hour before night fell, covering at least five hundred miles over Algeria, I did not see a dirt track or a building or a tower or a fence—not a single mark of humanity. Great dunes of sand rolled north like a groundswell from a distant storm, a masterpiece of bas-relief, line after bending line, sharp as razors. As the sun set, they turned sandy red in the light and plum in the shadows, then blue, then silver-black under a crescent moon. The caravans crossed all this somehow. It must have been an otherworldly trek for the slaves taken from the enveloping jungle and marched across the sere expanses of earth's bare crust.

I finished my Air France baguette and cordon bleu and fell asleep, waking up a few hours later coming in for a landing over what looked like forest with spot fires burning everywhere. We landed in Douala with applause and walked across the tarmac to the terminal. The air was humid and smoky.

Waiting in line at the open-air customs counter, sweating and coming out of my sleep, I had the fluttering fear that what I was doing was an act of psychosis. I had obsessed so much over Edward that I had now raided my bank account and flown to Africa to find him. I swiped a mosquito off my neck and shuffled up to endure the interrogative glares of the customs officers, then stepped into the chaos outside. I knew to come out of the terminal like a self-guided missile, striding with summoned confidence, looking for Walter holding a sign with my name. I made a pass through the crowd from end to end. *Damn, where is he?* I came back through it again, my facade of assuredness quickly wearing thin. I could not slow down or look confused; the hustlers were already tailing me.

I couldn't bear to think that Walter might have bailed on me. So clear was our plan, worked out over email, that I didn't even have his phone number on me. I now cursed myself for such a ridiculous mistake. Walter was my lifeline on this trip.

"Let me carry your bags," a hustler implored. Another of them motioned to a café. "Why don't you wait there?"

I couldn't keep circling around. I sighed and sat down at the café as they surrounded me, asking to buy them beers. I leaned in to two of the most persistent and told them that I would, if they would get the rest to back off.

They did, and I drank my own beer quickly and pushed my way back into the throng. Just as I was giving up hope, I saw small scrap of cardboard with "Mozingo" written on it.

Walter had a warm, smiling face and came in for a bear hug like an old friend. "Oh my," he said. "I had a *big* fight with the police getting into the parking lot."

We dashed to the car with the young men demanding money all the way. We closed the doors and sped off, the hustlers' curses swirling like moths in our exhaust. Walter had arranged for a hotel room in Buea, the university town where he teaches and the cultural center of the Anglophone side of Cameroon, a hybrid country that had been cobbled together from British and French colonies. It was a bare box with a window, a skeletal mattress, no toilet paper, raw wires hanging from the ceiling, and a shower drain with a bucket of water. The walls were powder blue with big cracks that were crystallized with salt. But it was secure and relatively clean and the TV worked. After I took a quick bucket shower, Walter and I drank some Scotch I had bought at the duty-free shop in Paris.

He was a slight man, forty-two years old, with a neatly trimmed beard, mirthful eyes, and an inscrutability, which all combined to remind me of the King of Hearts. He had young children, was finishing up his PhD from Leiden University in the Netherlands, and, like myself, had an overactive mind that liked a little whiskey to help him fall asleep.

The next day, Walter picked me up, and we took a taxi up the hill. Buea was a long and narrow city that clung to the highway as it ascended seven miles like a taut wire, barely bending or changing tilt. From the backseat I had to lean forward to see the immensity of Mt. Cameroon looming high above, like a gray tsunami about to crash down. The place felt like a roadside boomtown, with tin hut shops, street vendors with wooden carts, and concrete, half-finished two-story office buildings with rebar spearing the sky.

"I'd like to find anyone with my name or a variation of it and see if they know anything about it," I was telling Walter.

He scratched his temples. "There is a famous playwright I know named Victor Musinga, M-U-S-I-N-G-A. I will call him."

"Perfect."

"You know, in Swahili, *Mzungu* means 'white man.'"

"I've heard that."

Near the top of the road the taxi climbed a steep hill into a pleasant neighborhood of big palm trees and tin-roofed colonial buildings, many set on stilts apparently to ride out lava flows. The forest rose precipitously beyond, with the black and brown volcanic peak high above. The National Archives squatted on the top of the hill, a low-slung midcentury building with red moss on the roof.

I knew the archives would not date back to anywhere near the seventeenth century, as Cameroon was not colonized until the last few years of the nineteenth century and writing didn't exist here before that. But I hoped they would give me more details about where the slave trade had flourished and how it worked on this side of the Atlantic.

The chief archivist, a bespectacled, elderly man named Primus, guided me to a little wooden desk in a damp, bare room. A quintessentially colonial sign above said, "No Smoking by order of the Antiquities Commission."

"What would you like to look at?" he asked.

"I'd like to look at anything documenting the slave trade."

"Okay, give me a few minutes." With a quaint froglike voice, Primus was the warm and helpful antithesis to the dreaded African bureaucrat I was expecting.

I looked out the louvered windows. This was where the Germans had established their colonial headquarters and ruled from 1901 until the end of World War I, when Britain took over the western part of the colony and France took over the rest. The painted stone buildings, with tetrahedral roofs, spires, and finials, gave it a Bavarian feel, a faded little bit of Berchtesgaden carved out of the equatorial forest.

Primus brought me a stack of brown folders and I started paging through them. What I found were mostly records of the English trying to extinguish an economy of internal slavery they had helped create centuries before. Slavery in Cameroon lasted well into the 1950s, particularly along the route that once brought slaves from the interior to the British ships anchored in Old Calabar. I paged through sheaves full of "Certificates of Freedom," much like Edward's of 1672.

"Agnes Mba Bessongu (female) of Nguti, Mbo area, has claimed her freedom today, and it is granted her. She is not the slave of Tanyi Besong or Supe Family, OR ANYONE ELSE." It was signed by the district officer of the Mamfe division and dated May 5, 1953.

In another note to the same district officer, a man complained that members of his family were sold into slavery in 1954 and that police needed to investigate.

Primus came in with a book. "You might be interested in this."

It was called *Slave Settlements in the Banyang Country, 1800–1950*, by two of Cameroon's foremost historians, Victor Julius Ngoh and E. S. D. Fomin. Banyang Country was an area of deep-forested gorges in which trade routes from the inland savannah known as the Grassfields converged on their way to Mamfe, the river market town where the slaves were loaded on canoes and sent to Old Calabar. I read, "Slaves in this transaction came largely from the grassfields and were sold and resold by dealers as they moved coastwards. . . . Under the influence of the trans-Atlantic slave trade, slave dealing became rife in Banyang country." While slaves were transported down from the Grassfields to Old Calabar, English goods were transported up: salt, gin, Danish guns, whiskey, Manchester cloth, towels, gunpowder, spoons, and pots. I was struck by how little I knew about the effects of the transatlantic slave trade on Africa itself.

One interesting point the authors made was that iron mined in the Grassfields was found on the coast as early as the sixteenth century, meaning these trade routes existed in one way or another at the time Edward left Africa. Perhaps he came from the Grassfields.

The Banyang people considered the slaves in their midst to be wretched souls possessed of evil spirits and rejected by their own societies. They used them to do risky but vital tasks such as harvesting nuts from tall palms or painstaking work like processing palm oil. The masters feared the witchcraft of their captives and kept them in settlements outside of the villages. These *kesem* settlements provided a buffer against outside slave raiders, but also gave the slaves an autonomy they never had in the Americas.

> The slave was never under the direct surveillance of the master as was the case in the ancient Roman and 18th Century capitalist world systems. The slave could own property and pass it to his children. . . . The male slave built and owned a house in which he lived with his family.
>
> The Banyang bought female slaves not for direct use but for the purpose of giving wives to their male slaves. According to some

informants, the marrying of slave wives to male slaves was done as a reward for meritorious services by a male slave to the master. But the truth is that it was cheaper and a surer way of getting more slaves who could be exploited for sale and labour. The trans-Atlantic slave trade lasted the way it did (400 years) and could not have created the havoc it caused in Africa if the new world slavers were humane enough to try to increase the stock of slaves through procreation.

A caste of slaves existed long after the slave trade and the local practice of slavery were outlawed. If you came from one of the settlements, you were seen as a slave. Even today, the Banyang people did not knowingly marry descendants of slaves, and they will likely divorce their spouse if they learn he or she came from a *kesem*. Even where color was not an issue, the stigma of slavery persisted in a pariah class.

This all made a letter in the file, dated July 3, 1957, more poignant. John Abane Arreyneke, a pupil at a school in the Banyang region, complained to the district officer that people were calling him and his friends slaves: "I had heard [that] from many people even in the school where we were told by our teachers that there are no more slaves in the world. That there were slaves so William Wilberforce convinced that slavery was a blot on civilization. He made slavery to be stopped in the British Empire. But I see no reason why the people in Mbang Area always call others slaves while slavery had been stopped by Wilberforce." He named the towns where this was happening and asked the officer to send the paperwork to make an official complaint.

It would later become a punishable offense to remind slave descendants of their origins. But the British officer didn't see it as such when he wrote back to the boy: "While the law prevents the actual practice of slavery it does not prevent people calling each other 'slaves,' any more than it prevents them calling each other 'fools.' If you don't like being called a slave by your companions at school you will have to prevent them from doing so by whatever means you have at your disposal."

I dug through more files, reading and scanning for my name. I came upon the account of a Swede named Knut Vilhelm Knutson who explored Mt. Cameroon and surrounding areas in 1885, and this: "On the 3rd January 1885 Mr. Waldau and I went with Molla Mosingi to hunt monkeys and wild hogs near the small Cameroon peak." He skipped ahead in his account to tell how Mosingi accidentally shot someone on a previous venture. "Molla Mosingi was very afraid the man should die, and that would have caused him a great deal of trouble. Molla's father, called 'Beggar King Mosingi' because he always begged tobacco, must pay a good deal of money for his Molla's carelessness." Mosingi was the chief of the village of Soppo.

This was very promising.

I paged through the last files in the afternoon, thanked Primus, and stepped out into the brilliant equatorial light. The smoke had cleared and yellow butterflies swirled around banana plants and rain-washed coconut palms. The air was fresh up here at three thousand feet. Mt. Cameroon swelled up ten thousand more above me, and you could almost lose your balance looking up at it. The craters atop the massif were still active, and its many recent eruptions left a jumble of brown and black and red lava flows, while tendrils of green threaded up gullies from the forest at its midsection. I walked down to the main road in a mild state of revery and flagged a taxi, heading to the university.

A quarter mile down the road, the driver picked up two young men, then a big woman, who wedged in so tight next to me I could feel all of our hip bones locked in place from one side of the car to another.

I had an appointment with a linguist, Ayu'Nwi Neba, but he sighed when I arrived at his office and acted as if I had just dropped in unannounced. Five students stood around him, and he made it clear I was interrupting whatever he was doing with them. "In Cameroon we have two hundred Bantu languages," he began. "The hypothesis is that they originated from the Grassfields. Now your name. Mu is Class 1, coastal narrow Bantu. . . . Mu has become nasal. . . . The tendency now is to reduce words to one or two syllables in Cameroon. If you meet an M you can guess it used to be Mu. Now Mo is Class 6. That is different."

The students were staring blankly at me as I tried to take notes.

"*Sing* might be a bird. And most words end in *a*. But that doesn't mean your name is the same. It could be *zing* or *jhing*.

"I don't know what the name means. It is fossilized. It might be lost. Some of the languages have changed to *Ma*. It's very complicated. Some native speakers say an *s* as if it is an *r*. *Musinga* is *Muringa*. *Z* is pronounced *jh*."

"Really, *Muringa*? That doesn't seem like a natural jump to make."

"Only a linguist can determine these things."

I'd been down this rabbit hole many times before with a particular brand of academic who loved to show that nothing was what it seemed but refused to show what it actually was. I suspected if I continued I would learn that *Mozingo* came off the tongue like *Yakamoto*. Only his expertise could answer the question, except that it couldn't.

The next morning, I trudged up the misty slopes of Mt. Cameroon with a young Bakweri guide named Samuel. I had wanted to come to the mountain for a reason. This region was roughly where anthropologists believed one of the world's great migrations began three thousand years ago, similar to the one that brought peoples from Asia over the land bridge in Alaska to populate the Americas. It is thought that forest-clearance and slash-and-burn farming in the Grassfields and savannahs just to the north of here proved to be so bountiful that the population of Bantu-speaking peoples expanded suddenly. Running out of arable land, groups cleaved off around 1500 BC and set out looking for more. These groups eventually outgrew the belt of savannah altogether and pushed southeast into the alien territory of the Congo forests, settling along the great river and its myriad tributaries, dominating the scattered hunter-gatherer groups that Europeans would call pygmies. Unable to sustain as large a population in the forest, they radiated outward for more than a millennium, into new savannah to the south and east, ultimately reaching the Kenyan coast of the Indian Ocean and the Cape of Good Hope on the southern tip of the continent. Their language evolved into many new ones along the way: Zulu in South Africa, Shona in

Zimbabwe, Lingala in the Democratic Republic of Congo, Umbundu in Angola, Swahili in Kenya, all Bantu.

Each language appeared to have variants of *Mozingo*. Among others, I found a Francis Mazinga looking for an IT job on an online job board in Malawi, a Mazinga Institute in Kenya, a village of Mosingo in southern Sudan, a medical researcher named Louis Adolf Muzinga Lumfe in South Africa, and a Sudanese refugee named Mazinga Yona Alebe. There was a dialect of Kikongo called Mazinga, a onetime king of Rwanda named Yuhi Musinga, and of course my friend the basketball player Monga Maluku Mozingo in the Democratic Republic of Congo, whom I had reached by phone but who didn't know anything about the name.

So whether Edward Mozingo had left Africa from Old Calabar or the Congo River mouth or the sand island of Luanda in Angola, his ancestors, my ancestors, had likely been here several thousand years ago.

The air was overcast as we began our climb, and became smoky again with the dry season's burning of the fields. The trail mounted the slope more steeply than a stairway, with slippery roots and loose chunks of red lava rock giving way underfoot. We traversed charred fields, then plots of bananas and cocoyam, and came to a complex of dilapidated stone warehouses with rusted tin roofs. "This is the prison," Samuel said flatly.

The buildings looked like they had been burned out from the inside. The blackened window frames had no panes and were blocked with rotted wooden studs and chicken wire. The prisoners saw us and immediately wedged their faces into the openings. "White man, give me something!" "Please anything!" "I'm hungry!" "Charity please!" When I ignored them, the taunts began, and demands. "Look at me, sir! Sir, look at me!"

The insults and threats faded as we rose into the forest. *Nice start to a hike*, I thought. A Bakweri woman silently tended a little clearing, planting cocoyam. She did not glance up at us as we passed. Giant ficuses levitated in the fog beyond her. Red ants motored across the trail in straight slots an inch wide and deep, their traffic so furious that, without even leaning down, I could actually hear it.

Until the last years of the nineteenth century, when my recent ancestors were skulking around Bloomington, Illinois, selling horserad-ish, Mt. Cameroon offered an impregnable redoubt against the white men in ships far below. From the foothills several thousand feet above sea level, the Bakweris could see all the way down to the creeks and estu-aries of the gulf, spotting potential invaders and slavers, preemptively attacking them or disappearing into the forests. They hunted monkeys, porcupines, and antelopes, trapped elephants in pits, and grew exotic Asian plantains as their staple crop. They lived in bark houses with surplus crops to trade and raised livestock in well-fenced areas within their villages.

Baptist missionaries from the coast were the first to bring word of the Bakweri to the rest of the whites. Near the base of the mountain in 1858, they had made a beachhead on the black sand bay they called Victoria. Nearly four hundred years after Fernão do Pó sailed by, Europeans were still on the outside edge trying to look in; what went on just miles inland was a mystery. The Bakweris began trading their food to them, while keeping the interior blocked, and accumulated an arsenal of flintlock guns in exchange. The American cocoyam brought by the missionaries replaced plantains as the staple. But the missionaries' efforts to convert the Bakweri to Christianity were thwarted. The king, Kuva, refused to allow a new faith to be introduced in his realm, and his people did not dare to be baptized.

German colonizers immediately set their sights on the mountain when they took control of Cameroon in the 1880s during Europe's "Scramble for Africa." The elevation would offer an inimitable military vantage of the coast, as well as cooler temperatures and fewer disease-transmitting mosquitoes. Volcanic soil and heavy rain made the terrain some of the richest in Africa. In the lower reaches, the Germans carved out plantations for palm oil, rubber, tea, cocoa, and banana. But above 1,500 feet or so, the Bakweri were well fortified and rightly unfriendly to their aims.

Like the British in Virginia with Powhatan, the Germans thought they could outsmart King Kuva. "A spy was sent, piloted by one of those subjects whose chief had been deceived by a couple bottles of rum, some heads of tobacco and a few bags of rice and stock fish," wrote the historian P. M. Kale in 1939. Presented with the liquor, "Kuva looked at his feet, drew his long beard and ordered that the drink should be served. He sipped long shots, and his eyes sparkled. Then he replied to the whiteman, through the same interpreter, that he was glad to have him as a friend, and that they could discuss matters. . . . At the time of exchanging friendly thoughts, the whiteman, in a most cunning way, asked Kuva to give him a portion of land on which to build. By this he said, they would live at close quarters and meet any time. Kuva sternly refused telling the 'spy' that the area of land that he ruled came under him through the 'Spear' and if the whiteman wanted to get a share of it, he would better not pretend any diplomacy, but get ready with his own 'spear.'"

The white man hastened back to the German base in Victoria, narrated what "the monster said," and "the Germans got ready, for the first time in their lives perhaps, to meet African warriors."

They climbed back up the mountain and found themselves under a barrage of gunfire from a rock barricade. The fusillade was so fierce that it rained down boughs and branches from the forest canopy, sending the Germans scrambling back to the coast.

It took them three years to conquer Kuva and his people. The Germans removed the Bakweri from much of their land and placed them in reservations near the plantations, where they were forced to work. But the new overlords found them to be despondent and dissolute subjects and had to import laborers from other parts, particularly Igbo from neighboring Nigeria. The Bakweri became an impoverished minority on what had been their own soil, and when the British took over after World War I, they described the situation to the League of Nations this way: "Uprooted from the homes of their forebears, settled willy-nilly on strange soil, deprived of their old-time hunting grounds, and fishing rights, the Bakweri have retained but a small sense of tribal unity or cohesion." Many mixed with the newcomers, and by the 1940s anthropologists were predicting the tribe's extinction.

The British debated returning the land to the Bakweri, but ultimately ruled that out. Tribal leaders tried to wrest their lands back, sending off petitions all over, and were granted a hearing at the United Nations but couldn't afford the trip. British Cameroon's "independence" and union with the larger French Cameroon, in 1961, didn't further their cause, as the one-party government kept a tight grip on the lucrative plantations.

A wind picked up off the ocean and the clouds sifted through the canopy, allowing in an occasional glint of sunlight as we climbed. When I stopped huffing and actually looked around, the forest was striking, an effulgence of green. Ferns twisted up through the gray voids and light filtered through the foliage as if through stained glass. Birds pinged and whooped and insects sputtered like wind-up toys. It almost felt as if I could see the whole place growing and rotting and breathing and feeding on itself. It looked so beautiful. If only rain forests weren't such miserable places to actually be in.

At six thousand feet we reached our destination. The forest abruptly opened into a cold windblown brown savannah arching up to the red, brown, and black ridges. The change was as sudden as if we simply walked out a door. Recent lava flows had apparently caused the catastrophic transformation, mowing down the brush from the upper slopes. The mountain last erupted in 2000, sending streams of magma within a mile of the coast. On the older, more decomposed lava flows, grasses planted by the Europeans for the cattle mixed with sedge. I saw the same grasses on every empty hillside in California, where the Spanish seeded it for their cattle.

I turned and gazed out at the lowlands, freezing in my drenched shirt. The rugged landscape set the clouds swirling. I got faint and fleeting views of the twenty-mile-long downsweep of land, all the way to the estuary, glimmering in the sun. I had never seen such a long swoop of earth. I pictured sweaty Germans in tall hats charging up it in a phalanx. The haze lifted over the Wouri River Valley and the line of the shore, but blocked the volcano across the channel on the island named after Fernão do Pó.

Samuel picked up a bunch of fern branches. "Up at this area is the God of the Mountain. And the God of the Mountain was called Efassa Moto, half human and half stone," he said. His accent was very difficult to understand. English was his third language, after Bakweri and the regional pidgin imported by English missionaries from Jamaica. "In those days when the mountain was going to erupt, our great-grandparents had this belief that the God of the Mountain is angry. So in those days they were using *habeenos* to be sacrificed to appease the God."

"What's a *habeeno*?"

"*Habeenos*, a type of white person."

"Ah-hah."

"They were using *habeenos* to appease the God. At first they hiked up here to this spot. They would kill the *habeeno* here. They would go back to the village. They would sit together as one family. They share a bottle of palm wine together. They know they have appeased the God. In case of any eruption, everything would stay up on the mountain.

"Today we don't use *habeenos* anymore to do the sacrifice. We use a white goat, a white cock, palm wine, and a bottle of whiskey. If we were doing a tour in which we were going to spend the night on the mountain, I would ask you to buy that."

"I have one question," I said. "Before white people came here, what did they sacrifice?"

"There have always been *habeenos* here."

By the time I met up with Walter again that evening I had figured out what *habeenos* were. We were meeting the playwright Victor Musinga, and while we waited I told Walter about the hike. "So did they really stop sacrificing albinos?" I asked.

Walter had a way of listening to people as if he were taking great pleasure from it, then rubbing his chin, tilting forward, and retorting, always a degree removed, as if it were all a bit of a game in which he was marveling at human behavior. "No, they just did a sacrifice in the year 2000. The lava was threatening the road by the oil facilities. The chiefs had two albinos sacrificed. The police even looked into it. It was terrible, *very terrible*."

"How do you know this?" I asked.

"I saw it," he said, eyes wide with a wry smile.

I pushed the point, incredulous, and he said the murders were all over the news and undeniable.

Victor Musinga strode up the hotel driveway in a yellow print shirt with bright blue birds and satin blue pants. He was a tall, wiry man in his sixties. We jumped in a minitaxi to find a place to get some beer. On the way we passed a white bus from the Musango line that caught my eye, as did the Obama restaurant. Sporadic drops of rain began pelting the dusty windshield.

"You know, America is trying to control the Gulf of Guinea for the oil," Walter said. "They are building one of the biggest embassies in the world in Yaounde."

I didn't doubt this. A load of State Department people were on my flight from Paris. "Did you expect something different from the United States?" I asked.

"It's not about what we expect, but about what they project, that they are this benevolent nation, out to help. They are here to take our resources."

"What do people think about Obama?"

"Obama is a legend throughout all of Africa."

"Well, it's his government, right?

"Is it?" Walter asked. "I don't know if he controls such things."

We pulled into the parking lot of a restaurant with groups eating and drinking in their own little cabanas. As we sat the rain came down harder and smelled of clay. The waitress served us Castel beer in bottles and gave us an opener fashioned out of a stick and two wooden screws.

"So, Victor," Walter said. "This *mzungu* is looking to find out about his name, Musingo," as he pronounced it.

Victor leaned back in his chair, said, "Ah, yes," and looked at me curiously.

"You know, it was probably never spelled in Africa by the time my ancestor left," I told him, as there was no written language in these parts. "So here and in America, there are variants. Our names have to be related."

He had shown little interest in me so far, but now he lit up. "This reminds me. I was inspired by *Roots*. I was in the States then. I was a visiting lecturer once at Bloomsburg University of Pennsylvania. What was his name?"

"Alex Haley?"

"Yes, what he did was amazing, very inspiring. People here like to have a connection to America."

"So tell me about your name," I said.

He put his hands behind his neck and leaned back in his chair. "I am from Kumba, just north of here. I am Balundu, and our language is Bafaw. This was the name given to my father. Here in Africa, we give names according to circumstances. My grandfather got in trouble with the law and was in prison for a while. He was released the day my father was born. Musinga is a thread, something that binds. The thread hooked my grandfather in prison. It was cut off. And this new thread now bound him to his son."

I had heard from John Thornton, the expert on Angola history, that there the name had a similarly linear meaning, but more in the sense of something twisting and turning. Queen Nzinga of Ndogo was supposedly named because she was born with the umbilical cord around her neck. But a simple thread—I couldn't have invented anything more symbolic.

"So why did you get the name from your father?" I asked. "I thought it was more common here to inherit the surname of a maternal uncle than from your father."

"I got everything from my father. My father was headmaster at a school. He groomed me."

Walter explained about the matrilineal society. "Your heirs are not your children here," he said. "Your sister's child is the only clear person to succeed you." This was not a matriarchal society, where women ruled the family and tribe. Men could marry as many women as they could afford to keep. Walter, who came from the Kom, a matrilineal society, described the motive of inheritance going down a female line: "It's only the mother who knows where the child really comes from." So simple, and yet so cynical. The father could only be sure of his blood relation to his sister's children.

Walter got his surname, Nkwi, from his mother's brother, whom he barely knew. Ostensibly, he should receive his inheritance from him too.

He laughed out loud at that prospect. "This nonsense cannot last for long," he said. "My estate goes to my children."

We ordered more beer, talked awhile longer, and watched the lightning.

Victor leaned in after a thought. "What you're doing is very important," he said. "Africa does not do this. That is how you become a society, with documents you can look and see where you come from, and learn." He sipped his beer. "You are coming to the source."

Chapter 17

The Path of the Python

Just after dawn we were screaming down the lower slopes of the mountain through an orange and smoky light, Congo music thumping, a back window with rubber linings and seals whistling in the slipstream.

"Listen, we don't need to go this fast," I said.

The driver, John, was a husky young man in his twenties with wraparound shades and a quietly truculent manner. He nodded just enough to acknowledge he'd heard what I said, but not to agree with it.

"This man is a professional driver," Walter offered, smiling at the irony.

"Come on, we're going to kill someone. *Please*," I said. "We're in no rush." But my protests were to no avail. Plantations blurred by, oil palms, rubber trees, bananas, tea, and sugar, in a war of violent braking and acceleration. We hurtled up behind motorcycles going a quarter of our speed, bleating the horn, and shot past little roadside bars, over a wide muddy river with canoes hauling sand, ascending into a green valley with giant silver baobab trees. We hurtled around bends within inches of little packs of children in uniform walking to school, into a land of high knobby mountains.

Walter explained that the French used forced labor to build this road. "They paid the chiefs to recruit the labor force, and the chief would

239

force people of low standing to do the work as tribute. The conditions were inhumane and many people died. It wasn't just roads. Once you reached the age of paying taxes you were forced to work on the plantation."

We were heading northeast to the Grassfields, which was such a prolific source of slaves that coastal kings in Douala and Calabar, 130 miles apart, competed to procure them. Walter was from the heart of the region and had good connections from a book he had written about his people in the Kingdom of Kom. We were headed to meet the king. I hoped to talk to him about the history of his people and to see if he knew of my name. Then we planned to follow the old slave routes west through the Banyang Country to the river town of Mamfe, where slaves were loaded on canoes and sent to Old Calabar. I was tinkering with the idea of hiring a canoe and floating down the Cross River to Old Calabar myself. But Walter didn't seem so keen on the idea. "Nigeria is not safe, man."

The rally race continued as we flew up to a bend marked with multiple 50 kph signs. Our speedometer read 120 kph. Then I saw a small white sign that said, "Ici 7 Morts."

Gripping the handle above my window, I jammed my foot into the floorboard as if I had the brake and yelled, "Goddamn, slow down!" John slowed negligibly for the curve, and the tires barely held on as we rounded it. He was palpably angry with me now.

Soon the forest and plantations gave way to dry-grass fields planted with fruit trees and bunches of blue-green raffia palms, with thatched-roof houses and garden plots scattered about. I started to notice small compounds of two to eight or so mud buildings with steep pyramidal copper roofs, like shiny witches' hats lined up in rows. "Chief's wives," Walter explained. "Each one is for one wife's family. The traditional elites have multiple wives."

Some of the compounds were well built, with cinder block, modern windows, and satellite dishes, while others were made of mud-brick and dreary looking, just ground lifted into three dimensions. The quality didn't seem to correlate to the number of wives in the compound. "Some inherit them," Walter said. "If your brother dies and has four wives, they are your four wives. Some do it for prestige. I cannot manage one. There are some with five. And a king might have fifty."

We were now at the nebulous edge of the Muslim world, just a hundred miles from the coast. Maps of the old Arab trade showed two routes heading north from Cameroon across the desert to the Libyan port of Tripoli. Influences from Sudanese culture to the northeast mixed here with native animism and the Christianity that arrived with Europeans from the south.

"Are Christians ever polygamists?" I asked Walter.

"No, very, very rare. *Very*, very rare. But there are some."

"So your father wasn't a polygamist because of that?"

"Yes, but mostly because *his* father was a Catholic and monogamist."

We climbed steep switchbacks to a high hilly plateau. "This is the beginning of the Grassfields," Walter said grandly.

I hadn't even heard of the place a year before, but now it was a fabled land in my mind. The air was hazy, and from a distance the dry brown grass and stands of eucalyptus reminded me of southern California. I had John stop so I could relax for a moment and take in the view. A clear creek lined with elephant grass trickled through a patchwork of garden plots of every color. Banana leaves luffed in a balmy breeze, and children played in the shade of a tree next to their thatched hut. It was a beatific scene and, for a moment, I imagined it broken by slave raiders coming and dragging those children into oblivion. What a horror that must have been. Having children of my own made it hard to fathom.

From there we drove to a research station where foreign anthropologists stay, and picked up a Toyota Land Cruiser and a new driver, Ernest, heading farther into the grassy mountains of Kom. Ernest was a lanky young man whose name fit his personality.

"You know Ernest has an international driver's license," Walter told me. "This is very rare. He drove in Abidjan." I was glad to hear it.

The fertile meadowland around us had allowed the native population to expand, and it grew so crowded that it set off the Bantu migration and drew slavers from both north and south. It had been attractive to the European colonizers for the same reason: a breadbasket and labor pool only two hundred miles by road from the coast. Even today Kom produced more people than it could hold, and plantations throughout the country were worked by Kom laborers.

A light rain fell sporadically as we reached the mountains.

I gazed out the window at older women picking cassava from the slopes. Another group of women walked along the shoulder of the narrow road with bundles of firewood on their backs.

"We are in Lakom now, Kom country," Walter said. "Kom is 280 square miles, one-point-two million people of many different ethnicities now. Perhaps we can stay in my parents' house."

Walter's father was eighty and still worked as a yard laborer at a monastery. His mother grew yams and corn and cassava in the mountains. Walter had done well in school and had dreamed of going to the university, but his family couldn't afford to send him. So he had gone to work for a year with an uncle on a Dutch plantation in the coastal forest, earning about $30 a month. He then got a job as a hospital janitor, and after two and a half years had saved enough to go to the university.

I reflected on my own youth, where all the obstacles seemed self-induced. Walter came from a village of subsistence farmers with no electricity, and by sheer force of will and intellect he was about to get his PhD from a prestigious university in Europe. The American Dream that had eluded my family for three centuries he had found in Cameroon. And Cameroon, while nothing like the failed states in the region, was no beacon of opportunity. It was low on the United Nations Human Development Index, with a life expectancy of fifty years, six years average schooling, and $2,197 per capita income.

I asked Walter what the king's role was in Kom and whether his authority was recognized by the national government. He explained that the *fon* is the spiritual leader of the people but that his power has been greatly eroded and he doesn't govern them. The *fon* had absolute power until the British set up their colonial administration and became the titular owners of all the land in Kom.

I asked if the current *fon* had many wives.

"Whoooo," he responded. Until the 1970s, Walter explained, it was said the *fon* could point at a girl and she belonged to the *fon*. "But then controversy over the suggestion that he had hundreds of wives led a UN mission to interview him and he claimed to have only three hundred. But he really had only about eighty. The delegation told the wives that any who wished to leave could do so, and about forty did."

"How many does he have now?" I asked.

"This one, he might have fifty. No one really knows. He does not even know them all. . . . The *fon* is a practicing Roman Catholic. It is difficult to reconcile such ambiguities in someone with many wives who remains a Catholic. When I looked at his baptism card, it showed he never got married in church."

"So is the marriage just ceremonial?" I asked. "Do the women have other men on the side?"

He put his hands up and smiled coyly, as if it were anybody's guess. "These women all have children."

Suddenly, coming around a bend, Ernest lost control of the Land Cruiser and we spun off the road and lurched violently into a deep ditch, careening up the far side, bouncing hard off rocks, and coming to a rest in deep mud under a mango tree.

Walter turned to me with wide eyes and said, "Well, I am a *little* stressed now."

Ernest looked *very* stressed. He put the jeep in reverse and tried to gun out of the mud, but we only dug in deeper. Men came out of their huts, and the driver of another car stopped to try to help.

They put sticks and rocks under the tires. Earnest floored the engine as Walter and I and the men rocked the vehicle from side to side. The spinning tires put up an acrid smoke but got no grip. Finally, after a good half hour, the driver of the other car took charge, putting it into reverse and punching it. He jolted down the center of the ditch, getting momentum, and, miraculously, spun back onto the road.

We were back on our way to meet the king.

Higher in the mountains, as the rain let up, we descended a thousand feet into the Valley of Too Many Bends and came up on the other side through plots of pumpkin and flowering coffee and through the village of Njinikom, where Walter grew up. We continued to the pleasant little town of Fundong, where we stopped to get a bottle of local Casanova wine to offer the *fon*. Following a rutted dirt and rock road into the mountains, we passed old stone colonial buildings with signs announcing "Cash and Accounting Office" and "Secretary" over the doors. From there the road climbed more steeply through ranchland, and we slowed to the pace of a mule.

"You see the strategy, it's very difficult to get to the palace," Walter said. "The longest tribal resistance against the Germans came from the Kom, seven months. The Germans couldn't even find the palace." Near the mountain's peak we came into a lush cloud forest. "When the Germans finally did locate the palace, the *fon* had moved higher into the mountains. They looted all the artwork he had."

The road ended at a cluster of mud-brick and stone buildings. The king apparently drove an Audi coupe, which inexplicably got up the mountain.

Several young men in ill-fitting, threadbare sweaters and sweatshirts ran up and greeted Walter and Ernest. It was cold now, with the light fading and a wind coming up. We were at 6,300 feet. The men were barefoot or wore plastic flip-flops. They guided us past the wives' quarters, a dozen or so long rectangular buildings with black walls and peaked tin roofs. Women cooked on fires outside. Reaching an open plaza, we were at the king's court.

In the shadows, the king sat in a brick pergola, glowering and gripping his cane.

Three stadium-style rows of steps surrounded the courtyard, backed by stone longhouses, with eaves held up by columns of intricately carved wood. We joined four men and a woman waiting for an audience with the *fon* on benches under the eaves. Walter and Ernest put on black stocking caps, similar to the type you might rob a bank with. This was protocol when talking with the king. "Do I need one?" I asked.

"No, only Kom."

The king's throne was just a wood chair covered in a blanket.

The palace guard motioned to Walter, who bowed as he walked across the courtyard to the side of his throne. I hadn't expected such formality. Walter talked to the eighty-year-old *fon* for five minutes and waved me to come over. I suddenly got nervous. This whole scene was so strangely off the grid of my known world.

"Make sure to bow as you cross," Ernest whispered.

I walked low across the paving stones, performing my first bow since square-dancing in the third grade. The *fon* stared at me impassively with clenched lips. A glass Baltimore Orioles mug sat on a little shelf next to his chair, along with a small brown bottle of Marula Fruit Cream Liqueur and a bag of Bic disposable razors. He spoke in Kom as Walter translated. "He said he is happy you came and he apologizes that the palace is dirty."

"Tell him thank you and, no, it is very nice."

I asked Walter to tell him a little of my story and ask him if he knew anything about the Mozingo name. Walter started speaking to him in Kom and I heard him say "Mozingo."

The king pushed out his lower lip and shook his head. "He doesn't know anything of this name," Walter said.

Walter resumed speaking to the *fon* and then turned to me and said, "Okay, you can go back."

As I shuffled back to the bench, the *fon* motioned to the woman waiting on the other side of the throne. "She's one of the princesses," Ernest whispered. She got on her knees before the *fon,* cupping her hands in front of her mouth, and he poured Marula Cream into them and also directly into her mouth. "A blessing," Ernest explained. This is what the others waiting were also here for. The *fon* invited Walter to receive a blessing, and Ernest gasped in giddy excitement for him.

Then Walter waved to me, and Ernest gasped again. "He wants to bless you!"

I knelt before the *fon* and the Marula tasted like Baileys Irish Cream, a welcome surprise.

When I rejoined Walter on the bench, he said, "That is a very high honor. He never does that to people he does not know."

We were then taken to a dark bare room to eat some stew. The young men in sweaters appeared, and Walter explained that they were princes. He advised that I should give them some money. I gave them $20.

With the *fon* having fifty wives, I calculated that there could be upward of two hundred princes. I chuckled, recalling the speculation that Edward was an African prince.

As we returned to the Land Cruiser, Walter explained some of the history he and the *fon* had discussed. "The story is that the Kom followed the path of a python here. They had been living to the north, when the Fulani people, thought to have originated in Senegal, nearly two thousand miles west, had started jihad in about 1804.

"The jihad drove the Kom to a place where they cohabitated with the Babessi people, and over time the Kom population began overwhelming that of the Babessi. So the chief of Babessi devised a plan to trick the chief of Kom. The Babessi chief argued that the populations of both people were growing too large and would overcome the chiefs. They would both build a hut and they would put many of their own kinsmen in their hut and burn it. The *fon* of the Kom constructed his hut the traditional way, with one door, but the *fon* of the Babessi constructed his hut with two doors. Both huts were set ablaze, but the Babessi escaped out of the back door.

"When the Kom realized what had happened, he told his people he was going to commit suicide by hanging himself in the forest and that when his body decomposed, all the maggots would turn to fish in a pool of water. The Babessi hunter will discover the pool of water full of fish and go to his *fon* and a royal hunt would be organized. But no Kom should go fishing. For right as they would go fishing, the pool would turn upside down, and everyone would drown. From there the path of the python, the dead *fon* incarnate, would develop. The Kom would follow his path through the grass until it disappeared, in Nkar, where the Kom people stayed. After some time, it appeared again and they went on to Noni, where they settled for a while. Then they went to Djottin, and then to Akeh, and then here, to Lakom."

He pointed to where the trail we were walking bent back down to the road. "That is where the python path ended."

I asked him what he knew of the documented history of the people. "The jihads of 1804 did occur, and many of the peoples up there fled to the Grassfields. The people already here were dispelled or absorbed. Throughout the nineteenth century, the Kom waged a war of expansion, subjugating weaker neighbors and bringing ten kingdoms under them."

We walked up to a ridge where you could look down the Valley of Too Many Bends. I lingered while the rest walked back toward the cars.

I had crossed the sea to find Edward's homeland and his past, as if those two notions were fixed in time and space. But of course, he and his ancestors had their own pasts, and movements, and lost homelands. The thread I was following from across the world in California did not end or begin here. It went back forever, to the Rift Valley, Gondwanaland, the primordial soup. But the only accounts of Africa at the time Edward left it were distorted, seen through the spyglass of slave traders, and missionaries, most of whom had barely stepped foot in the interior, had little understanding of the people, and knew nothing of their history. And with no written record before those spyglass accounts, the thread simply blurred and wobbled out of view beyond that.

Chapter 18

Take Me to Old Calabar

The pavement ended after the village of Bali. We were dropping off the Bamenda plateau into a gorge of dense, primordial rain forest. Baobab trees lorded above the canopy like silver-skinned giants, and the jungle bugs sawed and screamed.

The road narrowed into a thin ribbon of ruts and mud holes. Nothing but high-clearance vehicles or motorcycles could pass. We had Dennis at the wheel today, a family man in his late forties, and a truly good driver. The Chinese were building a trans-African highway through here, from Mombasa on the Indian Ocean to Nigeria on the Atlantic. Every half hour or so we came upon a stretch of wide road cut in the middle of the forest, with dump trucks and excavators parked alongside and quarries dug out of the mountainside. Glum Chinese laborers watched us as we lurched by. We passed the occasional mud hut with blackened doorjambs and women and children sitting outside. The children would scream and wave in delight, while the women stared stoically, perhaps as their ancestors did when the slave convoys passed through.

This place would soon leap forward hundreds of years, for better or worse.

In the early afternoon we entered a valley of oil palms and stopped in the old slave-trading town of Widikum. There was only one restaurant, an open-air wooden stand, on the red mud road. We parked and sat down at the table. The proprietress, a big woman with a colorful skirt, opened the lid on an aluminum pot. "Porcupine," Walter said.

I had expected that this might be the case. Porcupine was a staple in these parts, as was monkey. Consuming them was illegal, but federal rule was marginal out here, and the people had no other source of meat.

I leaned into the pot and grabbed a piece. Up close, it looked more like skin and gristle than meat. The outside was black and mottled like a dog's snout and covered in little black hairs. My stomach flexed.

"We just shot it yesterday," the woman said.

I ripped a piece off with my teeth and thought cleansing thoughts— the cold ocean, a gin martini—until it was all the way down. I glanced at Walter's piece, which looked more like goat meat, which I generally liked. "Maybe I should have grabbed the ribs," I said.

"No, that is a very good piece you have," he said. "I'll take it." He gave me a chunk of his in exchange, which tasted like spare ribs.

Farther down the road, we washed down lunch with glasses of palm wine that put me to sleep in the backseat.

At the end of the day, we pulled into Mamfe and found a hotel in an old colonial neighborhood right on a bluff above the Cross River. Women were washing laundry on the rocks, and canoes with and without motors were ferrying bananas, cocoa gourds, vegetables, sand, jugs of gasoline. Mamfe was a point of embarkation for the villages in the vast lowland forests to the west. Calabar lay on the other side of that wilderness, roughly 250 miles downstream.

Walter said he had once met a man from here who was a judge and knew the history better than anyone else. He described him to the hotel manager. "Judge Edjua, yes. He lives just up the road," the man said.

We walked up there just after dark. The judge lived in a Western-style house with louvered windows and tile. His wife opened the door. The judge was seventy-five and sat in a chair in plaid shorts, holding a carved cane and watching television. He looked robust and sported shockingly black hair for his age. He vaguely remembered Walter, who explained that they had met once before. Inviting us to sit, he opened a bottle of red wine from Napa, explaining that one of his six living children, a daughter, worked as a nurse in California. We talked about

America for a while, and then what I was doing here, and we came to the subject of the slave trade.

"It is not true that slaves were not strong so they were captured," he explained. "The towns at night, the invaders came and set the houses on fire. People ran out into the dark. Armed men captured and tied them up and took them to the river. In this kind of attack you can't say the men were inferior.

"My father, Phillip Edjua, was a slave trader. He would buy the slaves and sell them down the river."

"Your father?" I asked, startled.

"Yes, before I was born, into the 1920s."

"Where would the slaves go?" I asked.

"To Calabar."

"But the Atlantic slave trade was over by then."

"This is just what I know," he responded. "The slaves came from the north of the Grassfields. They walked them here and put them in canoes."

This was astounding, that a man drinking Napa wine with a daughter in California was the son of slave trader.

"I asked my father about the circumstances by which slaves were captured. He said there were many. A child of a noble family might be made a slave if it is someone who did funny things, a sex maniac or something. This is an incongruous fellow. The plan is to get rid of him. He goes down to Calabar with a friend. 'You stay here. I will come back.' He is taken to places he can never recognize and never come back.

"There was a man named Akoini."

"Yes," Walter said. "We knew of him in Kom. He was legendary."

"He would take two or three children in a bag. He came to the river to sell. I was told this direct by Akoini's son."

"And your father bought them?"

"Yes. This was not the same as slavery in America. I grew up in Widikum. Some slaves were kept by their slave masters. They develop a relationship with the family. Your father might be a slave master. He may have slaves on his land that are good. He may give them land with palm nuts.

"As a magistrate, I dealt with cases where the younger generation was trying to get rid of slaves who were given land. You cannot. If the slave was good he protected your family. That is a consideration the children might not know. There could be a respect between the slave and slave master.

"I visited my father's slave, Menge Tambong. He was a freed man. My father freed him. He recognized we were the slave master's children and he showed great respect."

"Amazing," Walter said.

Before I left, I asked the judge about my name, and he said it probably came from the coast, around Rio del Rey, between Mt. Cameroon and Calabar. He also told us that the canoes that brought the slaves to Calabar had launched from a spot a few miles down the river. "Yes, just under the bridge, where the canoes are still today," he said.

I determined that I'd head there the next day to look into hiring a motorized canoe to take me to Calabar.

As Walter and I walked back to our hotel in the swampy night, Walter explained, "Akoini was Kom. He brought his children here. But you see how when you get oral history everything tends to get exaggerated. Three boys in a bag, how is this possible? The version I heard in the Grassfields was the same except that he didn't carry them in a bag, but he lured them along with fried peanuts."

This kidnapping was described as far back as the 1780s, by the British surgeon Alexander Falconbridge, who worked on slave ships coming to Old Calabar and elsewhere. "I was likewise told by a negroe woman that as she was on her return home, one evening, from some neighbors . . . she was kidnapped," he wrote. "The transaction happened a considerable way up the country, and she had passed through the hands of several purchasers before she reached the ship. A man and his son, according to their own information, were seized by professed kidnappers, while they were planting yams, and sold for slaves."

Falconbridge didn't know of Mamfe but was told of a slave "fair" upriver "more than 200 miles from the sea coast." The captive Africans he questioned said they had traveled far to arrive at the fair.

"Many negroes . . . asserted that they have travelled during the revolution of several moons (their usual method of calculating time)."

As we ate fried chicken and french fries at an outdoor café, Walter poured a dash of beer on the ground before he ate. I gave him a curious look. "For my ancestors," he explained. "There is a serious link between the present and the past. The Kom believe they live through their ancestors. My name Nkwi came from a very important ancestor, George Nkwi, my father's maternal uncle. He died just before I was born.

"Amongst the Kom, ancestors are resurrected, one, in naming, and two, in libations. I pour a libation on the ground before I eat for my ancestors and the ancestors of this land."

I gnawed at my chicken and listened.

"It is believed that ancestors live in the ground and can see you."

"How does this fit with your Catholicism?" I asked.

"I hardly ever pray to the Western God," he said. "Catholic doesn't mean you believe in anything."

"I guess this is true," I said. "My dad doesn't believe in God, but he still claims to be Catholic."

"God is all that is good. But what does he look like? It is your ancestors."

I mulled this over.

"Very interesting. . . . Because we are all created by them?"

He broke up his chicken leg and picked at it. "My kids are never sick," he said. "I see my neighbors' children. They are always going to the hospital with malaria. I am blessed by my ancestors."

At three in the morning, I woke up in a knot of sweaty sheets to hear two herons calling each other across the river in great honks. My room was crawling with fleas, the air like a dog's breath. I opened the window and looked out. The river gurgled through the rocks below and roosters crowed far off, the faint sounds magnifying the swallowing silence of the jungle night. Infinite stars washed a perfect blackness.

A man's voice started crying out from the forest, beginning soft and low and lifting to fill the void, achingly sad and strong. It took me awhile to realize he was the town crier, and his singing conveyed the news of births and deaths and judgments of the prior day. Not so long ago, he might have called out the names of those who had disappeared down the river. In my half-awake state, his lilting voice seemed as if coming from antiquity.

That morning Walter and I drove down the river to where the canoes launched. We met a canoe pilot who took us out for a jaunt downstream as he decided if he could take me all the way to Calabar. He told me the river used to be filled with hippos, but when the canoes were equipped with outboard motors, the noise drove them into more isolated creeks. The plank-hewn canoes could easily hold twenty people, but mostly carried produce from the small farms carved out of the forest and jugs of cheap gasoline from across the border. The river was still a thoroughfare for commerce between Cameroon and eastern Nigeria.

We passed a raft loaded with planks of mahogany, cedar, and walnut. "The people will set up a tent on it and cook and eat and go to Calabar," said the pilot. "It might take two weeks."

"How long would it take you to get there?"

"Two days."

"Is it dangerous?"

"Eehhhh . . ." He was thinking. "No."

"So can you take me there?"

He pondered this for a moment. "Yes," he said, but not convincingly.

The canoes didn't usually go all the way to Calabar, especially at this time of year, when the river was low. A couple sections of rapids were dangerous.

Back on the bank under the bridge, the pilot conferred with his friends. One man said he did it all the time and was sure we could make it. I came close to saying "Let's go," but Walter thought the trip would be foolhardy and would not be traveling with me if I went.

The thought of traversing this ancient rain forest in a canoe, along the same river the slaves drifted down, was intoxicatingly appealing to me. But the pilot now seemed fairly certain he didn't want to do it, and the thought struck me that if something went wrong, I might find myself stranded in *a bad way*. So we headed back to the coast in the

Land Cruiser instead, on a red trench of mud and clay that cut through the buzzing lowland bush. The route sidled the monkey forests of the Monenguba Mountains, and lunch in the village of Nguti was predictably monkey in a pepper soup.

Many of the homes along this road had graves right in front of them. "When their children are ready to go to school, they bathe them on the graves so their ancestors protect them," Walter said.

The next day we descended some coastal mountains to Likulu Bay and a scattering of homes that composed the village of Bimbia, in the heart of what was once one of the main coastal kingdoms that traded with the Europeans. The territory was nearly empty now, reverting to tall grass and forest.

Two local men guided us through a bamboo grove to the ruins of what they said was a slave fort. I had never read of a slave fort in Bimbia, but these remains certainly looked very old and European. Piles of gray brick lay next to standing columns mottled with lichen, and a few cobblestone walls with arched windows and doorframes still stood upright. A stone staircase rose to a fallen second floor. There appeared to have been a whole complex of buildings following the slope to the water, all now hidden under the canopy. Walter said he too did not know of a slave fort in Bimbia. I began to suspect it was the ruins of an early English mission in Cameroon.

The men said hunters always knew this was here, but that the community had just recently cut the trail to get to it, hoping it might draw tourists. "A group of black American tourists came here," one of the men was saying. "They were crying, 'My grandfather might have been here.'"

Walter returned to Buea to get some work done. In the middle of the night, I set off alone on the ferry for Old Calabar, which turned out to be a busy modern city. I checked out a slave museum, then took a water taxi up the Cross River a ways and had dinner and palm wine with Ivor Miller, an American anthropologist studying how secret Nigerian societies were re-created by slaves in Cuba and survive in both Calabar and Havana today. "There were no large kingdoms around here, so each village was governed by a secret society called Ekpe," he said. "Ekpe means leopard, which is a sign of royalty. Every village had an Ekpe lodge that decided matters of trade and justice and land use."

"So what form did they take in Cuba?"

"There they are called Abakuá. Free black artisans in Havana started it. They had a formal initiation and titles and an oath of secrecy. People have likened them to the Masons. But their original function was to purchase slaves . . . out of slavery."

"Have you been to the societies in both places?"

"Yeah, I learned about this first in Cuba, where they have long been part of the liberation movement. But I haven't been initiated there. I was initiated here and am kind of ambassador to the Caribbean Ekpe."

These bits of African culture that survive in America always fascinated me, and I wished I could find some African tradition that came down with our name to the present.

"Are the similarities between the two really that clear?" I asked.

He took a swig of palm wine.

"It's amazing. The Abakuá retained what they brought from Africa with a remarkable kind of orthodoxy. And Ekpe in Calabar will listen to speech and music by Abakuá and actually understand it. They recognize the rhythm, and many of the words."

We walked to an outside bar and continued our talk into the night.

The next morning at dawn, as I was standing at the back of the line to take the ferry back to Cameroon, a ferry worker came up to me and said, "Come, sir, come."

I groaned, wondering what elaborate African version of colonial bureaucracy I was going to be dragged through, having had a long interview with the Nigerian intelligence service the day before. "I'm good." I said. "I've got everything handled."

"Come, come," he insisted.

I realized I had no choice but to follow him. At the front of the line, he said, "Stand here."

It became distressingly clear that my assumption about bureaucracy had been dead wrong: they were going to board me, the sole white person on these docks, before the two hundred African people in line. A middle-aged woman in a black church dress standing in line broke into a rightful fury. "Why are you boarding him first!" she screamed at the man.

"Madam," he said.

"Why are *you* boarding *him* first?" she demanded. A younger woman traveling with her chimed in in agreement.

"Calm down," the man said, waving his hands downward.

"Look, I don't want this," I said, mortified.

"Is it because of the color of his skin?" the older woman yelled.

"Ma'am, please be quiet."

I backed away, but two ferry workers said, "No, no, no, come, sir! Come, sir!" and ushered me in.

As I found a seat up top, a crew member came up to me and said, "Welcome, sir, is the air-conditioning all right? Just tell me if it's not."

The crew member who had brought me to the front of the line came up to me and said, "Don't apologize to anyone. Don't talk to anyone."

The two women had followed him up. "I don't understand this thinking, sir. What is this *thinking*?" the older woman asked him.

"Please be quiet, ma'am," he said as they took seats. He returned to the stairwell, where he lurked to see if they molested me.

I leaned over toward them. "Look, I agree with you," I said. "I was just standing at the back of the line and he just came. I didn't know what he wanted. This is very embarrassing. I'm sorry."

"You see, thank you," the older woman said.

I still felt guilty, as I should have foreseen what was happening.

The man came back to me. "You don't need to talk to them."

"He didn't even ask for it," the younger woman chided him. "She was just asking, 'What is this mentality?'"

That afternoon, I rode a motorcycle back to Bimbia and paid a couple of young fishermen to take me out to uninhabited Nicolls Island in the bay. Local lore held that the kings kept unruly slaves on the island before they were sold to the Europeans. When the transatlantic trade was banned, British warships from their base on the offshore island of Fernando Po used Nicolls Island to hide behind before attacking outgoing slave ships. In 1837, they stopped a Portuguese slaver, the *Cobra de Africa*, as it left Bimbia headed for Cuba with 110 slaves, including a four-foot-three-inch, nine-year-old boy whose name they spelled Mahsingah. They took the slaves to Freetown, Sierra Leone, founded by British abolitionists specifically for freed slaves.

We crossed the waters in a dugout as a gusty wind whipped chop against the side and sprayed us. The two fishermen paddled quickly. We landed under trees on a little black sand beach, and they told me there were artifacts of the slave trade on the ridge above. We hiked up the broken lava slopes and picked through the scree, finding two old bottles of thick green glass and pieces of ceramic plates and cups. The bottles looked handblown, but who knew how old they were.

The bay was as beautiful as any I had ever seen, surrounded by cliffs shimmering with emerald foliage. It was hard to envision the perdition that once reigned here. Slaves waiting to be purchased were usually starving and shackled, knowing nothing about the strange white men purchasing them, or where they were going. But they seemed to know they would be forever severed from all they ever knew. The ship surgeon Falconbridge wrote that many went insane and tried to drown themselves:

> While I was one day ashore at Bonny [about eighty miles west of Calabar], I saw a middle aged stout woman, who had been brought down from a fair the preceding day, chained to the post of a black trader's door, in a state of furious insanity. On board a ship in Bonny River, I saw a young negroe woman chained to the deck, who had lost her senses . . . In a former voyage, on board a ship to which I belonged, we were obliged to confine a female negroe, of about twenty three years of age, on her becoming a lunatic. She was afterwards sold during one of her lucid intervals.

He watched one woman eagerly seize "some dirt from off an African yam, and put it in her mouth, seeming to rejoice at the opportunity of possessing some of her native earth."

There was a sadness in the solitude of the place now, in each sigh of the wind. It felt like a spot even the spirits abandoned. The fishermen took me back to the beach where I jumped into the warm water alone.

Swimming in distant lands was baptismal, infusing me with the essence of the place in a way treading across it could not. I did it in Virginia and Indiana. If Raven Creek had been deep enough, I would have done it there in Kentucky. I floated on my back and listened to the metallic sift of the sand roll back and forth with the tidal surge. The Atlantic smelled and tasted the same as it did in the estuaries of Virginia, brackish and algal. I hadn't found any hard information about Edward, but I felt that I had crossed a sensory breach, taking a major step, however intangible, toward understanding his story.

Walter rejoined me and we spent my last morning in Cameroon walking through overgrown, snake-infested cemeteries, looking for Mozingos. We found all sorts of Mousingas and Musingas, as well as glassy-eyed young men ominously following us around. Flying out, I knew my best chance of finding the place of Edward's birth still lay ahead, in Angola.

Chapter 19

In Memory of the
First Baptized, 1491

The only way I could get an invitation to Angola was by hiring a registered tour guide for a few days, which I did, further draining my accounts in pursuit of Edward. While I was at home making my preparations for the next trip, my dad called me one afternoon. I was in the kitchen doing the dishes, and for some reason, seeing his number on my cell phone at that time of day, I knew immediately what he had to say. I didn't want to pick up.

When I did, there was a long pause, and then my dad simply said, "Joe died."

He could barely talk, and neither could I. He gave me the particulars. "Okay. I'll call you tonight," I managed.

His older brother, my uncle Joe, weighed close to four hundred pounds most of his life and had stents throughout his heart, missing toes from diabetes, and a colostomy bag from colon cancer. It was amazing that he had lived so long; he just passed his seventieth birthday, unconscious in the hospital. He'd never married, so we were his closest family. When he retired from working as an information technology manager for the City of Los Angeles, he had moved into a double-wide mobile home near my parents' home. When we visited him, he took my son on golf cart rides into the hills behind his neighborhood and,

259

in the past few months, our daughter too. He took photos as we taught Blake how to swim in the community pool and drove up to our house for every birthday party, just as he had always been there for me and my brother when were young. He used to bring us See's Candies, but lately he would bring a cake from the locally famous V. G. Donut & Bakery, where he probably spent too much time. He was a gentle soul, whom I would miss dearly, and I wanted desperately to think I would see him again. But by most measures of the word I was an atheist, and I couldn't see how I ever would.

Just four days after his funeral, I sat on a piece of driftwood on a desolate bay in northern Angola. The finality of my uncle's passing had yet to sink in, but it clawed across my consciousness. I was exhausted from three days of travel and an eight-hour time difference. We had two hundred miles of dusty, bone-rattling road to cover that day. The ocean was surprisingly cool for being just seven degrees south of the equator. The land rolled gently, a dry savannah with stands of thorny trees and fan palms, almost black in the midday sun. A square white jaw of cliff jutted into the blue-gray sea.

Translucent ghost crabs skittered across the sand with their claws in the air as if they were ready to beat down the surf. When the water retreated, they chased it away as if they had bullied it into submission. They gamboled around until a bigger wave rolled up and wiped them all away. I couldn't tell where they went, but one by one they popped out of holes, ready to fight again. Why were they doing this? I could have come to this beach a hundred years ago, or perhaps thousands of years ago, and seen the same endless pantomime of life and death.

The thought of death had terrified me since I became a father, both my children's and my own. I had been struggling with its specter more sharply since the Haiti earthquake. A girl screaming for her mother as the woman was pulled dead from the rubble and thrown into a rusty wheelbarrow. How can that be possible? My uncle's departure drilled home that death is a resounding omission, a lacking, as impossible to grasp as air. We lash out in the face of death for a future to cling to—

heaven, reincarnation, transmigration. *We'll see him soon.* I just couldn't believe in that future. I did find slight comfort, though, in what Walter had told me about how his people thought of their ancestors. They were God, in that they were the Creator, and we became part of God in death, as our descendants went on. They were part of the soul within us, they had to be.

On this trip, I was headed to M'banza Kongo, in modern-day Angola, traveling with Paul Wesson, a British expat who operated as the only real guide in the country. While his invitation letter got me my visa, it turned out his dual-gas-tank Land Cruiser was the only way I could have gotten around, given the lack of gas stations in the country.

Angola ironically ranked as one of the most expensive countries in the world to live and travel in, thanks to the oil boom there. A hamburger and a Coke cost $30; a dreary hotel room in the capital of Luanda ran more than $300. And still it remained one of the poorest countries in the world, just below Haiti on the UN Development Index.

I had seen the effects of the boom the day before in Luanda, a bewildering amalgam of fetid slums and towering glass skyscrapers. The onslaught of oil cash was fast obliterating the old colonial tile roofs and cast-iron balconies near the bay. Paul said a good condo in town ran for about $1.5 million. The streets were jammed with imported SUVs that cost three times what they do in the United States.

The boom was a free-for-all. The blue-glass skyscrapers were served by narrow lanes of broken pavement or dirt. No one took credit cards. Traffic simply locked up for much of the day, and there was nowhere to park. Paul and I circled for an hour to find a spot near my guesthouse. He said normally if he had a meeting, his driver dropped him off and looped around until he was done. Many of the middle class as well as expats had moved to master-planned communities sprouting up in the scrublands south of Luanda.

We had coffee at Club Naval, a yacht club on Luanda Island. Across a weedy vacant lot, docks were filled with speedboats with names like *Spicy*, *Bella Vida*, *Miss Texas*, and *Paradise*. Angolan children sailed small boats in the polluted green-brown water. Across the bay a sweep of beach where the slaves departed nearly three hundred years ago curved below the long porticos and red-tile roofs along the main avenue, the Marginal. Above that, concrete and glass edifices climbed the hills into the Ciudad Alta section. At least nineteen tower cranes pierced the skyline.

I tried to envision what Luanda would have looked like during the peak of the slave trade: reeking slave pens on the shore, the Brazilian ships they called *tumbeiros*, floating tombs, anchored at bay. In his book *Way of Death*, Joseph C. Miller described the destitution of both the Africans and the Portuguese who found themselves here:

> The traders often entered as desperate men, driven to Angola to recoup their fortunes after failures elsewhere. . . . They settled temporarily in the commercial quarter of the lower city; then within weeks or months the majority was carried off to the European graveyard on town's edge. . . . A few expatriates survived the fevers and enjoyed sufficient success handling goods and services in the town to leave for Brazil after a few years. Many more survivors found that their fortune again eluded them at Luanda and headed instead for the backlands to trade for slaves or, still unable to succeed even there, to cast their lot with the Africans. Only a Luso-African minority [the *pombeiros*] and their slaves accepted Luanda as their home. To nearly everyone else it was a place where every variety of flotsam and jetsam from three continents washed up on the shore, including not only people but also merchandise, spoiled wines, bad rum, flimsy textiles, faulty guns, and other goods unsalable elsewhere in the world but sent to Angola for dumping on African markets. The stench of decay and death was everywhere.

A promontory flanked the bottom of the bay and tapered down to the land bridge that linked Luanda Island to the city. At the tip of the bluff, the crenellated walls of the fort, built in 1618, stood squat in the spiny scrub, the preeminent symbol of Europe's dismal four-hundred-year-long reign here. I wondered if Edward looked up from one of those stinking pens and pondered that very castle.

The Kingdom of Kongo had nominally claimed the mainland here before the Portuguese took it in 1576. It kept the six-mile barrier island where it collected its *nzimbu* shells until they seized that in 1649. The colonists didn't begin settling the interior until the late nineteenth century, when they used forced labor to build large sugar, coffee, and cotton plantations. All along, the traders, soldiers, missionaries, and settlers were mostly men who, sleeping with and marrying African women over four centuries, produced a sizable population of *mestiços* (about 250,000 today). After World War II, Portugal encouraged families to settle in Angola, and in the next thirty years the white population rose from 44,000 to over 400,000. Nearly all of them left in a mass exodus when Angola won its independence in 1974 and descended into twenty-seven years of civil war. But now they were returning by the thousands to take advantage of business opportunities as the country boomed.

After coffee, we went up the hill to meet Simao Souindoula, a prominent historian and head of the UNESCO Slave Route project in Angola. He was a big, paunchy man with a gray goatee and booming voice. When I told him about my quest, he said, "In the Kongo region, this is a very common name. The word can mean *life* or *journey*. It's a twisting journey, it's got complications. The difference between *Nzinga* and *Mozinga* is just a matter of pronunciation. If one says *zinga zinga*, it means someone is having problems. Queen Nzinga was called that because the umbilical cord was wrapped around her neck."

"Yes, I heard that. But she was not from Kongo. She was from Ndongo."

"Yes, but Kikongo and Kimbundu are very similar languages, like Spanish and Portuguese. Ndongo was once a vassal to Kongo and paid a tribute to the king."

"Where were the slaves coming from in 1644?" I asked.

"Everywhere—Kongo, Ndongo, Matamba. This was all Angola produced. Luanda didn't do anything except warehouse slaves from the interior. Slaves were held throughout the city. Even churches were used to hold them."

I asked if he knew anything about why Edward would have kept the name. "The pope decided the slaves should be baptized as they left, and they often were given a new Christian name, but kept their surname to keep some identity," he responded. "Nzinga was a royal name, so it was even more important." I nodded but I didn't understand why the slave captains would allow this.

"You are from a royal family," he added.

"So do you think he was Kongo or Mbundu?" I asked.

"Kongo. This is where that name started. You must go there."

"We're headed there tomorrow," I said.

At last I had found what seemed a sure thread to follow.

Thornton and his wife, Linda Heywood, the American professors who knew as much as anyone about the slave trade from Angola, had already told me the patterns of the trade in the early 1640s suggested Edward was from the Kongo. The fact that the name was pronounced with an M was further evidence, as that was the pronunciation still in use in the Kongo at the time of his arrival in Jamestown, whereas the N pronunciation was the norm by then in Ndongo, as evidenced by Queen Nzinga.

Souindoula made a call to the top cultural official in M'banza Kongo, the historic capital of the Kongo Kingdom, which was three hundred miles to the northeast, near the border with the Democratic Republic of Congo. He told him to greet me when we arrived and arrange anything I needed. Paul mentioned later that he heard him tell the man, in Portuguese, "Hey, we have a brother here from America. Unfortunately he is white."

And so there Paul and I were, driving up the coast on a bright day after a drizzly marine layer burned off, moving slowly. The solid red line on my map turned out to be two wheel tracks through a battered badland of hardened clay and jutting chunks of old asphalt. It looked like it might actually be smoother driving over the open land. The rare spots of plain old washboard came as a short respite for my wincing back. I had expected a paved highway, as this was the main coastal road and connected the capital to the port city of Soyo, on the mouth of the Congo River, where vast amounts of oil were drilled offshore. And I expected to see villages and towns. But this part of the country was ravaged by the war and depopulated. Bridges were blown up, plantations abandoned, and roads mined. I had never seen such empty expanses of fertile, grassy land. The only signs of humanity were the road and the blue tsetse fly nets in the dust-caked trees. We'd travel an hour without seeing a soul, and then come upon a cluster of crude brush huts with rawboned families sitting listlessly under scraggly branches, then rattle back into the great wide open. Truckers who broke down waited for help sometimes for days. They carried bedrolls, food, water, and mosquito nets. "They're out here for a week sometimes," Paul said. "I've seen them rebuild an entire engine right there in the dirt."

Paul grew up in Hampshire, England, and moved to Angola in 1982, when he was twenty-five. He had lived through twenty years of war here, more than half of his adult life. He had told me this earlier on the phone, and I wondered if he had come here as a mercenary. It took a little convincing before I bought his story that he moved here to work as a commercial manager for Land Rover. He said his future looked limited in England, and it was all adventure here. Not to mention, the fighting was well outside Luanda, except for a brief siege in which he took refuge on a friend's yacht in the Atlantic.

Paul wore khaki shorts and a khaki shirt emblazoned with the logo of his company, Eco-Tur. Driving, he had a serious, rugged profile that reminded me of the actor Tom Wilkinson, but when he sat down to dinner in a canary-yellow Brazil football jersey and jeans, he changed persona, becoming vaguely reminiscent of Ricky Gervais. He clearly loved being out in the bush and drove the mangled road with cool precision.

The baobab trees were much shorter and fatter here than in Cameroon, with swollen trunks branching into stunted little arms and wispy crowns of foliage. They bent in every direction, and evoked human forms: a couple in a sinuous dance, children wrestling, a surly alpha male harrumphing, a woman yelling at her kids, an old man scrambling to get bees out of his hair.

By now I thought the chances were good that a young boy named Mozingo had played in a long-vanished village somewhere in these hills. From what I read, the villages were often surrounded by a hedge or palisade to keep out lions and leopards and stampeding elephants. The boy might have followed his mother into the field at sunrise to pull up cassava and vegetables, then returned to pound grain into flour. As he grew older he would have helped his father retie the grass roof, tap palm wine, and pound bark and leaves into cloth. They might have treaded quietly together through the high rasping grass, hunting antelope, zebra, and buffalo.

I could almost make out the silhouettes of a man and a boy in the forms of the baobabs, taking delicate steps through the heat shimmer in the distance. I envisioned a boy who grew to old age on Pantico Run, near Farmers Fork, with his set of ceramic plates, his candlestick and feather mattress, his two guns, and his fiddle. What a colossal bridge for a single life to have crossed.

The road turned inland at the sun-beaten colonial town of N'Zeto, strewn with colorful little homes with verandas, shutters, and tile roofs. The commercial district was faded and largely abandoned. A few buildings were riddled with bullet holes. We found a graveyard on a bluff over the river mouth and looked on the stones for variations of my name, but realized it had only interred the Portuguese. At least no one stalked us in this cemetery. We crossed a roaring river on an old metal bridge that could take only one vehicle at a time, and headed up into the mountains. The terrain turned lush and rugged as green valleys wended under rocky outcroppings and mesas. Sprawling acacias spread over the road like lampshades. In the ocher late afternoon light, the hillscape reminded me of Italy. We began to see clusters of houses. The Kongo people lived in long rectangular homes made of mud-brick walls and grass roofs and often painted their doors and window jambs bright blue. They cooked in communal outdoor ovens made of clay. They had fruit trees and livestock and little farms, all tightly hemmed in. The surrounding land was too dangerous to settle, as it was studded with land mines.

We rolled into M'banza Kongo at dusk. From the kingdom's early conversion to Christianity to independence from Portugal, the town had been called São Salvador. The accounts and illustrations I had seen of the royal city described it as perched high atop a mountain. In reality, it spread over the top of a gentle sloping hill that rose only about four hundred feet from the valley below.

We checked into the Hotel Estrela do Kongo, in the center of town, just up the road from the stone cathedral built in 1534.

After dinner, I poured the last whiskey I salvaged from a bottle that broke during the jarring ride. I sat on my bed and read some papers, piecing together a coherent story from what I knew about Kongo in the years of Edward's presumed departure.

The kingdom survived various invasions and civil wars and was probably more centralized than it had ever been. But it was openly fighting in the north with its most powerful vassal, the ruler of the province of Soyo, where a brisk trade in slaves ran out of its port of Mpinda at the mouth of the Congo River. The Count of Soyo had declared independence from the Kongo king, Garcia II, in São Salvador, and both rulers were vying for the military support of the Dutch to fight each other and the Portuguese. The Dutch were at war with Spain and Portugal and had been attacking their holdings across the Atlantic. They took the rich sugar colony of Pernambuco, Brazil, in 1630, the castle at São Jorge da Mina in 1637, and the fort in Luanda in 1641. And they established new colonies on Curaçao in the southern Caribbean and St. Eustatius in the north, and New Netherland on the east coast of North America. By then the Dutch had already been trading in the Soyo port of Mpinda for years, reporting, "Here is no lack of ivory or slaves."

The Dutch signed a military alliance with the Kongo king against the Portuguese in 1642, which they hoped would "reestablish the slave trade" that had fallen off since 1639. The seceding Count of Soyo complained that weaponry they gave the Kongo king was used against his people as much as against the Portuguese. Both the count and the king sent diplomats to Luanda and across the seas to Brazil and north to Amsterdam to secure further allegiance with the Dutch. As gifts, they brought loads of slaves, often freeborn Kongo caught up in the turmoil of war.

Heywood and Thornton, digging through the records of the Dutch West India Company in The Hague, found numerous instances of slave-gift diplomacy. "Between the Dutch capture of Luanda and the end of

1643, [King] Garcia II sent the Company 1,200 slaves, along with a personal gift of 170 slaves to the director," they wrote. "In addition there were gifts from other Kongolese nobles, including smaller gifts from the Count of Soyo." A Dutch commercial factor in Luanda in 1642 informed the West India Company in Brazil that any Kongo who fled from combat was "reduced to slavery with his whole family." Garcia II, like his predecessor more than a century earlier, even lamented in a letter that slaves had become his country's very currency "in place of gold and silver and other things that serve as money in other places."

"In our simplicity, we gave place to that from which grows all the evils of our country," he wrote in 1643, perhaps the very year Edward left Africa.

I shuffled through some emails from Thornton and Heywood that I had printed.

Because Mozingo is not a place-name like Angola or Kongo, or simply the word Negro, they said it must be an actual personal name, which "suggests to us Edward was a noble and literate," Heywood wrote.

He had a reason and the intellectual means to keep the name.

"Kongo was a literate country in the seventeenth century, in that there were regular schools, though as elsewhere only people of a certain class attended school or became literate," Thornton wrote. "The Jesuits opened a college in São Salvador in 1625.

"Edward in English is equal to Duarte in Portuguese. . . . We think Duarte Mozinga was probably a lower level noble in Kongo. His noble position was probably a military one, and he was probably captured in a war and deported as a POW. In Kongo the army had two components, the archers and the heavy infantry. Archers were usually recruited en masse from the peasants of the country, and battles opened with the mass discharge of arrows against the enemy. . . . After this the heavy infantry would advance. They were armed with shields that went from the neck to the knee and carried curved bladed swords. The heavy infantry was considered to be noble and lived, we think, at public expense on salary."

Years ago, Thornton had conveyed this to one of the Mozingos, who had reached out to him while researching Edward. This is how the

"Bantu warrior" theory entered the family lore of the few willing to hear it. I wasn't sure Edward could have been old enough to be a soldier. But it was possible, or he might have been working on a baggage train following the soldiers, which were easy pickings.

But how did he come to have his name? Christianity had taken root in much of Kongo by that time and many people were baptized and boasted both Christian and African names. As I had learned earlier, African surnames mostly did not pass down from father to children like paternal family names in the West. More often, a person had a pair of given names indicating paternal descent. In this system, I would be "Joe son of Dave, son of Joe," and my son would be "Blake son of Joe, son of Dave, son of Joe." I glanced through Thornton's paper "Central African Names and African-American Naming Patterns," and ran across something that startled me.

In 1624, Garcia II's father was crowned king, representing "a new lineage" to the throne. To prove he had royal blood in him, he traced his lineage back a century and a half to the revered first Christian king of Kongo, doing so through his name, which was spelled by a Jesuit missionary at the time "Mobemba am-Camga, à-Mubîca, à-Zumba, à-Mobemba, à-Mozinga à ncu-à-Mutino." Translated: Mobemba, son of Camga, who was son of Mubîca, who was son of Zumba, who was son of Mobemba, who was son of Mozinga a Nkuwu the king.

I felt a key unlocking the door.

Earlier, it had seemed far-fetched to me that a man in Edward's time would have felt his name carried any currency, 138 years after that first Christian king had died. But here was a new king, just twenty years before Edward landed in Jamestown, trying to sanctify his own blood with the name, spelled at the time Mozinga.

In the morning Paul and I drove to the government center to meet the official whom Simao had called. The city was small, with a population of only 67,000, even though it was more than half a millennium old and the capital of the oil-rich province of Zaire. Acacias and fig trees shaded smoothly tarred streets, everything stained red with the laterite dust.

The midcentury buildings of the government complex sat among well-tended lawns and king palms. We met the official, a thin academic-looking man with a tan corduroy jacket and spectacles, and he sent for an assistant to take us to the elders who could talk about the kingdom's history.

We drove to the royal palace, which happened to be right next to our hotel. The Portuguese built it for their puppet king in the early 1900s, long after they took control of the region. It had a peaked tin roof and wraparound verandas and struck me as the epitome of tropical colonial architecture. I envisioned being met by a man with a gin-blossom nose and pith helmet.

We were standing on the same piece of land where, half a millennium before, Captain Rui de Sousa and his entourage were greeted with trumpeters and lance bearers and dancing women, and King Mozinga took up a handful of dirt, the same iron-red laterite, and rubbed it down the captain's breast as a sign of respect.

A man greeted us and pointed to the trees at the front of the yard. "Those are the sacred trees," he said. "Justice used to be dispensed there."

He took us into a meeting hall behind the palace, where four elders of the royal council enthusiastically greeted us and invited us to sit with them at a table. They were a dapper group, wearing wire-rimmed sunglasses and Aloha shirts with African motifs. They looked at my passport and conversed.

Paul struggled to understand them; apparently their Portuguese was rough.

"Yes, this name comes from here. This is equal to Nzinga," one said.

"It suffered a variation. Mujingo, we still have that name here," said another.

"In proper Kikongo, it is Nzinga. But the Portuguese couldn't say that."

I asked them what it meant, and they all immediately started drawing loose loops on the table with their fingers. This was untainted by translation. "It means a cord, something that binds people together."

A cord. The thread that had bound Mozingos for 368 years was now coming back full circle in my being here.

They gave me a tutorial in the lineage of the king and directed us to a local history professor, Pedro Gabriel. We met him in his cramped office, next to a discothèque called Delirius. He was a serious man in a charcoal suit and blood-red shirt, with good Portuguese, and he vigorously agreed that Mozinga was one way the name of the early kings would have been pronounced. "There were three main clans," he said. "Nzinga, Nunda, and Mpanza. The kings originated from this clan, Nzinga."

I asked if there were any old records in the city.

"No, the Jagas burned everything in the sixteenth century and the city was abandoned for many years in the seventeenth century."

I had read how this band of people, the Jagas, ransacked the country, how the nobility dispersed, how little oral tradition had survived from the old kingdom, and how most Kongo people learned of it from textbooks written by Catholic missionaries during the colonial period. Later the civil war drove many Kongo people to Zaire (once the Belgian Congo, now the Democratic Republic of Congo) and Congo-Brazzaville (the former French Congo), and even still they were finding themselves unceremoniously repatriated to Angola. As with the Powhatans, the only surviving accounts of their early history came from their European conquerors.

Gabriel said the slaves from here were taken by the Ndongo and that many Nzingas went that way, and many others were sold directly to the Portuguese and Dutch at the ports of Luanda and Mpinda, near the mouth of the Congo River.

"The slaves needed to be baptized to give the people more fear of the people they were working for," he said. "So if they were going to disobey them, they were going to disobey God."

He said Edward, either as Duarte or Eduardo in Portuguese, was a very common Christian name, so it was quite possible he got that name in Africa, not in Virginia. The Portuguese would have treated someone with a royal name with more respect, he said.

"Even as a slave?" I asked.

"Yes, it would be an honor to sell an aristocrat. It would increase the value of the slave: 'This is no ordinary slave. This family is from such and such family.'"

This ran counter to one article I had read about the plantation owners not wanting freeborn Kongos, particularly royal ones, because they were not accustomed to a life of hard labor. But in those early records, people's observations varied widely.

We ate African cuisine for lunch, my first in Angola, as hotels and restaurants mostly served Portuguese food. We shared beef stew, a big fried fish, and cassava.

Gabriel said he would find us a Nzinga to ask about the name and took us to a secondary school, where I assumed he knew a teacher of that name. We waited in the principal's office until he came in tugging along a mortified-looking teenage boy, who stared at Paul and me like we were white cannibals. His name was Masadi Nzinga Victor, and he didn't know anything about the name except that it came from his late grandmother. I told Gabriel to forget dragging out any others.

We walked down to the ruin of the cathedral, thought to be the first in sub-Saharan Africa. All four red stone walls still stood, with a big arching entrance. And we drove to a post office to look through the Angola phone book, which was a quarter the size of my local directory, even in a country of 18.5 million people. I found two Mazingos as well as numerous Mazingas, Muxingas, Mazangos, and lots of Nzingas.

Lying in bed later, unable to sleep, I conjured my ancestors having a giant party in a field that stretched to the horizon. The Swedes were standing around looking uncomfortable, forming a widening fan of towheaded people going off to infinity. My grandfather Elmer Ternquist sat in his lounger in front of them, reading his National Geographic. My grandmother and great-aunt, the Manents and Eschardies, stood next to him, drinking wine with the French, who fanned out from the Swedes. My uncle Joe helped my grandma Helen bring food to the table, where the smaller groups of Brits and Irish complained about the pickled herring. Spencer sidled up to them, trying to fit in, trying to ignore his great-grandfather standing nearby, ruining his image. Edward stood back a ways, serene, head high, his arm proudly interlocked with Margaret's.

Now and then an obvious fact of life hits like a revelation, and this one hit me then: every person, every leaf, every fish, every dog and virus traces back to the beginning of life. Lineages might die off going forward, but going back, every single one of us is linked to the very beginning. No new chain of life has started for millions of years as far as we know. Somewhere along the way this word Mozingo emerged and attached itself to one of these chains. Occasionally when I signed my name at the grocery store or read it on my gas bill, or watched Blake run around the T-ball field with it emblazoned on his uniform, it staggered me to think that those three syllables came out of the jungles and savannahs so many centuries ago. I thought of that town crier in Mamfe. I wondered when the first sound of Mozingo had pierced the ancestral night.

In the gray of early morning, Paul and I flew back down the mountain listening to "Dark Side of the Moon." *The lunatic is in my head.*

Paul was explaining how elephants and zebras and other mammals moved east during the civil war. The largest elephant ever recorded had been shot in Angola in 1956. There were so few roads and people in the hinterland today that no one really knew if elephants were coming back, or if some populations had never left. "That's virgin bush," he said.

I planned to check out a couple of historical sites the next day in Luanda, before catching my plane back home that night, but I had a nagging feeling that instead I should go to Soyo, another rattling, tortoise-paced 150 miles to the north. An instinct told me Edward might have left from the port of Mpinda there. It made sense, with the war between Soyo and the kingdom the year of his departure, Mpinda's status as Kongo's main coastal slave market, and his name connected to the king whom the Count of Soyo was battling. It was Soyo of Luanda, which I'd already seen.

The present-day city of Soyo sits at the mouth of the Congo with a small but bustling modern port. The exact location of the nearby port of Mpinda was said to be lost, swallowed by the jungle. Both were at least six hours to the north, which made the timing very tight for making my flight out of Luanda, twelve hours from Soyo if all went well. *But when will I ever be so close again?* I thought. "Let's ask someone coming down how the road is," I said.

Paul asked a motorcycle cop.

"Bad, he says."

Then he asked a truck driver coming south. "He said it's a little improved."

One thing I appreciated about Paul was that, although he had much more lucrative business to handle back in Luanda, he still had the itch of curiosity and adventure at age fifty-four. He wanted to see how Soyo had changed since he was last there a few years back. I calculated the likelihood that I would be able to make my flight the next night, and the connecting one in Lisbon, and the next in London, and then Washington and Dallas.

"Fuck it, let's go," I said. I didn't want to leave Africa without seeing the mighty Congo River or looking out at the vast Atlantic as Edward would have seen it at his departure.

We bounced along dry green hills, wet lowlands and lily ponds, by an old Russian tank half-buried in cracked hardened mud and red flags marking land mines, past thatched villages and a little girl holding up a dead monkey to sell, through giant wild mango groves into rising humidity and thickening jungle, blazing by trucks manned by Chinese drivers, vast road cuts for the new highway, soldiers at checkpoints sitting in camping tents, begging cars for rides, oil wells flaring natural gas in the bush, and finally into the bustling little city of Soyo.

Taxis and motorcycles swarmed the streets. I'd never seen a place at once so busy and so isolated, a modern frontier town. The shopkeepers did their business out of cast-off shipping containers, fashioned with doors and windows and painted every color. The dirt track we had taken was the only road in. Clearly, the port served as Soyo's main link to the outside world.

We turned onto a paved road that snaked along a tributary of the river, passing auto body yards, pharmacies, billboards, fish markets, one-stool beauty salons, and one-pot restaurants. Just past a modern luxury hotel the road straightened and then curved to the left, and there it was, a vast glittering blue bay: the mouth of the Congo, the second most powerful river in the world.

Paul parked in the sand by the side of the road leading down to a beach along the river. I ripped my swim trunks from my bag and changed.

IN MEMORY OF THE FIRST BAPTIZED, 1491

This moment demanded baptism. This was the Congo. A light offshore breeze raked the water's surface. As I walked out onto the beach, a yellow butterfly floated up in the sky.

The river was magnificent. Here at its mouth it certainly didn't square with the menacing image that's come to us in literature, the "immense snake uncoiled," in Joseph Conrad's words, venturing up which was a bloodcurdling journey into the primordial, like "traveling back to the earliest beginnings of the world."

A lifeguard in a red bathing suit watched over the beach. Two teenage boys were laughing and mock-fighting nearby. A young man in urban clothes rested on a piece of driftwood gazing out, lost in thought. The warm wind over cool ocean morphed distant boats into strange hourglass figures. On the opposite shore six miles away, I could make out the mangrove jungle of the old Belgian Congo. The faintest blue outline of mountains serrated the horizon.

I shuffled into the river up to my thighs, the water gleaming a translucent orange, glinting with flecks of pyrite and leaf matter. The current tugged hard, even at this massive breadth. No wonder the explorer Diogo Cão ran across reddish sea and islands of vegetation in the Atlantic long before he saw land. Only the Amazon drained more volume. The boys were drifting closer to me, taking turns doing cartwheels into the river. I dove in and turned onto my back, gazing up through the sun-dappled orange.

My chest wanted to open wide, to turn inside out. I had come so far in my search for Edward, and now, floating in the tepid current of the Congo, I felt a sudden nostalgia, as if I were reconvening with someone close I had left behind. In all of this time—time off from the real work of news reporting, time away from my wife and son and newborn daughter, making two trips to Africa—the search had seemed a quixotic detour from real life at points along the way. Here, now, having come so close to the likely point of Edward's departure, I knew that my pursuit of him had in some way restored part of me, a germinal layer that had been buried by my habits, by the grown-up routines that balanced out the highs and lows, and kept me on a track. I was at a point in my life where that person—the boy who played for hours in the Way Back, who painted in

275

his garage—no longer thwarted me. I did not need to keep him locked in the attic so I could focus on relationships and skills to find my place in the world. I did not want to skate blithely on exigencies to the end. Now I was coming on forty years old and it was time to let him back out before my rituals calcified and exiled him forever, and I died wondering where he went.

I realized that boy was both born of me and passed on to me; I had seen signs that he had lived in my ancestors before I was born. That struggle within my father compelled him to quit dentistry for a spell to write a novel. He wrote and painted and relentlessly traveled his entire adult life and is still going. His imagination never sat still. I didn't know much about his dad, but I knew that as an orphan with no money he drove across the country on a motorcycle in the early 1930s. That was nothing but an act of imagination, as every voluntary journey into the unknown is.

So much of me, I knew, came from my mother and her family, but this part came from my father, and the many Mozingo fathers before him.

I looked out at the ocean as a tanker was dropping over the horizon, watching its tower recede beyond earth's curvature, just as the *pombeiros* must have watched the masts of the slaving ships drop away with their cargo.

On the other end lay various ports in South America and the Caribbean. The former Dutch colony of St. Eustatius sat 5,500 miles due west-northwest from here. By the 1660s it was a slave transshipment point, and somewhere in its history the high rim of the island's central peak got a name, Mazinga. Escaped slaves holed up in the bush of Mazinga, nearly two thousand feet over the channel between the island and St. Kitts. No one knew how it got this name or when.

I had reported from Barbados and Trinidad when covering the Caribbean for the *Miami Herald*, and I could see the thread's spool unwinding from here to the crystalline waters of those shores, where the Earl of Warwick's ships awaited, on to the lonely pines and marshes of Jamestown, to the creek called Pantico Run. From there it traveled to the pastures of the Piedmont, rolling up into the Blue Ridge Mountains, on to the braiding tendrils of Raven Creek and the benchlands and forest stands of Decatur County, into the red prairie surrounding Bloomington, across Missouri, Kansas, Colorado, New Mexico, and Arizona, to the faded Art Deco buildings of Hollywood, the master-planned 1960s ranch homes of Dana Point, and my 1920s bungalow home outside of Los Angeles, where Noaki was waking Blake about now for preschool, Lucia soundly snoring. This was the simple vision I had been looking for.

Seeing it now, I understood that my family of course did not rise from an immaculate conception. As part of America's promise, we can attempt to do better than our ancestors did or take different paths, to reinvent ourselves. We can also do worse, as Edward's grandchildren did. But we never start from scratch. The past lives within us all, in every hair and cell and spiral of DNA, in young psyches seared by parents, whose own psyches were seared the same way. I saw almost everything about myself, good and bad, in my son. (Lucia was too little to know.) I twisted in my sheets some nights worried that I passed him my introversion, as if I could have prevented it, and prayed he had a milder case. My ancestors—the Swedish ones in regards to that particular trait—might have done the same in their stone huts in Småland. Childhood, this linking of two generations, remains at the core of who we are. We get to the middle of our lives and find even the most adult of our friends are still reacting in one way or another to their childhoods. When I was younger, I had subconsciously expected to be a new person when I grew up, as if a separate adult would just be grafted onto my youth. But there is a tenacious continuity. We are all bound together by these fibrils of lineage, each family its own, but each also interconnected with all humanity. We understand ourselves better seeing this. A great burden lifts in knowing we didn't create ourselves from a blank slate but emerged from many long and tortuous roads. If you come to appreciate just how many turns that backstory holds, you will not wake up one day to find the sun shining and the stars all aflame. Having a "Bantu warrior," or warrior's son, in my lineage was not so strange at all.

Getting back to the Land Cruiser, I toweled off and said to Paul, "Let's go find Mpinda."

We searched the sandy roads of a countryside shady with palms and fruit trees. Small cinder-block homes and mud-and-thatch huts were tucked among them. Women were starting their cooking fires and calling their youngest to come in. It felt almost like forest, but every parcel was cultivated. We found a beautiful white stone church, Santo António Mpinda, with a rectory and school, set on immaculately raked ground, and we asked a young priest where the old port was. He gestured down the hill behind the church. But he said we could not go there; it was too difficult, fallen trees blocked the way. He said he planned to have them cleared tomorrow because he was holding a pilgrimage in two days to commemorate the slaves who left from Mpinda. We could come then.

I would have loved to witness that. But it would have cost me thousands of dollars to change my many flights home. I had the next hour of light to see it, or never see it at all. I asked if he would just tell us where it was, but he wouldn't say.

A barefoot boy was standing next to him, and we asked him if he knew where it was. He nodded yes.

"It is too difficult, the car cannot go down there," the priest said.

"We can walk. Is it far?"

"It's just difficult."

"Okay, let's go," I told Paul.

The barefoot boy came running after us, with his friend. His name was Antonio, age nine. His friend was Gordensio, thirteen. They would take us to the port.

They climbed in back of the Land Cruiser and pointed to the right, where the road forked. The track was narrower than the car now, and the wheels were driving through weeds, which made me nervous. "Paul, can you ask them about any land mines around here?"

I heard them say simply "No." "They say there aren't any," Paul confirmed.

I was not entirely convinced. My muscles were tight.

IN MEMORY OF THE FIRST BAPTIZED, 1491

We came to a clearing where a sinewy old man was tending his cassava plot, and the boys suddenly looked confused. Paul asked the man where the port was, and he gestured up and around. "Wrong spot," he told me.

We went back up and turned back onto the road we had turned off at the fork. Soon we passed a government sign that said, "Area Historico Cultural do Antigo Porto." I was heartened.

When the road narrowed to a mere footpath, we parked. A little monument stood there, with a cross of gray marble, inscribed in Portuguese, "In Memory of the First Baptized," dated April 3, 1491.

Three other boys joined us. They had been giddily running after the car ever since their two friends got in. The light was growing softer, the palm trees basking in an amber wash. We waved hello to a man high in one tree, tapping sap for wine.

We followed the footpath down a steepening ravine until it ended at a clear stream. Paul said he'd wait there. I took my shoes off, rolled up my pants, and walked into the stream with the boys following. Heading into a thick mangrove forest, the stream poured into a still channel, bubbles and twigs inching up it almost imperceptibly. The tide was coming in. As we continued down the channel, other channels joined it. The water rose over my knees, and my feet sank into the silty bottom up to my ankles. I hoped there were no alligators or hippos. Or leeches.

The boys tried to spear a crab with a sharpened stick but missed. An old dugout canoe sat rotting, half buried at the junction of another small channel.

We came to a mudflat where the channel met a bigger one that I suspect was the main tributary. As we crossed the flat, the sulfurous mud sucked at our feet with great slurps that had the boys giggling madly. My legs were black up to my knees. I inspected for leeches.

I thought about how boys like this, laughing at funny sounds, their mothers waiting for them to come home for dinner, were hauled from this place in shackles, never to see their families again.

"*Onde porto?*" I asked.

They all pointed to the ground.

"Here?" *It can't be here,* I thought, the water must have been deeper where the European boats anchored. I started down the bigger channel, slogging in search of a deeper lagoon. My pants were drenched above my knees now. I'd start swimming if I needed to.

The boys hung back, watching me curiously from the mudflat.

"*Porto aqui?*" I shouted back again.

"*Sim, sim, sim, aqui,*" they said, pointing again to the mudflat.

Maybe a lagoon here had filled with silt over centuries, I thought. Or maybe the traders took advantage of this disorienting circuit of small channels, rowing slaves down converging mangrove tunnels until they reached deep water. The way back would not be so easy, as the tunnels narrowed and spidered off. An escaping slave would have to thread a thicket of passageways simply to get to dry land, much less his home.

The sun was setting in the northwest. I was drenched with tidewater and sweat. I knew I had to stop.

As I turned back, mosquitoes descended in squadrons, biting through my shirt and boring into my neck and legs. The canopy of mangroves closed in with the gathering dark. That old feeling of eeriness was coming on, and the thread was fading from view.

Epilogue

anielle's fiancé Jason Bell stands at the white altar on Croatan Beach in a cream-colored suit. He has a shaved head and a sprawling shoulder span and chest. He could easily pass as an NFL linebacker and is routinely mistaken for a Charger in San Diego and asked to sign autographs. The irony is that he has never been an athlete and doesn't even lift weights.

The wind is keening north, glazing the sand and driving silty waves over the low seawall that protects the harbor outlet. The hotels of Virginia Beach jut up on the other side of the channel. The sky is smoky from raging wildfires in North Carolina.

I find my seat among about fifty people. Danielle's many aunts and uncles are here, for the most part beaming and exuding happiness for her. Jason's friends and family members show up in equal numbers, brimming with warmth and excitement.

Danielle's mother seems the only one burdened with a bad history. She walks across the sand in a yellow dress with her sisters rubbing her neck and whispering in her ear, consoling her.

I had wondered whether Danielle's father would come around at the last moment and walk his daughter down the aisle. He did give her $5,000 to pay for the wedding and stopped ranting and cursing about it, she told me. But in the end, he said he was too busy to attend. I knew that her grandfather, Bud, would not show, but Bud's wife Shirley is here. She ran up to Jason with open arms when they first met back in Greensburg.

Danielle strides across the beach barefoot in a diaphanous white dress, trailing her younger brother and three bridesmaids.

Her brother walks her up the aisle and the service begins.

Danielle's mom watches the ceremony with her head tilted down, as if she is at a funeral. When the bride and groom kiss, she doesn't clap with the others, or even look up. At the reception, I stay away from Danielle's family members. I know I am toxic to many of them after my articles.

I introduce myself to Jason's mother and tell her I'm writing a book. She tells me she knows that her son is a strong, unflappable guy, but she says she worries that he's going to get hurt, not by Danielle, but by the simmering hatred of some of her family.

"I think Danielle seems to be dragging them into the light," I say.

"Well, it doesn't seem to be working," she says.

"Her mom came here at least. At first she wasn't going to."

Her brow cinches up in a knot and she glances to the side. "Hmm."

"You don't think so?" I ask.

"I went up to her and tried to tell her she was not losing a daughter, but gaining a whole new family. You know what she told me? She said, 'I took her on a cruise, and I just feel she royally screwed me.'"

"Wow" is the only response I can muster.

The toasts begin; the love and admiration for the newlyweds resonates strongly. One of Jason's two older brothers, Shawn, a forty-year-old Navy SEAL, dapper in a white silk shirt, takes the microphone.

"They call me a man of few words," he starts.

Those in the party who know him laugh in agreement.

He swivels uncomfortably before the emotion of what he wants to say lifts him up.

"Jason is probably the most generous person, the most loving person, you'll ever meet in your life. I used to torment him. . . . We used to beat him up, pick on him. . . . We all played sports. He played the cello."

The crowd laughs again, and Jason calls out, "Man!"

"I was so proud of him," Shawn continues, his voice catching, "when he followed in my footsteps and joined the Navy, and took on one of the most unpioneered communities, the submariner field. There are very few African Americans, and my brother he did it, and I was so proud of him when he did that. . . .

"One thing about Jason is he's so genuine, and me, I'm a man of few words, and I've been called emotionless, whatever, and Jason brings your heart out."

He chokes up hard.

"And whenever we talk, you say, 'I love you, man.' Every conversation."

He puts his hand in his pocket awkwardly. "That's why I love you."

Jason wipes his eyes as he steps in for a bear hug, and then Shawn regroups and finishes.

"All right so," Shawn says, "God's blessed me with a couple gifts, and one of them is, I can see people's hearts, you know, in two seconds or two minutes. When I met Danielle, I had heard a lot about her, and within five seconds I knew her. I knew she was the one. I could see her heart, and it was pure."

An osprey hovers over the water, hunting fish. I walk along the glistening white beach at Archer's Hope, where the Spanish first launched their expedition to build a settlement in Virginia in 1570. College Creek undercuts a white cliff, sloughing off vertical layers. Pines perch right on the edge, roots exposed. The creek hooks away and opens up into the James River, bending south, and then east to the Atlantic. It is my first view of the river where America began. A smattering of wispy clouds sets off a deep blue morning sky. The heat does strange things to the light on the cool water, as it did on the Congo. It looks like the middle of the river is roiling with giant fish, and farther downstream it's as if magnified trees are floating in the air above the river.

I talk to a family fishing for croaker and channel cats, and then go down the road to Jamestown, tracing the steps Edward would have followed when he came to court here on October 5, 1672. I drive along the long neck of land and across the marshy isthmus to the island, where I park and pay the National Park fee. A gangway leads visitors over the swamp where the settlers once got their pitch tar.

Epilogue

The malarial settlement went to ruins after the governor moved the capital to Williamsburg. Now the island is an archaeological site and tourist attraction. The only colonial building that remained remotely intact was the redbrick church built in 1639, which has now been restored. The log palisades of the fort have been rebuilt and the replica frame of one of the old homes was erected. A commanding century-old statue of Captain John Smith gazes across the river.

I hunt around the "Back Streete" area, where the settlement spread out beyond the palisade walls, reading placards, trying to find the spot of the old statehouse where court was held and where Edward won his freedom. I had read that in the 1640s, the house of a John Harvey served as the statehouse, and that Swann's Tavern stood nearby, where people stayed when they came to the island for court or the assembly. I wonder if they let a black man stay there in 1672 on his visit to plead his case. Edward may have traveled down from the Northern Neck with Colonel Walker's daughters and their husbands. Maybe they vouched for him at the tavern, like they seem to have done in court. I walk west along the seawall, where the wharves once teemed with the shipments of tobacco and slaves, to the other side of the palisade.

In the archaeological museum, I find my answer: the building itself stands on the site of the statehouse, built in 1665. I step back outside to where the docent told me the courthouse entrance once was. A tern nest on the ground is staked off with police tape, and the birds seemed unbothered by the people stepping all around them.

The entrance looked out on the wide river arching south, level with the pines. I walk to the seawall. After Edward won his freedom, he would have walked out and seen this same view, the slowing coursing tidal river, the low green banks fading off into the vast continent his descendants would one day cross, chasing the elusive American Dream.

Acknowledgments

Special thanks for being so generous with their time goes to Ann L. Miller, John Thornton, Linda Heywood, Benjamin Woolley, Walter Gam Nkwi, Ralph Austen, Larry Gragg, Ira Berlin, Paul Heinegg, Barbara A. Farner, Walter Hellebrand, Simao Souindoula, Philip D. Morgan, Samie Melton, Rhodie Mozingo, Wiley Mozingo, Amy Osting, Tom Mozingo, Melicent Remy, Kathy Ross, and, of course, Uncle Joe.

A Note on Sources

I relied upon a broad array of sources to piece together the historical passages in this book, including original source documents, academic articles, biographies, and local history books. Much of the genealogical material was found in the Library of Virginia and local courthouses, libraries, and historical societies throughout Virginia, Kentucky, Indiana, and Illinois.

For the passage on the founding and early years of Jamestown, I drew heavily on the firsthand accounts of the settlement compiled in *Jamestown Narratives: Eyewitness Accounts of the Virginia Colony*, edited by Edward Wright Haile, and *The Complete Works of Captain John Smith (1580–1631) in Three Volumes*, edited by Philip L. Barbour. *Cavaliers and Pioneers: Abstracts of Virginia Land Patents and Grants*, edited by Neil Marion Nugent, was a good reference for digging for common settlers in the colony. Two contemporary books provided valuable context: *Savage Kingdom: The True Story of Jamestown, 1607, and the Settlement of America* by Benjamin Woolley and *A Land As God Made It: Jamestown and the Birth of America* by James Horn. Also useful were *Savagism and Civility: Indians and Englishmen in Colonial Virginia* by Bernard Sheehan and *The Growth of Political Institutions in Virginia, 1634 to 1676* by Warren M. Billings.

For the history on the earliest slaves arriving in Virginia and subsequent race relations in the colony, the original documents compiled in the four-volume *Documents Illustrative of the History of the Slave Trade to America*, edited by Elizabeth Donnan, were indispensable. So too were the genealogical records amassed by Paul Heinegg and published on his website freeafricanamericans.com. The slave ship records gathered in the Trans-Atlantic Slave Trade Database—run by David Eltis at Emory University and available online at slavevoyages.org—was a tremendous resource. I also relied on the following books: *Many Thousands Gone: The First Two Centuries of Slavery in North America* by Ira Berlin; *American Slavery, American Freedom* by Edmund S. Morgan; *Foul Means: The Formation of a Slave Society in Virginia, 1660–1740* by Anthony S. Parent, Jr.; *Before the Mayflower: A History of the Negro in America, 1619–1964* by Lerone Bennett, Jr.; *Slave Counterpoint: Black Culture in the Eighteenth-Century Chesapeake & Low Country* by Philip D. Morgan; *The African American Experience: Black History and Culture through Speeches, Letters, Editorials, Poems, Songs, and Stories*, edited by Kai Wright; '*Myne Owne Ground': Race and Freedom on Virginia's Eastern Shore, 1640–1676* by T. H. Breen and Stephen Innes; *Landon Carter's Uneasy Kingdom: Revolution and Rebellion on a Virginia Plantation* by Rhys Isaac; *The Free Negro in Virginia, 1619–1865* by John Henderson Russell; and *The Free Negro in North Carolina, 1790–1860* by John Hope Franklin.

For the more granular details I needed in trying to piece together Edward's specific journey to Virginia I found numerous scholarly articles and books helpful: *The Rich Papers, Letters from Bermuda, 1615–1646*, edited by Vernon A. Ives; "'To Procure Negroes': The English Slave Trade to Barbados, 1627–1660" by Larry Gragg; *Atlantic Virginia: Inter-colonial Relations in the Seventeenth Century* by April Lee Hatfield; *White Servitude and Black Slavery in Barbados, 1627–1715* by Hilary McD. Beckles; *Providence Island, 1630–1641* by Karen Ordahl Kupperman; and *Warwick Castle and its Earls: From Saxon Times to the Present Day* by Frances Evelyn Maynard Greville Warwick.

A description of how public records, including Edward Mozingo's order of freedom, were kept from colonial Virginia through the Civil War was provided in *The Common Wealth: Treasures from the Collections of the Library of Virginia*, edited by Sandra Gioia Treadway and Edward D. C. Campbell, Jr.

The sections on the Mozingos moving west from Virginia drew upon numerous sources, most notably: *James Madison, A Biography* by Ralph

Ketcham; *Diary of Col. Francis Taylor*, transcribed by Barbara A. Farner at Gunston Hall Plantation; *Boone, A Biography* by Robert Morgan; *History of Pioneer Kentucky* by Robert S. Cotterill; *History of Kentucky* by William Elsey Connelley and Ellis Merton Coulter; *How the West Was Lost, The Transformation of Kentucky from Daniel Boone to Henry Clay* by Stephen Aron; *American Notes for General Circulation* by Charles Dickens; *The Indiana Way, a State History* by James H. Madison; *Herndon's Lincoln* by William Henry Herndon and Jesse William Weik; *Lincoln's Youth, Indiana Years, 1816–1830* by Louis A. Warren; *History of Decatur County, Indiana* by Lewis Albert Harding; *Democracy in America* by Alexis de Tocqueville; *The Struggle for the Michigan Road* by Geneal Prather; and *Rural Life in Indiana, 1800–1950* by Barbara J. Steinson.

For the story of the Atlantic slave trade, the aforementioned Trans-Atlantic Slave Database and *Documents Illustrative of the History of the Slave Trade* were immensely helpful. Firsthand accounts of the trade came from: *A New Account of Some Parts of Guinea, and the Slave Trade* by William Snelgrave; *An Account of the Slave Trade on the Coast of Africa* by Alexander Falconbridge; and *The Portuguese in West Africa, 1415–1670, A Documentary History*, edited by Malyn Newitt. I drew heavily from the following: *The Slave Trade: The Story of the Atlantic Slave Trade, 1440–1870* by Hugh Thomas; *Central Africans, Atlantic Creoles and the Foundation of the Americas, 1585–1660* by Linda M. Heywood and John K. Thornton; *Africa and Africans in the Making of the Atlantic World, 1800* by John Thornton; and *Prince Henry 'the Navigator': A Life* by Peter Russell. I also found illuminating *The Transatlantic Slave Trade, A History* by James A. Rawley; *Saltwater Slavery, A Middle Passage from Africa to American Diaspora* by Stephanie E. Smallwood; *The Atlantic Slave Trade* by Herbert S. Klein; *The River Congo* by Peter Forbath; *Way of Death, Merchant Capitalism and the Angolan Slave Trade, 1730–1830* by Joseph C. Miller; *The Atlantic Slave Trade* by Johannes Postma; *Enslaving Spirits: The Portuguese-Brazilian Alcohol Trade at Luanda and its Hinterland, c. 1550–1830* by José C. Curto; "Trans-Saharan Trade and the West African Discovery of the Mediterranean World" by Pekka Masonen; *Slave Trading and Slavery in the Dutch Colonial Empire: A Global Comparison* by Rip Van Welie; and *The Queen's Slave Trader: John Hawkyns, Elizabeth I,* and the Trafficking of Human Souls by Nick Hazelwood. Particularly useful to my specific search was Heywood's *Slavery and Its Transformation in the Kingdom of Kongo: 1491–1800*.

Books and articles that follow provided a glimpse of the internal dynamics of Africa during and after the slave trade: *Recreating Africa: Culture, Kinship and Religion in the African-Portuguese World, 1441–1770* by James H. Sweet; *The Kingdom of Kongo: Civil War and Transition* by Thornton; "Beyond Decline: The Kingdom of Kongo in the Eighteenth and Nineteenth Centuries" by Susan Herlin Broadhead; *The Kingdom of Kongo* by Anne Hilton; *Kingdom on Mount Cameroon: Studies in the History of the Cameroon Coast, 1500–1970* by Edwin Ardener; *Slave Settlements in the Banyang Country, 1800–1950* by E.S.D. Fomin and Victor Julius Ngoh; *Swedish Ventures in Cameroon, 1883–1923* by Knut Vilhelm Knutson and George Waldau; *A History of the Cameroon* by Tambi Eyongetah Mbuagbaw, Robert Brain, and Robin Palmer; and *Middlemen of the Cameroons Rivers: The Duala and their Hinterland, c. 1600–c. 1960* by Ralph A. Austen and Jonathan Derrick. Most critical to my ultimate findings was Thornton's "Central African Names and African-American Naming Patterns."

Index

Index

League of Nations, 233
Lemme, Ada Mozingo, 154, 160
Library of Virginia, 53, 91, 176
Licking River, 104–5
Light in August (Faulkner), 107–10,
   142–43, 151
Lincoln, Abraham, 31, 149–50, 152, 161
Locust, Valentine, 122
London, 43, 274
   colonial Virginia and, 33, 36, 38–39
   slave trade and, 6, 44
Los Angeles, Calif., 13–14, 16–18,
   24–25, 63, 143, 156, 158, 166,
   198, 260, 277
   blacks in, 16–17
Los Angeles, University of California at
   (UCLA), 17, 25, 63, 156, 158
Los Angeles Central Library, 26, 58, 60
Los Angeles Times:
   J. Mozingo's employment at, 12–13,
     27, 58
   J. Mozingo's stories in, 193–96
Luanda, 231, 273–74
   fighting in, 216–17, 265
   J. Mozingo's trip to, 261–62, 273
   Netherlands and, 267–68
   slave trade and, 216–17, 219–20,
     262–63, 271
Lumfe, Louis Adolf Muzinga, 231

McIlwaine, Henry Reed, 77
Madison, Ambrose, 92
Madison, Ind., 147, 150, 152, 161
Madison, James, Jr., 91–94
   on groundhogs, 97–98
   Kentucky and, 102–3
   personal letters of, 96–98
   slaves of, 59, 96, 98
   S. Mozingo and, 58–59, 64, 91, 96,
     98, 112, 147
   Taylors and, 59, 91, 93–94, 96–97,
     157
Madison, James, Sr., 59, 93, 96
Madjingo, 220
Maharaj, Davan, 12–13
Maiden, London, 179–80
Malebo Pool, 216, 218
Mamfe:
   J. Mozingo's trip to, 249–52
   slave trade and, 9, 226–27, 240,
     250–51
   town crier of, 252–53, 273

Mark, Gareth, 48–49
Mason, Thomas, 179–80
Mazinga (island peak), 276
Mazinga, Francis, 231
Mazinga Institute, 231
Mazingo (village), 220
Mazingo, Sherrie, 24–26
M'banza Kongo, 211–12, 214, 216
   J. Mozingo's trip to, 261, 264–67,
     269–72
Melton, Samie, 51–54
   DNA project and, 52–53
   E. Mozingo and, 30, 197
   S. Mozingo and, 30–31, 51–52, 60
Melungeons, 28–29, 120, 180
Mexicans, Mexico, 16, 19, 21–23, 33, 43,
   158, 190, 215
Miami Herald, 27, 276
Miller, Ann, 96, 98–99
Miller, Ivor, 254–55
Miller, Joseph C., 262
*Minutes of the Council and General Court
   of Colonial Virginia* (McIlwaine),
   26–27, 77
Mississippi River, Mississippi River
   Valley, 89–90, 101, 154–55, 161
Missouri, 103, 152, 276–77
   Mozingos in, 14, 61, 154–55
mixed-race people, 9, 28–29, 86, 150,
   216, 263
   E. Mozingo and, 61, 69–71, 187
   Faulkner and, 107–10
   Indiana and, 151, 169–70, 176
   North Carolina and, 63, 116, 119–21,
     123–25, 132, 136, 144
   as pariah class, 48, 87, 105, 142, 144,
     146
   S. Mozingo and, 51, 60–61, 107
   Virginia and, 46–48, 179–80, 182,
     184, 187–88
Mongom, Philip, 63
Mont Zingeau, 22, 195
Moody, Dr., 151
Mormons, 26, 56–57
Mosingi, Beggar King, 229
Mosingi, Molla, 229
Mt. Cameroon, 4, 209–10, 225, 229–32,
   251
   Bakweri and, 230–32, 234–35
   German colonizers and, 232, 234
   J. Mozingo's hike on, 230–31, 234–35
Mount Olive, N.C., 130, 137–38

Index

Index

Virginia (*cont.*)
  racism and, 47–49, 51, 120–21,
    180–82, 189
  slave trade and, 6, 27, 41–48, 69–70,
    92–93, 106, 119, 179, 218–19,
    222, 284
  Taylor and, 95–96
  Tidewater of, 45–46, 70–71, 89, 101–2
  tobacco and, 39, 43, 45–46, 48, 59,
    61, 69, 72–73, 89–90, 93–94, 110,
    113, 284
Virginia Beach, Va., 200, 281
Virginia Company, 33, 38–40

Wake County, N.C., 122
Walker, Jerry, 79–83
Walker, John, 53, 77–82
  death of, 27, 31–32, 48, 73, 77
  E. Mozingo and, 27, 31–32, 41, 44,
    68, 77–78, 81, 173, 183, 185, 284
  J. Mozingo's Walkerton trip and,
    80–82
  land owned by, 45–46, 73, 75, 82
  marriages of, 45–46
Walker, Sarah Fleete, 45–46
  E. Mozingo and, 27, 31–32, 48, 77
Walker, Thomas, 78–79, 81
Walker, Virginia Henley, 80
Walker, William, 82
Walkerton, Va., 78–83
Warsaw, Va.:
  E. Mozingo and, 66–68, 73–74, 76
  J. Mozingo's trip to, 66–68, 71, 73–76,
    83
  tobacco and, 72–73

Warwick County, Va., 41–42, 44, 46, 70
Washington, George, 56
Watkins, Katherine, 47
Wayne County, N.C., 116, 123, 127,
  131–32
Wayne Memorial Park, 131–32
Way of Death (Miller), 262
Wesson, Paul:
  J. Mozingo's Angola trip and, 261,
    264–66, 269–70, 272–74, 277–79
  J. Mozingo's Kongo trip and, 264–67,
    269–70, 272
  J. Mozingo's Mpinda trip and,
    277–79
  J. Mozingo's Soyo trip and, 273–74
West Africa, 9, 42, 63, 208–9, 218, 220
Westmoreland, Westmoreland County,
  Va., 48–49, 61, 69, 179
White, William, 35–36
white supremacy, 190–92, 196–98
Widikum, 248–50
Wilberforce, William, 228
Wilderness, Battle of the, 91
William and Mary Quarterly, 213
Williamsburg, Va., 59, 76, 92, 284
Wilson, Mary, 86–87
Wingfield, Edward Maria, 34
Wired, 27–28, 68
World War I, 155, 226
World War II, 17, 19, 63, 175, 263
Wright, Richard, 137

York River, 40–41, 45

Zurara, Gomes Eanes de, 206–8, 213

About the Author

Joe Mozingo is a projects reporter for the *Los Angeles Times*. He won a Robert F. Kennedy Award for his coverage of the earthquake in Haiti and helped lead a *Miami Herald* reporting team whose investigation into the crash of the space shuttle *Columbia* was a finalist for the Pulitzer Prize. *The Fiddler on Pantico Run* was named a finalist for the J. Anthony Lukas Work-in-Progress Award, administered by Columbia University and Harvard's Nieman Foundation. He lives in Southern California with his wife and two children.

Printed in the United States
By Bookmasters